THE IRISH COUNTRYWOMEN'S ASSOCIATION

A HISTORY

1910-2000

Aileen Heverin is from Clonmel, Co. Tipperary. She now spends her time between Donegal and Galway, where she completed her degree in Geography and Economics in 1982. She is married to John and they have five children. Aileen previously worked for Aer Lingus and is now involved with voluntary and charitable organisations, taking a particular interest in issues that affect women. She took on the research and writing of this book as a member of the ad hoc History Committee of the ICA.

The Irish Countrywomen's Association

A History

1910-2000

Aileen Heverin

The Irish Countrywomen's Association
AND
Wolfhound Press

First Published in 2000 by
Wolfhound Press
68 Mountjoy Square
Dublin 1, Ireland
Tel: (353-1) 874 0354
Fax: (353-1) 872 0207

British Library Cataloguing in Publication Data
A catalogue record for this book is available from the British Library

ISBN 0-86327-818-3

5 4 3 2 1

Photographs: ICA archive
Typesetting: Wolfhound Press
Cover Design: Azure Design
Printed in the Republic of Ireland by ColourBooks, Dublin

CONTENTS

ACKNOWLEDGEMENT TO W.K. KELLOGG FOUNDATION 6

PREFACE
Breda Raggett, National President, ICA 7

INTRODUCTION: WOMEN WORKING TOGETHER THROUGH ICA 9

1: BIRTH OF THE SOCIETY OF UNITED IRISHWOMEN 17

2: THE EARLY YEARS 33

3: SUMMER SCHOOLS AND COUNTRY WORKERS 60

4: 1930S AND THE BIRTH OF ICA 72

5: STRUCTURE OF ICA 84

6: THE 'EMERGENCY' AND ITS AFTERMATH 90

7: RURAL WATER, ELECTRICITY AND DEVELOPMENT
IN THE 1950S 105

8: AN GRIANÁN 120

9: ICA IN A CHANGING SOCIETY: 1960S 129

10: THE WOMEN'S DECADE: 1970S 146

11: 1980 ONWARDS 167

CONCLUSION: DEEDS, NOT WORDS 183

APPENDIX: PERSONALITIES AND PRESIDENTS OF ICA 196

NOTES 231

ACKNOWLEDGEMENT TO
W.K. KELLOGG FOUNDATION

In 1993, the Irish Countrywomen's Association decided to collect and catalogue the available records and material of the organisation, founded in 1910 throughout the countryside.

This archival material was to be the basis for a history of the association, which would assess the members' contribution to the improved status of women down through those years.

In order to achieve this aim, financial support was needed. In the past, the W.K. Kellogg Foundation, realising the importance for the women of Ireland of the work of the Irish Countrywomen's Association, had funded the Adult Education College and the Horticultural College at An Grianán, Termonfechin, Co. Louth. Once again, the ICA approached the Kellogg Foundation for sponsorship, and once again Kellogg responded most generously. The result of that sponsorship is twofold: the history of the Irish Countrywomen's Association has been written by Aileen Heverin, and the nationwide material has been archived through two FÁS schemes and donated to the National Library of Ireland to facilitate future scholarly research.

To all who have assisted in this Trojan work — FÁS, Bank of Ireland, the National Library, the ICA Federations and Guilds, my colleagues on the History Committee, Kathleen Delap, Karen Carleton and Aileen Heverin — and to our main sponsors, the W.K. Kellogg Foundation, I extend my very sincere thanks for their support and confidence in this important project.

Sheila O'Donnellan
Chairman
Ad Hoc History Committee

PREFACE

The publication of the 90-year history of the ICA presents an opportunity for members to feel a quiet surge of pride at what has been achieved. The organisation has made a difference — a profound, measurable and marvellous difference – to the way generations of Irish women live their lives. The ICA was central to the setting up of the co-operative and credit union movements, in consumer and health affairs. And that's not even half the story.

At its simplest — and most effective — the ICA provided a forum for women to talk to each other about their needs, hopes and dreams. They gained strength from each other and grew together. We were blessed with some very fine leaders.

These women have made an exceptional contribution to enriching the lives of the communities within which they lived and to advancing the role of Irish women. This publication is a fitting tribute to their memory. It also presents us with an opportunity to celebrate our successes, reflect upon them and be inspired by them.

I am deeply honoured to lead this organisation as the first National President of the new millennium. Irish society has changed dramatically — and for the better for Irish women. However, there are new challenges. In stark contrast to the situation that prevailed in 1910, most of our people now live in urban areas. Rural communities often live in greater isolation and have difficulty accessing basic services such as transport, banking and health services. Many urban areas lack the kind of services needed to build healthy communities. Prosperity too brings its own challenges; people lead more pressurised lives, placing greater strain on relationships. Research indicates that parents tend to feel less sure about how to give direction to their children. Children lead shorter childhoods.

At the same time there are greater opportunities presented to us through technology. And a diversity is offered through the new multicultural nature of our society.

With over 1,000 guilds (branches) throughout the country there are few organisations as well placed as the ICA to extend the hand of friendship to people of different cultural backgrounds, to represent the needs of women and their families, and to influence policy at all levels. My ambition is that as an organisation we would leave as proud a legacy for the women of the next century as our predecessors did for us in the last one.

Breda Raggett
National President
Irish Countrywomen's Association

INTRODUCTION
WOMEN WORKING TOGETHER THROUGH ICA

The history of the Society of United Irishwomen, (UI, later to become ICA), from its foundation in 1910 is a history reflective of women in Ireland in the twentieth century. As Ireland was predominantly rural, it is a history of the branches spread throughout the twenty-six counties and an account of members active in their local communities, in the context of events in Ireland during the period. The ICA archives reveal information about women's experiences which is not recorded in other historical sources, and its records give a unique and valuable insight into Irish women's social history from 1910 to the present. The idea of groups of women coming together — women on the farm, women in the home, women living in remote and isolated areas — to discuss their needs and become involved in the social, educational and cultural life of the country was a radical one for the era.

Theirs is not a history in isolation, but a history tied up with social, economic and political developments in Ireland. Much writing about the history of women in Ireland has focused on leading personalities at the expense of the silent majority — most Irishwomen who have any historical presence have worked with male-dominated organisations, so that women's history has been viewed through the political concerns of men. Recent work is beginning to change this:

> Women's history clearly reveals the importance of the powerless in contributing to the success of those who became powerful. This contribution has at times been deliberately played down, and not just simply undervalued.[1]

As the oldest and largest women's organisation in Ireland, ICA could never have been considered radical in its policies, and indeed has frequently clashed with the feminist movement. However, on examining the work of ICA, we see that all its actions have been for the betterment of women, and it has worked to empower women through education and through addressing specific grievances. The aim of the feminist movement is to give each woman the freedom to explore her own potential and the right to be accepted as a full person with rights and responsibilities equal to those of men; in fact, this corresponds to much of the work of ICA.

The founders of the Society of United Irishwomen demanded the right to knowledge, self-determination and responsibility which would allow them to be better mothers and have a positive influence on their children. ICA, with its thousand guilds spread throughout every county in Ireland, has worked since 1910 to empower women, cultivating a community tradition amongst its members, and encouraging them to organise in response to local needs.

Although often cloaked in tradition, women have used apparently conventional organisations such as ICA and IHA (Irish Housewives Association) to improve the lives of their families and communities, to extend the space for women's activity, and thus to combat the oppression of women.

ICA has been a vehicle for change, though the changes are seen by many as coming too slowly — but countrywomen know that seeds take time to germinate.

WOMEN WORKING TOGETHER

ICA has served as a meeting ground for women from differing social and religious backgrounds. It adopted strategies appropriate to its time, and has thus always been in a position to discuss issues of concern to all women in an environment free from religious and political supervision. In 1911, Horace Plunkett wrote, 'So far as women's knowledge and influence will avail, they will strive for a higher standard of material comfort and physical well-being in the country home, a more advanced agricultural economy and a social existence a little more in harmony with the intellect and temperament of our people.' ICA's work since then has proven the truth of his words.

In its struggle to improve the quality of rural life, ICA succeeded on many fronts now forgotten or taken for granted — running water, rural electrification, farm home advisory services, and above all the opportunity it gave thousands of women to leave their homes and engage in social activity with other women.

In contrast to the 1937 Constitution which sought to imprison women within the family, ICA worked to expand and develop their role in the family so that it influenced society as a whole. As such, ICA was virtually unassailable by the patriarchal institutions which excluded women from public life, yet it managed to offer women an avenue through which to fight for a better life, and the confidence to voice their opinions in the development of public policy.

LEADERSHIP AND PUBLIC SPEAKING

As Esther Bishop wrote of the ICA in 1950:

> All training for leadership has to begin by building up self-confidence and then using it through taking responsibility for small and familiar things. ICA guilds have provided a valuable training ground, with further opportunities through summer schools and college. It was quickly realised that one of the greatest ordeals facing an Irishwoman was to be asked to speak in public, and so every effort was made to provide training to efface the terrors from that ordeal. Starting at branch level and beginning in the very simplest way through a 'Roll-call' on a given subject, to which all had to contribute, through verse speaking and drama to discussion groups and debates and finally to classes in public speaking, the work went on and showed results surprisingly rapidly.[2]

EMIGRATION AND QUALITY OF LIFE

Recognising that housewives were in need of representation on many fronts, ICA called on the government to introduce specific social welfare reforms, fought to improve the quality of life and to increase women's earning power in order to combat emigration. Ireland differed from other countries in the early twentieth century in that the majority of its emigrants were women, leaving a low ratio of women to men in rural Ireland.

Ellice Pilkington, ICA's first organiser, made an impassioned plea to stem emigration by improving the quality of rural life:

> The starved soul of womanhood is crying out over the world for an intellectual life and for more chance of earning a living. If Ireland will not listen to this cry, its daughters will go on slipping silently away to other countries as they have been doing – all the best of them, all the bravest, all those most mentally alive, all those who would have made

the best wives and mothers — and they will leave at home the timid, the stupid and the dull to help in the deterioration of the race to breed sons as sluggish as themselves.

Such was the determination of the founders of ICA to act and improve the lives of women in Ireland.

When married men emigrated, as they frequently did in the 1950s, women were left in to run the farm and rear the family alone — often for years on end with brief visits from the men. These essentially lone-parent families were headed by women who had to earn a living as well as running the family, in the process providing a strong role-model for their children. Coincidence or otherwise, this was a period of great growth for the ICA, with the founding of the Adult Education college, development officers, the campaign for amenities such as running water and electricity, but above all the networking, support and friendship between guilds throughout Ireland.

STATUS OF WOMEN

The relative decision-making power of women and men can be seen in the spread of electricity and water to rural households. Just as leisure appliances such as radios, or in more recent times television and hi-fi, spread more rapidly among consumers than labour-saving devices such as washing machines, so electricity — which was associated with leisure — spread more rapidly to rural households than running water. The fact that leisure products were used by men, while household appliances and water are primarily of benefit to women, is an important consideration. This reveals much about the status of women in rural Ireland, and reflects prevailing values and attitudes.

In 1967, the UN Commission on the Status of Women asked women's organisations to examine the status of women in their own countries. ICA participated in an ad-hoc committee formed with nine other women's groups to investigate discrimination against women in Ireland. The resulting memorandum called among other things for the establishment of a Commission on the Status of Women. This became a reality in 1970, with three ICA members among the 13 appointees (Kathleen Delap, Alice McTiernan and Kathleen Gleeson). By 1972 the Commission for the Status of Women in Ireland had produced a report with 49 recommendations. This report marked a watershed for the development of women's rights and their admission to the political agenda.

By 1976, 39 of these recommendations had been implemented. Several factors assisted the success of this measure — the consciousness-raising work of ICA among rural women, the fact that the report came at a time when entrenched attitudes were changing, and Ireland's membership of the EEC in 1973.

In 1993 the second Commission on the Status of Women (which included Joy McCormick of the ICA) produced a report recommending many changes for rural women, such as improved transport plans, introduction of mobile health centres, that the work of women on farms be categorised and counted for statistical and policy purposes, that training and education needs of rural women be met. Again, ICA is represented on the committee monitoring implementation of these recommendations.

REALITY OF IRISHWOMEN'S LIVES

The dominant ideology of the 1937 Constitution placed women in the home as mothers and housekeepers, yet provided no advice, no financial support or guidance on how women should fulfil that role. The state remained indifferent to women in the home, and even to violence against women and children. The reality of the violent and harsh nature of many women's lives was not allowed to upset the imagined ideal of Irish family life.

However, the idea that the archaic practices in rural Ireland were inherently positive did not go down well with ICA members. In 1940, Alice Courtayne wrote, 'The romantic and sentimental lovers of the land are beyond classification. They have one thing positively in common. None of them derive their livelihood from the land. Few of them even live on it.' As Alice Ryan, ICA President in 1952, noted 'Rural life, in the minds of many, corresponds to the catechism definition of purgatory — a state in which people should suffer for a time before they go to the heaven of a town.'

Aware of the loneliness experienced by many women living in the countryside, the ICA gave members the opportunity to meet for weekly classes in domestic science, traditional handcrafts and farming skills. Lectures and debates as well as music, drama and dance were organised to recruit new members and provide some light relief from the everyday drudgery of life. Women were also encouraged to get involved in local government, and many guilds campaigned on issues such as the introduction of school meals and nursing schemes in their areas.

Muriel Gahan, describing the lives of women in 1950, was adamant that the countrywoman was not an abstraction in print:

Mrs Conneely with half a dozen children to rear on five acres of rock in Connemara, Mrs McCarthy of the midlands, trying to run a big farm with insufficient help and cut off from her sister countrywomen six days of the week. Mary McBride in Donegal, home from service and restless with the thought of opportunities that might be waiting for her in another country, too many of them in the house, her younger sister wondering when she too will get away. Nancy O'Sullivan raising chickens in Waterford, her fingers itching to make something pretty for her home, but she doesn't know how. And Mrs Clogherty, sitting — just sitting — as I saw her in her little house in Kerry not so long ago, an empty room, no sign of food, no belongings except her spinning wheel, idle in the corner because she was without the means to buy wool.[3]

Mary O'Donnell also described 'forgotten women':

Kathleen McKenna, Annagola, who was able to wash a week's sheets, shirts and swaddling, bake bread and clean a house all on Monday, while Birdy McMahon of Faulkland walked to Monaghan for a sack of flour two days before her eighth child was born.

John D. Sheridan wrote in the *Irish Independent* in 1963:

In the farmhouse kitchen a woman is up to her elbows in a bucket of mash, a baby yells blue murder from a pram, a toddler on the floor is trying to find nourishment in a sod of turf while strangling the cat. Somewhere outside a chorus of hungry hens is squawking like teenagers at a pop concert and from the yard 'himself' is shouting for details of the clown who let out the cows. The woman says 'God, give me patience', looks at the clock and wonders whether she should try to feed the hens before settling the baby, before starting the dinner for the children at school. She is wife, mother, cook, needlewoman, nurse and gardener.

It was important that these descriptions of women's lives in various parts of the country be heard. This was the reality of their everyday experience, and it was to this scenario that ICA addressed its energy. It was important to look at how women lived and organised, their interests and priorities, strengths and in-securities. Evidence of the many roles of women emerged — women in the home, women on the farm, women administering local services, women in adult education and women in voluntary self-help. These women lived on the land, and wanted to improve their standard of living and their environment.

MODERN FEMINISM

With the development of the feminist movement in the 1970s, ICA came under criticism for being 'stuffy', conservative, and not doing enough for Irish women. Its unquestioning support for the institu-tion of the family brought the association into conflict with younger feminists, while the ICA felt that its history, its size and the scope of its activities were not being taken into account. Mamo McDonald, ICA President, responded from the ICA perspective:

> There was a Women's Movement started when most of them were not even thought of. In 1910, poverty was the over-riding problem especially in rural Ireland. Many people lived in hovels, the infant mortality rate was shocking and most rural women endured a life of drudgery, hardship and deprivation, with abysmally low status and opportunity. The pioneering UI addressed these problems and insti-gated programmes on nutrition, hygiene and childcare.
>
> ... On a practical level, ICA has helped liberate women by help-ing to get water and electricity in all rural homes, establishing income-generating projects for women, set up farm guesthouses, establish craft and services co-operatives and gain a voice on decision-making bodies. Within the guilds, ICA has provided mutual support and consciousness-raising among women. Members come together to discuss issues relevant to them, clarify their thinking, articulate their ideas and develop the capacity to make judgements. Those who have to cope with tragedy, worry or even the lesser human problems find consolation, loyalty, friendship and support.
>
> ... Those demanding contraception have made their point, but in 1910, poultry and not the pill was foremost in the minds of Irish countrywomen, and the ICA was there to assist. For all the publicity which our more militant sisters can generate, the ICA has a more revolutionary and direct bearing on the vast majority of Irish women.

On the same debate, Nell McCafferty commented wryly:

> For most of the twentieth century, rural women had to fetch water
> from the well to meet all their household needs. For some the night-
> mare still continues. ICA was instrumental in the 1960s in having
> water and electricity piped into country homes. It was, arguably, the
> most significant improvement in our lives since the foundation of the
> state. In the 1970s, however, the ICA's cheeky younger sisters, city
> born and bred, dismissed the association out of hand for failing to
> support the demand for legalised contraception. The young ones had
> not realised what the mature woman knows only too well from
> Tipperary to Addis Ababa — that we can live without sex, but not
> without water.[4]

1
BIRTH OF THE SOCIETY OF UNITED IRISHWOMEN

The Society of United Irishwomen was founded in 1910 and later changed its name to the Irish Countrywomen's Association. In Ireland at the time, women were idealised as homemakers and childbearers in rhetoric, yet in reality the constraints of long hours and family responsibilities precluded everything but the need to survive for most women. At the beginning of the century, life was tough in the Irish countryside. Housing conditions were poor, with most families living in one- or two-roomed cottages — cramped, squalid living conditions without light or water, privacy or independence. This inevitably brought great stress, as well as a high infant mortality rate, with large under-nourished families striving to make ends meet in unhygienic conditions. When serious illness struck, the stark choice was between the Poor-law hospital and the grave. This rural Ireland was crying out for improvement, and thus in 1910 the UI was founded, motivated by the ideal of 'better living' for rural women.

INSPIRATION

The introduction to Sarah McNamara's *Those Intrepid United Irishwomen* puts the ICA agenda very clearly:

> Myles na gCopaleen (Brian O'Nolan) once described the ICA as 'tweedy old dears with ascendancy notions'. This image may be shared by many people, but it is unfair and inaccurate. The ICA today is a thriving organisation which offers practical help to women in their everyday lives. It also gives them a shared identity and sense of comradeship. Although primarily a rural organisation, the ICA occupies itself with issues which concern women all over Ireland.[1]

It is unsurprising today to find women in the forefront of public life, politically active and campaigning for social change. Ninety years ago, this was not the case. Women occupied a low place in the hierarchy of a male-dominated society. Their function was to bear children: in law they were mere chattels. They were subservient, viewed as possessions, and dependent on men. The wives of wealthy men were engaged in an endless whirl of social functions, oblivious to the plight of their poorer sisters who struggled to survive against the bleak background of social division and deprivation.

UI members faced up to the challenges of rural life in the early twentieth century. They were firm believers in self help and community co-operation. Free of political or religious dogma, they were ecumenical long before ecumenism gained its current popularity. Many of the early leaders and members were from the upper classes, but the UI sought to be as class-free as possible.

For many women, UI and ICA offered an introduction to vocational training and an insight to cultural education. UI was founded, organised and promoted by the upper echelons of society and the ascendancy class, presumably because the ordinary Irish middle and poorer classes were mostly uneducated, somewhat down-trodden, with the inferiority complex which often accompanies poverty and lack of privilege. UI's success in raising the status of rural women is all the more meritorious, for that reason.[2]

Who were these women who founded the UI? They were mostly from the middle and upper classes — the classes which generally involved themselves in women's issues. They saw themselves as responsible not only to and for women but also to their country.[3]

In Ireland at the time, there was an enthusiasm for social change, an atmosphere of self-help, and the UI was an expression of this self-help and enthusiasm directed at rural life. These ascendancy women who founded the UI were patriotic in a practical way. Fr Finlay wrote in the preface to the UI's publication in 1911, 'What Ireland would become will be determined by what her people do for themselves — government has much power to hinder but small power to help the energies of a nation; it may second national effort but cannot create it.'[4]

An important source of inspiration was the address of George Russell (AE) to the AGM of the Irish Agricultural Organisation (IAOS) in December 1909, at a time when Ireland had come through great turmoil and was trying to recover its richness of life:[5]

To what extent it will do so depends on the stimulus and directions to the forces within it. What Ireland will become will depend on what her people would do for themselves. We must go on imagining better than the best we know — self-help above all other kinds of help, knowing that if we strove passionately after this righteousness all other kinds of help would be at our service. No country has grown to greatness mainly by the acts of some great ruler but by the aggregate activities of all its people. Therefore, every Irish community should make its own ideals and should work for them — we cannot build up a rural civilisation in Ireland without the aid of Irish women. Such a community would soon generate a passionate devotion to its own ideals and interests; it would kindle and quicken the intellect of every person in the community; it would create the atmosphere in which national genius would emerge and find opportunities for its activities. The clan ought to be the antechamber of the nation and the training for its statesmen. What opportunity leadership in the councils of such a rural community would give to the best minds! A vast network of living progressive organisations will cover Ireland, democratic in constitution and governed by the aristocracy of intellect and character.... We are dreaming of nothing impossible, a national purpose is the most unconquerable and victorious of all things on earth. Nations are not built so by the repetition of words but by the organising of intellect forces.

These passionate pleas did not fall on deaf ears, and so profound was the impression made on the women attending that AGM of the IAOS in 1909 that they came out of the meeting determined to embark immediately on the organising work. The UI was conceived following a conversation between Anita Lett of Davidstown and Mrs Alex Rudd of Clonhaston on the train journey home from Dublin to Enniscorthy. Anita Lett poured out the ideas and Mabel Rudd listened. Both agreed to do something positive and further plans were made, or as Rudd said with characteristic modesty 'before we reached Ferns she had talked me into it.'[6] On 8 May 1910 a meeting was called at Ballindara (Anita Lett's home) to organise a women's rural organisation. Horace Plunkett in welcoming the foundation of the UI looked to it to fulfil his most cherished ambition:

...the evolution of a healthy and progressive community life. The UI, dedicated to tackling relevant social issues, would show by example what could be achieved by self-help and organisation. Their work is particularly urgent in Ireland at the present time.[7]

Plunkett felt that the peaceful character of changes in agrarian ownership masked the revolutionary social change taking place in Ireland. In an agricultural country, the transfer of land from a few comparatively wealthy owners to a numerous body of relatively poor occupiers must have far-reaching political, economic and social consequences. 'The plain fact is that the whole structure of our rural society has been swept away on this by the power which upheld it for centuries.' To women's influence he looked 'for the brightening of the social sky in the grey dawn of peasant Ireland'.[8]

The UI's objective was to embrace the entire life of the rural community, in so far as those who wished to be good citizens had it within their power to improve their lives. UI planned to encourage women of all classes to meet on terms of perfect equality, although women of education, means and leisure would have to take the initiative and would very likely be continued in the leadership.

FOUNDING AIMS

At that Ballindara inaugural meeting, the aims of the proposed league of Irishwomen were presented by Anita Lett in a paper entitled 'The scheme explained'.[9] In her address she first outlined the reasons why such a body was needed in rural Ireland, arguing that if Irishwomen, regardless of class and creed, could unite for the 'common good of the country' much improvement could be made in rural life, the conditions of women greatly improved, emigration stemmed, and the whole country made more prosperous and its people more contented and happy.

She highlighted the deficiency of nursing and health care in rural areas (Anita herself was a nurse), and asked how many young lives had been sacrificed through ignorance of the most simple principles of nursing and nutrition. She stated that there were currently no nurses available for the poor, except maternity nurses who appeared to be generally distrusted. As a result, people who could ill afford to do so were forced to send specially for a doctor. Such a situation could be remedied by the provision of qualified nurses in rural districts and the education of women in health care matters. This would be a primary aim of the new organisation.

The next question she addressed was the rearing of children; many grew up delicate and vulnerable to tuberculosis because of inadequate care in childhood. She argued that many mothers were ignorant of the best way to care for and feed children, and she urged women to organise themselves and learn how best to serve the needs of their children. Another issue to be addressed in 'The Scheme' was that of education; people should be educated in ways that enhance not merely the productivity of rural life but also its quality. Lett stated that the dullness of rural life, the struggle for existence, often led to alcoholism, vagrancy and to an end in the asylum. Girls were constantly drifting to the cities because the country was dull and they were dazzled by the gayer life, but in her view a wholesome country life was far above a town one — as the girls generally found out too late. If the country, and conditions of life there, were made more attractive, its people would be more inclined to remain.

Another area in which the society interested itself was horticulture. Vegetables, with the exception of potatoes, cabbage and onions, were practically unknown to the bulk of the rural population. Fruit such as blackberries and rhubarb could be marketed co-operatively. Bee-keeping, poultry and egg production should also be encouraged, as should milk depots. This neglect of nutritious food was a disgrace, as vegetables and fruit could so easily be home-grown and this would also encourage people to have well-cultivated gardens.

'The scheme' also dealt with the way Irishwomen dressed. It was sad to see the miserable, shoddy clothes they wore, and Lett asked why they had abandoned their national costumes made of home-manufactured materials — which were more becoming, more durable and more respectable — in favour of inferior imported clothing 'made by sweated labour in Manchester, Birmingham and Germany'.

Anita Lett then went on to outline how the new organisation was to be governed. Branches were to be set up in every parish or group of parishes. These branches were to be affiliated to a county organisation, which would be connected to an All-Ireland branch to be established in Dublin. Although the organisation was to be a uniform body, local women would best know the needs of their districts and therefore would have a large degree of autonomy. She urged members to give generously of their time and imagination to the new organisation, adding that they must be united if they were to achieve their goals. Her paper ended on an optimistic and patriotic note:

> The model county (Wexford) has been a pioneer in many good works
> and there is no reason why it should not take the lead in this, but we

must go to work carefully and thoughtfully and we must not be discouraged if we do not see an immediate goal resulting. We want to build upon a sure and solid foundation and do work which will not only do good now but will bear fruit for future generations. We have the eyes of Irishwomen in all parts of Ireland on us, watching to see what we will do. So if we start this League, we should put our whole hearts into it and make it a success. In this way and this alone, can women bring the full force of their influence to bear on building up the future of Ireland. Let our motto be 'Faugh a ballagh' – and our politics as far as this League is concerned, should be summed up in one word: 'Ireland'.[10]

FIRST ACTIONS OF UI

Thus on 15 June 1910 in St. Aidan's Hall, Bree, Co. Wexford, the first branch of the UI was formed with the county families, farmers' wives and labourers' wives represented under the presidency of Lady Power. Rules were drawn up and the branch set to work to brighten the social life of the district by bringing the people together to a dance in the parish hall. A successful flower show was held at Bree, providing funds for working expenses.

The new society then asked to be allowed to send representatives to the AGM of IAOS in 1910, where they read a paper stating the aims and objectives of UI. One of the pioneer members, Ellice Pilkington (sister of Sir Thomas Esmonde, MP) has written: 'we stated our case very simply, saying that we were of the opinion that men could not make full use of their legislative and social organisations without our co-operation, any more than we could attain our ends without their assistance. We promised to help them if they would help us by encouraging us to start branches of our women's union close to their co-operative societies. A vote of assent was given to our proposal and we started at once to fulfil our part of the bargain.'[11]

AE moved the resolution that the UI be accepted within the co-operative movement. The Hon. A. Broderick seconded it and it was carried unanimously. Then the President of IAOS welcomed the UI and said they would give the society every support.[12]

By 30 November 1910, a provisional committee under Anita Lett's presidency was established, with: 'Mrs Alfred Hamilton (Vice-President), Miss Constance Pim (Hon. Sec.), the Countess of Fingall, The Hon. Mary Lawless, Mrs Stopford, Mrs Pilkington,

Mrs Stephen Spring-Rice, Mrs A.J. Crichton, Miss Helen Warren, Miss Helena Kelly, Miss Beatrice O'Brien, Miss Susan L. Mitchell, Miss Purdon. The treasurer was Mr E.A. Stopford'.[13]

Rules were drawn up based on those that had worked so well at Bree. An important resolution was passed to the effect that where societies dealing with the objectives of the UI were already in existence, they should be made use of as far as possible, so as to avoid conflict and overlapping.[14] After this it remained to find out whether the people they wished to help indeed wanted to be helped and above all, if they wanted to be helped by the UI.

This committee was empowered to undertake the organisation of branches. It held several meetings in Dublin and a great deal of individual work was done by members. Ellice Pilkington's own account of that organising is very interesting — and quite amazing when one remembers that it was 1910, taking into account the lack of transport and the time of year:

> On December 3rd I started for Dungloe, Co. Donegal, with a diminutive personal equipment, but with the best substitute that good-fellowship could give me — an organiser's bag and map lent by the secretary of IAOS, a thermos bottle and a passport in the old tongue given voluntarily by the president of the Gaelic League, Douglas Hyde. A herald in telegraphic form was dispatched before me by Fr Finlay. On arrival I found an independent capable community, a flourishing co-operative society with a manager who not only knew his work, but held the confidence of his people, a knitting industry in the hands of the women and girls, and all around them great possibilities for cottage gardening, dairying, and jam-making; a village hall for social meetings, a fine healthy race of men and women, bilingual, capable of enjoying intellectual pursuits and not ashamed to use their hands. And yet there was a silent sorrow here, for the curse of emigration was upon them. The young women and girls were slipping off one by one to the land of promise on the other side of the broad Atlantic, and only some of them came home again to listen mournfully to the sad sobbing of the sea on the dreary shore. The women did not speak to me of this but the men did.
>
> A meeting was held in the newly-opened village hall, where I gave the message the UI had sent me to deliver. The proposal to start a branch of the UI was welcomed enthusiastically and the men promised to safeguard the interest of the sister society and free the

women from the oppression of the 'truck' system. Members were elected to act on a committee and within a week the officers of this committee were appointed.

I left on December the 6th with these encouraging words in my ears: 'A good honest movement like this is sure to succeed.'[15]

Less than a year later, in 1911, there was a busy branch of the UI with over 200 members in Dungloe; two instructresses under the home improvement scheme were at work (dealing with household economy, home dairying and cottage gardening); the village hall was the centre for meetings of all kinds.

On 6 December, Anita Lett formed a second branch of the UI in Co. Wexford at Davidstown. And again Ellice Pilkington writes:

On the 7th and 8th I visited Oylegate and Glenbrien, and also Bree, where I was sent by the Executive committee to thank the women of Bree for the pioneer work they had done and to study the methods of their branch.

In January and February I visited Wicklow and Wexford and inaugurated branches at Oylegate, Glenbrien and Coolgreany.

Co. Wexford is admirably suited to, and quite ready for, branches of the UI in consequence of the progressive character of the people, their spirit of enterprise and their practical ability to create societies of their own, for their own purposes and avail themselves of every facility put at their disposal by the Department of Agriculture and IAOS.

On February 19th I started on a tour through Waterford, Tipperary, Cork and Clare, the results of which the future will show. At Kilkee I found a people with great advantages at their disposal, but needing the stimulus of the UI to induce them to make use of them. The hospitality of the people, from the parish priest to my hostess at the hotel, was unbounded. The problems of education, domestic economy and public health, which they will have to work upon, are such as to interest any body of capable women, to say nothing of the sturdy little group of patriots I left behind me in Kilkee Branch.

So far I have skimmed over the ground the UI has broken up. The ploughing, sowing and reaping rests with the branch members. I have no doubt that they will make full use of their committees for dealing with their local concerns.

> We had now proved that we were wanted, and could be useful in the
> country districts; the next task was to consolidate our central organisa-
> tion and frame it on the lines that would be permanent and practical.[16]

This is the background to the foundation of the UI in 1910. The
fact that it is still in existence ninety years later is testimony to the
solid foundations given it by the pioneering founder members.
Their hope that it would be 'permanent and practical' has been
achieved repeatedly, as is evident from the archival material of the
association.

MOTIVATION AND MOTTO

The name 'The Society of United Irishwomen' was the inspiration
of Susan Mitchell, founder member of UI and also sub-editor of the
Irish Homestead, the organ of the IAOS. Every assistance was
given to UI by the IAOS, who undertook to draw up a constitution
and to provide an office at their headquarters in Plunkett House to
begin with. However, to quote Sir Horace Plunkett, 'The United
Irishwomen are not a branch or department of the IAOS; they are
an independent association, but they come in to complete our work
at the point where we believe it to be at once most important and
most imperfect.'[17]

'The evolution of a healthy and progressive community life' —
what a task in 1910! No wonder the men had despaired of their
'better farming' and 'better business' alone bringing it about.
Nothing but a woman's dauntless spirit, a cause to which she was
utterly committed, and a programme dealing directly with needs as
she met them, could have made these pioneering countrywomen
confront the rural problems of the day. Facing prejudice of every
kind, these women succeeded under their chosen banner, 'Deeds
not Words'.

EXPANDING THE ROLE OF WOMEN

The founding members of the UI were predominantly middle class
Protestant women. Part of the reason lay in the general social
expectation that middle class women would direct their attentions
towards the less fortunate for the general benefit of both parties.
Thus Alma Gray, advising students at Alexandra College (a considerable number of UI members were Alexandra College educated)
on the duties of privilege, declared:

Practically I think every woman who has any margin of time or money to spare should complete her life by adding to her private duties the noble effort to advance God's kingdom beyond the bounds of her home ... even greater in importance is the strengthening and uplifting of our own personal character, so that we may fulfil the end to our creation, and be a help and blessing to those who are daily dependent on our love, care and companionship.[18]

Middle class women also had greater freedom to participate in activities beyond the strictly domestic. They had the time and were educated to see the needs of those around them. The stories of eight similar women who agitated for educational and social reform and the nationalist cause, changing the course of Irish history, are told by Cullen and Luddy in *Women, Power and Consciousness* where they state, 'The personal circumstances of all allowed them a freedom of action not shared by most Irish women. For most of their activist lives none of these women were encumbered by family responsibilities and seven of them were financially independent and intellectually independent. Their work was mostly class based, often with the explicit understanding that a social superior had a duty to help a social inferior.'[19]

It was from this background that most of the UI founder members originated. Ellice Pilkington was given the office of national organiser, while a certain number of ladies resident in or near Dublin undertook research and to procure information for the use of organisers — work which proved most valuable.

UI's VISION

Ellice Pilkington outlined the work of the UI under three headings:[20] 'Agriculture and Industries, Domestic Economy, and Social and Intellectual Development'.

 • In the field of agriculture and industries, the work of the UI was to encourage the development of the poultry industry, pig rearing and other industries which fell within the domain of women. Home dairying was also to be improved with the object of ensuring an adequate milk supply in rural districts. The UI would also encourage farmers to take a businesslike approach to farming by making use of agricultural shows, and would encourage cottage-gardening, beekeeping and even cider making. She elaborated on how women could revive cottage industries, such as basket-making, rush-plaiting, mat and hat making, embroidery, dressmaking, spinning, weaving, etc.

♦ Domestic economy involved raising the standard of home comfort. The UI would encourage personal neatness, thrift, healthy cooking and tidiness in the home. It would work with the Women's National Health Association to educate women on hygiene in the home and on health matters. Ellice also reiterated the UI's commitment to tackling the problem of rural nursing. Youth education would also be a concern of the UI, with particular emphasis on the education of girls — they should learn the value of work, pride in good work, and should be fully trained for professions.

♦ The social and intellectual brief of the society was of paramount importance. She acknowledged that emigration from the land was due to the monotony and dullness of country life as much as to economic necessity. The UI would seek to make country life more enjoyable by making good use of village halls for dances, lectures, concerts and debates. Libraries would be established, with Ellice's assurance that unsuitable literature would be eliminated. Music and art were two underdeveloped areas which would be given attention.

UI considered it essential that women in Ireland should make their wishes known, and felt that they had somewhat neglected their own interests by not putting them before the public more prominently. For this reason, they intended to seek improved representation on public bodies in order to make their point of view known in public affairs.

We have some women poor law guardians, for instance, but we want more of them; we want our voice heard when questions dealing with sanitation and public health are discussed by district and county council, and when schemes for agricultural improvement are considered by their committees; in short we want to benefit as much as men by the facilities offered us by our local government and by public departments. Patriotism for women is a thing of deeds, not words — it must be part of their daily lives. The most magnificent theories of men and the constructive work that they do cannot create national prosperity if the women do not help them in domestic details.

Ellice spoke for all the UI when she concluded:

We are tired of seeing our sons die in foreign countries because they are too poor to live in Ireland. We are maddened by the sad look in the eyes of the returned Irish-American girl who hates the discomfort of her Irish home. We are prematurely aged by too much hard, lonely work. We are sorry for our old people to whom we cannot give the care old age deserves. We are frightened by disease. We dread the horrors of the lunatic asylums. We are now awake to the fact that relief from all these troubles will only come to us from within ourselves. We must band together, join hands and hearts and work not half-heartedly and in sorrow but joyfully, at times merrily; ever looking to where the sun is breaking through the cloud. We have a great inheritance of youth and hope, and we have only to put out our hands to take it and to pass it on to our children when our day's work is done.

This was the vision of the UI at its foundation in 1910 — how much of that vision has been achieved in the ninety years since? Health, education, employment, economy and culture have all been immensely improved, yet 90 per cent of care-giving work is still done by women. Childcare facilities are poor. Women make up 40 per cent of the labour force, yet they receive only 65 per cent of the male wage. In positions of power, just 12 per cent of legislators are women.

CONSTITUTION AND RULES

The original constitution of the UI was drawn up in 1910. The Society consisted of a central union based in Dublin, and branches, the whole governed by an Executive Committee. The work of the central union was to organise the women of Ireland by the foundation of branches similar to those founded successfully by IAOS to organise the men. Branches were formed in rural districts, open to all the women in the neighbourhood, and were governed by a committee composed of the President, Vice-President, honorary treasurer, honorary secretary and twelve members. Each branch paid an affiliation fee to the central union of 5s. and each member of a branch paid a subscription of 6d. to her branch. The central union would serve also as a link between the branches when so formed. There were also individual members who joined the central union after being proposed and seconded by existing members and elected by a majority of votes at a meeting of the Executive Committee. Their annual subscription was 2s. 6d.

The constitution of UI was printed in 1911, and revised in 1913 as the rules of the UI. For example:

> Rule 4: 'The objects of the Society should be to organise women in the rural districts of Ireland for the improvement and brightening of the conditions of rural life, including domestic economy, sanitation and social and economic development, by doing all things necessary or expedient for the accomplishment of its objects.'
>
> Rule 7: 'Applicants for Membership must be Irish (a) by birth or marriage to an Irishman, and (b) must be naturalised as such by having their homes in Ireland.'
>
> Rule 49: 'Irrelevant Subjects — No question of party politics or sectarian discussion should be raised, nor shall any resolution which deals with irrelevant subjects be proposed at a General or Committee meeting of the Society.'

The 1990 constitution of the ICA retains similar clauses regarding the objectives of the association and what may be discussed at meetings.

The original programme included 'raising the standard of home life and comfort; improving the health of the rural population; creating and advancing women's home and agricultural pursuits (cookery, needlework, poultry, gardening, bee-keeping, goat keeping, cheese-making); encouraging healthy amusements such as dancing and games; initiating lectures and demonstrations in connection with women's work and interests; developing women's societies on co-operative lines such as provident and trading societies.' In practice, this involved training nurses, organising milk depots, improving the breeding of goats, organising nurses on remote island communities, encouraging market gardening and fresh egg production, charity dances to finance the treatment of sick children and negotiation with DATI (Department of Agriculture and Technical Instruction) to employ instructresses to provide practical teaching. UI left few aspects of rural life untouched.

BACKGROUND TO THE FOUNDATION OF UI

IRELAND IN 1910

Ireland on the eve of the twentieth century had a population of 4.5 million with 66 per cent in rural areas, mostly existing through farming, living as tenants on land often owned by absentee land-lords. Outside of the Belfast area, Ireland had few industries and Irish people had to emigrate to find employment. Agriculture was the most important industry in Ireland.

Out of a population of 5,000,000 people, 3,000,000 were directly involved in farming and another 1,000,000 were involved in servicing the farming community by processing or transporting their produce or supplying the farmer's needs. 'That made the whole question of land a matter of vital importance to everyone in the country.'[21]

Griffith's valuation of Ireland found that almost all the land belonged to 10,000 individuals, with some having enormous tracts of land and others a few hundred acres. Landlords divided their estates into farms and let them out to tenant farmers for a fixed annual rent. This rent was the source of the landlord's wealth. There were 600,000 tenant farmers with 30,000 of these rented farms containing over 100 acres. The majority of Irish farms were much smaller — on average between 15 and 50 acres. These smaller farms were run by the family with little outside help, apart from that provided by neighbours at harvest time. The men worked in the fields, ploughing, sowing and tending the animals. The women cooked, milked the cows, raised poultry and pigs, saved the turf and helped with other work when needed. In 1870 there were about 100,000 farmers with less than fifteen acres of land. These were the poorest section of the farming community. They were to be found in every part of Ireland but were most numerous in the western seaboard counties from Donegal to Cork. They lived in one- or two-roomed cottages, often with little furniture and an earthen floor that was difficult to keep dry. In general, they had a cow or two, a few pigs and chickens and grew mainly oats and potatoes. Because their farms were so small, they could not grow enough to feed themselves and also pay a rent to their landlord.

The poorest section of Irish rural society was made up of labourers. They had no land of their own but lived on the wages they earned working for landlords or bigger farmers.

The poverty of these people led to considerable unrest. In an attempt to stop this and to improve living standards, the govern-ment set up the Congested Districts Board (CDB) in 1893. Congested districts were areas where, because land was bad and farms small, there were too many people trying to make a living from farming alone. These areas were mostly in the west.

VOLUNTARY MOVEMENT

In 1889, Horace Plunkett founded his first co-operative society in Doneraile, to enable farmers to process their own produce, buy seeds in bulk, set high standards of quality and sell their products at the best prices. The movement spread, and in 1894 Plunkett formed the Irish Agricultural Organisation Society (IAOS) to co-ordinate the work of the local societies. The following year he launched a newspaper, the *Irish Homestead*, to spread his message.

IAOS was founded to bring new life and hope to the Irish countryside, with the slogan 'better farming, better business and better living'. Its aim was to strive for a higher standard of material comfort and physical well-being in the country home, a more advanced agricultural economy and a social existence in greater harmony with the intellect and the temperament of the Irish people.

This was followed by the setting up of the Department of Agriculture and Technical Instruction (DATI) in 1899 with Horace Plunkett as head.

WOMEN IN 1910

Throughout Europe, women began to emerge on the political stage in the early years of the twentieth century. Better education and job opportunities gave them confidence, while the growth of democratic ideas led them to demand equal citizenship with men.

> A woman's strength was commonly equated with her ability to put up with circumstances rather than alter them. The fact that husbands often tended to be considerably older than their wives further diminished the control which women exerted in their homes. However, women managed farms when husbands died while others ran hospitals and schools.[22]

Not all women accepted society's view that their only role was as wives and mothers:

♦ Many Irish women escaped through emigration. In other countries, emigration was more common among men than women, but men and women left Ireland in equal numbers.

♦ Other women found an outlet for their energies through voluntary work. They set up orphanages, visited prisons and opened refuges for prostitutes. Among Protestants, this kind of work was done by middle class married women, but among Catholics it gradually came to be done mainly by nuns.

♦ The number of nuns grew rapidly from 1850. It is possible that some able women saw the life of a nun as chance to build an independent existence for themselves. Many ran schools and hospitals with a freedom which would have been impossible had they been lay women.

EARLY WOMEN'S MOVEMENTS

Most of the pioneers of the women's movement were middle-class Protestants, who were probably better off and had contacts with similar movements in Britain. Isabella Tod in Belfast and Anna Haslam in Dublin led the Irish wing of a campaign to change the law on property rights. This campaign involved women in political activity and increased their awareness of the importance of voting. In 1876 Haslam and her husband founded the Irish Women's Suffrage and Local Government Association (IWSLGA). Around the same time a campaign began to improve education for women; one of the leaders of this movement was Anne Jellico who was responsible for establishing Alexandra College in 1866. After 1900, women's movements concentrated on demanding the right to vote.

In 1900, Maud Gonne founded Inighne na hÉireann, a nationalist organisation for women. Traditionally, women had been excluded from membership of nationalist organisations such as the Irish Republican Brotherhood (IRB). Inighne na hÉireann ran 'buy Irish' campaigns, held free classes for children in Irish, history and music, organised céilí and staged plays. Their first priority was the settlement of the national question rather than women's suffrage and their newspaper *Bean na hÉireann* was the first women's newspaper in Ireland.

In 1914, women nationalists set up their own organisation, Cumann na mBan, to complement the Irish Volunteers set up in 1913. In 1915 Inighne na hÉireann amalgamated with the new organisation so that Cumann na mBan became a wider movement.

The UI was formed, therefore, at a time when there was a revolution in land ownership, the beginning of a national quest for Irish language and culture, launch of the trade union movement, and tensions between Home Rulers and Unionists. Some people were involved in all of these movements but the vast majority of Irish women were concerned with their own survival and that of their families. With bare subsistence rather than any reasonable standard of living, a woman's dilemma was either emigration or a life of drudgery and hard work if she married.

2
THE EARLY YEARS

UI's FIRST TEN YEARS

The first detailed minute book of the association covering the years up to 1921,[1] gives a fascinating insight into the formative decade of UI. The very first statement of accounts, covering the period from 3 December 1910 to 31 December 1911, shows that there were 17 branches and 156 individual subscriptions, made up of 64 married women (each using her husband's name), 81 unmarried women with 9 titled women and 2 French women. It also shows that UI obtained funding that year of £800 — £500 from Pembroke Trust Charities Fund, £100 from Stanley Cochrane, £100 per Helen Warren and £100 anonymous.

Underlying all of UI's actions to achieve 'better living' was the threat of lack of funds — it depended on voluntary donations which were so unreliable that the organisers, whose numbers ranged from one to six depending on funds, were always on temporary notice.

'It was decided that the Organisers should be offered 2d. a mile for bicycle, and that they should travel 2nd. class from October to March, 3rd. class during the summer months.'[2] The most difficult challenge was to maximise funding, and every conceivable avenue was exhausted, as the Executive pursued development grants and donations to supplement the meagre amounts raised by the branches. During the first three years, funding went from £800 in 1911 to £731 4s 4d in 1912 and to £1249 5s 11d in 1913, but then in 1914 dropped to £244 12s 6d. It was then that UI was successful in getting funding from the Carnegie Trust over five years — £500 per year for three years, £300 the next year and then £200 the last year. The Congested Districts Board was also approached and contributed £41 13s 4d in 1914 and £103 in 1915 towards the organiser's expenses in Connemara following a very interesting report of Anita Lett's visit.

Mrs Lett gave a most interesting report of what she had seen and done. The islands are Lettermullen, Gorumna and Lettermore. She considered there was a great need for both an Irish-speaking instructress and a midwife on the islands. Industries to teach include basket-making, salting of fish, gardening, cocoa, etc. No milk in winter. Suggested two goats might be supplied to each of the five schools. Shopkeepers good to the people. No suitable place for midwife or instructress to live but Mrs Lett found the four walls of an unfinished house close to the causeway connecting the islands. She bought the house, but thinks it would take £100 to do it up. She said that Sir Roger Casement had written saying that Dr Douglas Hyde was going to the islands with three others on 19th instant and it was proposed that the UI should use that opportunity to inform CDB of all they had achieved.[3]

Other examples of fundraising attempts appear regularly in those early minute books. For example in February 1914 there were two Drawing-Room Meetings, one arranged by Lady Fingall and the other at the Irish Literary Society in London — the London committee having consented to pay expenses. It was also suggested that Lady Fingall go to the USA for funding and to promote the ideals of UI, though this proposed journey never materialised.

It was very difficult for the UI to plan as they never knew whether funds would be available, although Horace Plunkett advised them to do the job and money would follow. This advice was something the Executive could not carry out. Despite encouraging reports from two instructresses, for example, the UI was unable to formalise their employment. One instructress, Miss Hipwell said that, 'the branches took great interest in one another. Twenty-four gardens had been started, and the girls were keenly interested in the sewing classes. The young people get up the entertainment themselves.' Miss Hipwell had not had much opportunity of improving her Irish though she was willing to take a course during her holidays. Lady Arnott and Miss Spring-Rice expressed their willingness to subscribe £1 if necessary towards her board at the Irish College. In another item 'Miss Mangan reported that good progress was being made in sewing, cookery and gardening. In five or six villages the people got their own seeds this year. The sewing classes were mostly attended by girls from 14–30 but the older women came too. The girls made their own underclothing.' Nonetheless, whilst the committee was much pleased with these reports, they could only keep the instructresses on by the month.[4]

The Executive was stringent in its attitude to the UI's finances. In 1914 they were prepared to take legal action against a member who refused to produce a receipt for a thirty pound lodgement she had made. Financial constraints proved debilitating in that they diluted the campaigns to employ rural instructresses on a permanent basis, which led Fr Finlay to encourage the women to form credit unions to place the Society on a firmer business footing. Despite Plunkett's references to the female exclusiveness of better living, these women were also active on the business side — women's energies, they felt, should be directed towards the formation of agricultural industries and 'schemes of a productive rather than a purely educative nature'.

At one of the earlier meetings Anita Lett (at the time Vice-President of the Wexford Farmers Association) discussed the possibility of allowing women on Public Authority committees without having to go through the process of election. She felt that under current statutory procedures, women would not attract enough support to be elected. She asked that women be nominated directly to positions on important decision-making bodies. However, Mr J. Hickey of Enniscorthy who had an interest in the co-operative movement and politics disagreed. He told the meeting it would be out of the question for female members to sit on public bodies without being democratically elected in the same manner as everyone else. This desire to expand the role of women in rural Ireland was also reflected in attempts to push for the election of women as Poor Law Guardians, and to achieve representation on county agricultural boards and the All Ireland Farmers Convention. Their success in these areas, however, was limited. The UI, given the prevailing atmosphere of the time, was perhaps unwilling to arouse the considerable resistance there would have been to women taking on greater roles in public life and the association, as it evolved, carved out a more limited sphere for itself.

PUBLICITY

Browsing through that first minute book it is interesting to see how important it was to UI to keep its members informed — in the first year's accounts, there is an entry of '£3 6s 7d subscription to *The Irish Homestead* (Edited by AE, with Susan Mitchell sub-editor)' for distribution to the branches. It had then the largest circulation of any agricultural paper in Ireland. Then there were the library facilities from Plunkett House, with branches paying an annual subscription of 10/— which would entitle them to thirty books at a time for two to four months, all books bearing a UI bookplate on the cover. Up to January 1914, books were censored by Fr Finlay who then became too occupied. A Miss Kelly and a Mrs O'Connell, UI members, suggested that they could judge of their suitability. Their offer was not accepted and a Fr Sherwin consented to supervise the library books in future. Research of the minutes does not make it clear whether this censorship of books for UI members was self-imposed or an IAOS regulation.

The immediate response of the press to the foundation of UI was generally positive. Sarah McNamara in *Those Intrepid United Irishwomen* deals with this subject:

> The *Homestead* was particularly supportive; it compared the UI to the United Irishmen of the eighteenth century. It said that while the United Irishmen wanted to make Ireland free, the UI wanted to make Ireland happy. This clearly defined the non-political role of the UI. The *Homestead* said that the function of the UI was to contribute to the advancement of social and domestic life in rural Ireland. In doing so, the newspaper admitted that the organisation might meet some opposition: 'We have the slightest fear of feminist movements, a country where women have no influence gets along very badly. Men's movements, no matter how successful are only skeletons, unless intelligent womanhood mingles with them.' (*Enniscorthy Guardian* and the *Echo*, 11 June 1910, quoting the *Homestead*.)[5]

The newspaper went on to declare that when women's interests are limited to household affairs, their lives become barren and confined. The involvement of women in social movements would not only enhance the intellectual and social life of the home but would add to social and economic reform in the country as a whole. The *Homestead* concluded that the co-operative movement could only do so much on its own. It needed the active involvement of women and it urged its female readers to follow Mrs Lett and her colleagues.

It was inevitable that a programme so ambitious should provoke criticism if it did not actually arouse opposition. Horace Plunkett noted that it had been objected, by those who have a very imperfect knowledge of the scope and aim of this new movement, that it meant the launching of a superfluous organisation upon the already overcrowded waterways of Irish social service. Also the name UI is said to have given the impression in some quarters that a political motive lurked behind the declared objects of the association, which were purely social and economic.

In the 18 March 1911 issue of the *Irish Homestead*, the UI was taken to task by a correspondent for opting for a short training scheme for cottage nurses instead of the more intense one lasting three years. They chose one which was practical and thorough, to address the immediate needs of the countryside. The society was accused of trespassing on the work of Women's National Health Association (WNHA), and in order to allay any fears of duplication a special conference was held on 12 April 1911, with Lady Aberdeen present to discuss difficulties if any existed between the UI and WNHA. The UI was very conscious of not duplicating the good work already being done by the WNHA but rather sought to complement their work.

This criticism was answered in 1911 by the publication of *The United Irishwomen, their Place, Work and Ideals* by Horace Plunkett, Ellice Pilkington and AE with a preface by Rev. T.A. Finlay. Pilkington states:

> The very first day we appeared in public we were attacked on account of our want of training as nurses. The attack was, perhaps, justified because the training of most of us only amounted to this — some of us were mothers, some of us had devoted our lives to the nursing of aged relatives, some of us had seen men die in hospitals during war, and others were beginning lives in which they would be likely to meet with similar experiences. Whatever our lack of skill might be, we all knew what we intended to do and were determined to do it and therefore we never doubted but that we should find the way and secure the willing services of those who possessed the training that we lacked.

One of the first activities of the new organisation at Bree was the holding of a Flower and Industrial Show in August 1910. The show was well attended and the theme of the event was 'the welfare of the people'. The *Enniscorthy Echo* described how people of different classes mixed freely at the show: 'The distinctions of class were forgotten or if remembered, remembered as a necessary link in the social chain lacking one of which, the whole would be incomplete.'[6]

Bean na hÉireann, the newspaper of Inighne na hÉireann, also responded positively to the new organisation, seeing it as a broad body committed to dealing with relevant social ills. The women's newspaper was quick to dispel any notions that the UI was an elite exclusive group: 'The UI do not propose to establish committees of wealthy and patronising ladies ... who will award prizes for the best baked cake of soda bread ... the UI 's committees will be composed of people who want things reformed in their districts.'

Bean na hÉireann argued that the UI would instil a sense of pride and a commitment to the idea of self-help in rural communities. Country people had been patronised and spoon-fed for too long and as a result had become unable to help themselves. The newspaper stated that the UI sought to shake people out of this complacency. They would do so by urging them to take pride in their homes and districts. The UI would help rural people to look to their own resources and become less dependent on the state. *Bean na hÉireann* emphasised the fact that the UI, although a women's organisation, sought to advance the lives of both men and women. It criticised the exclusiveness of male bodies which excluded women from functions and establishments. In contrast, the UI would seek to be an all-encompassing organisation: 'They hope to enter the co-operative movement and work with men ... for the spiritual and material uplifting of Ireland. The UI will not withhold any interest that arises in connection with their movement from the men.'[7]

AE also heralded the new movement. In 'Ideals of the New Rural Society' he argued that rural development could only come about if rural people themselves worked collectively for a better future. He attacked what he saw as the cynical attitude of many Irish people, maintaining that this negativity helped perpetuate Irish national pessimism and self-doubt. It hindered progress and kept the country in a state of mediocrity. He believed that any change in the condition of rural life could not be effected without the help of Irishwomen. The problems facing women in rural Ireland should not be ignored or considered to be of less importance than those facing the wider rural community: 'It will help life little if we have the methods of the twentieth century in the fields, and those of the fifth century in the home.'[8]

Ellice Pilkington, UI's first organiser, claimed that the UI had been pushed into print prematurely with the publication of *The United Irishwomen — Their Place, Work and Ideals*. This pamphlet may have been in response to criticism of the UI. Indeed Mrs Lett and her colleagues did encounter much opposition to their efforts to build up the UI. Opposition to the involvement of women in public affairs was entrenched. In 1911, the parish priest of Ventry, Co. Kerry, remarked that 'a sure sign of the break-up of the planet was when women took to leaving their homes and talking in public.'[9]

The editor of the *Irish Homestead*, in his leader column on 25 November 1911, said that he took more pride in the fact that he helped the formation of the UI in some measure than in any other thing he had done since he began to write about building up a rural civilisation:

> This movement quietly as it has begun, would be recognised by historians in later years as marking a most psychological change in Irish nationality. Women would bring about the production of fine human beings while men would bring the production of national wealth ... women would restore national sanity and balance.

Publicity was important to UI, and one priority was the publication of articles on UI activities, in its own journal. On 1 May 1912 *The United Irishwomen*, a journal for Irish countrywomen, was launched. The first page states the objects of the society, also that the journal would be issued quarterly at a subscription of sixpence per annum, post free. The contents of that first publication were as follows:

1. UI — What they are and what they want to do
2. The Return of the Spiral, by Standish O'Grady
3. Hymn to the Daughters of Ireland
4. Irish poems
5. Review of Irish books, by Ethel Goddard Davidson
6. The Abbey Theatre
7. The work of the UI branches

The UI planned to use the magazine as a means of advertising the society while at the same time keeping its members informed. Hopes were high among this small dedicated band of women that regular publications would increase interest in the UI and that their numbers would increase accordingly. There was no shortage of enthusiasm or talent among these early pioneers and the success of their quarterly journal prompted them to publish monthly, changing the title to *The Irishwoman*. However, the monthly publication was short-lived, mainly due to war abroad and unrest at home.

In 1914, publication was suspended 'owing to the present unrest and the consequent impossibility of getting advertisements.'[10] Despite two attempts to keep it afloat, one by removing the Gaelic name from the cover to give it a wider appeal and secondly the offer by Executive members to contribute £5 each, publication was never resumed after the 1914-1918 war. However, from 1914 onwards the UI were regular contributors to the *Irish Homestead*.

While contributing to the *Irish Homestead*, the society was busy writing articles for publication in the country newspapers 'with the least political bias'. But the expense of having such articles typed and circulated to thirty papers was an insurmountable stumbling block and an appeal to editors to help with typing costs fell on deaf ears. The literary sub-committee was finally dissolved, having first passed the articles collected to the *Irish Homestead*.

Those Intrepid United Irishwomen quotes an article published in 1913:

> The aims of the UI are very wide and they may be summed up in one word — Patriotism — that is to say true patriotism, clear-eyed enough to recognise the national faults and failings and determined to overcome them and to replace them by national virtues. The UI mean to drive dirt, drink and thriftlessness from the country and to replace them by cleanliness, sobriety and self-respect. They aim at the rearing of a race of men and women whose beauty and strength will be in accord with the beauty of their native land and whose moral qualities shall fit them for true happiness. How? The rearing of the race is woman's business. UI will not attain their ideal unless all the women in the country join hands and say 'We will have it so and nothing will stop us'. If they do that, nothing will stop them. But, every single woman in Ireland must take her share in the work. UI cannot spare any of them. Rich or poor, Catholic or Protestant, Unionist or Home Ruler, each holds in her hand some gift that is necessary for the building of the race, and UI are out to see that no gift is lost through ignorance or apathy. They want Irish women to fight a more tremendous battle than men ever waged, for the glory of God and the honour of Erin.

Never losing sight of the value of the printed word, the UI was quick to accept when in 1919 the *Farmers' Gazette* placed space at its disposal for news and reports. Mrs Dermod O'Brien was appointed the first editor and this became the official organ of the ICA until the *Farmers' Gazette* ceased publication in 1963. The difficulty of obtaining a steady flow of UI news was then, as now, often acute, but increased activities together with increased membership must have considerably eased the lot of more recent editors.

1925 saw the publication of another UI magazine, again with a rather short life, although the Executive Committee expressed satisfaction with the first issue and even appointed paid assistance to the editor, Nora Reddin.[11]

In 1945 yet another effort was made to bring out a magazine, *The Irish Countrywoman*. This in fact never saw publication, but in the 1960s the ICA used the same title for its monthly magazine. It was not until 1954 that the association took its courage in both hands and produced an annual simply called *Ár Leabhar Féin* — Our Book — containing articles, stories, poems, drawings, photographs and progress reports on the working of the ICA. The annual went from strength to strength and became the means of encouraging members to write not only for their own magazine but also for other periodicals. From 1959, a second publication, *An Grianán News Quarterly*, kept the members in touch with the activities of the ICA college. The *Irish Countrywoman*, published monthly, took the place of *An Grianán News Quarterly*, the ICA notes in the *Farmers' Gazette* and the annual yearbook. ICA activities are freely reported in the national and provincial papers, and Radio Éireann was another valuable medium of publicity since 1935 when the UI became ICA. Members have taken part in feature programmes such as *Field and Farmhouse* and *Farmers' Forum* as well as being heard on news reports, *Provincial News Roundup, Who's News and Down the Country.*

THE SUFFRAGETTE MOVEMENT

The UI was founded against the background of increased migration from the land and intense poverty in rural Ireland. The last two decades of the nineteenth century had witnessed a revolution in Ireland — the Land League and the Land war causing the political mobilisation of agrarian unrest. Despite advances by Irish tenants in the late nineteenth century, life in rural Ireland remained one of hardship. Women were expected not to take an active role in political or national events. Indeed, they were not able even to vote. The 1898

Local Government Act did grant women the vote in local elections, but not in general elections. There were neither women's organisations nor bodies dealing with women's issues, with the exception of the Irish Women's Suffrage and Local Government Association. By 1910, however, other suffrage societies had been formed.

♦ In 1876, the Irish Women's Suffrage and Local Government Association was the first to mobilise support for women's rights to full citizenship.

♦ Then the Ladies Land League highlighted the radical potential of women activists in 1881/1882.

♦ In 1901 Inighne na hÉireann was formed to lobby for the vote for women and independence for Ireland, and published a newspaper, *Bean na hÉireann*.

♦ In 1902, the Women's Graduates Association was formed to campaign for access to higher education.

♦ In 1908, the Irish Women's Franchise League was set up, followed in 1911 by the Irish Women's Suffrage Federation.

The issue of votes for women came to the fore in 1910–12. Several bills to give the vote to women were introduced at Westminster but all were defeated because of disagreement within the political parties.

SITUATION OF WOMEN

Despite the vigorous activities of the various women's associations at the beginning of the century, according to Clear[12] the fundamental aspect of women's oppression had not been addressed — issues such as a woman's status in the family, unpaid labour in the home and lack of control over her body — and therefore there was no real change in the attitudes of a male-dominated society.

The life of an Irish countrywoman was characterised by hardship and deprivation. In fact, she was treated little better than a servant. Her day was spent feeding farm animals, doing physically hard farm work — footing turf, gathering seaweed, carrying large burdens — as well as preparing meals, washing, cleaning and keeping house with no water or electricity. It was customary for men to be fed first, and there was often little food left, resulting in many women being undernourished. In addition, recreational and social outlets for rural women were limited. In an article in *Bean na hÉireann* the situation of an Irish countrywoman is depicted:

The Irish girl flees the country because she knows that if she remains she will have to work as hard as any man; that she will have no gaiety in her free hours and that she will become an old woman before she is thirty.

The agenda for UI in 1910 was to urge the women of Ireland to work together to achieve better living conditions for all.

It is essential to Ireland that her rural population should be strong, healthy, and active. It must remain on the land, happily occupied, well employed, socially and intellectually developed. Here is permanent work for women to do and UI is the organisation best qualified to help them. We had no special training for doing what we intended to do and we, none of us, aspired to reform society or preach any gospel but that of domestic economy, good comradeship and truth.[13]

REGISTRATION AS A BENEVOLENT SOCIETY

Under the Friendly Society Act of 1896, UI became Registered Benevolent Society, no. 1230. The date of establishment of the society was given as 30 November 1910, and the date of registry as 8 May 1911. The trustees were Lady Arnott of 12, Merrion Square, Dublin, Wilfred Fitzgerald, esq. of 13, Raglan Road, Dublin and Harold Barbour, esq. of Dunmurry, Co. Antrim. The rules provided that all officials having charge of monies etc. should provide such security as the Executive committee deemed adequate. Constance Pim was honorary secretary and E.A. Stopford, treasurer. H.F. Norman, assistant secretary of IAOS, pointed out to Constance Pim that registration under the Friendly Society Act did not in itself give a society power to trade (This problem led eventually to the establishment of Country Markets Ltd. in 1947), and that an advantage of the Friendly Society Act was that it gave a society the possibility of appointing some person to represent it in legal action. This had for practical purposes the effect of legal incorporation.[14]

REGULARITY OF ATTENDANCE AT MEETINGS

Regular meetings setting sub-committees for specific issues were seen to be important. Executive members were asked to resign if they failed to attend three consecutive meetings. This was strictly enforced. Even at times of national unrest the Executive refused to rescind this rule except for the period of the 1914–18 war.

An important event occurred when Anita Lett was replaced by
Lady Fingall as President in 1913, but unfortunately the relevant
minute book is not available. One version of the event was given by
Sarah McNamara:

> In 1913, Anita Lett broke her leg from a fall from a horse. When she
> returned to the Executive Committee, she found that Lady Fingall had
> been installed as Chairman. There was a heated discussion during
> which Mrs Lett reportedly walked out. She had the support of the
> IAOS but this was not enough. Lady Fingall remained President of UI
> for the next thirty years.[15]

The *Irish Homestead* stated that Lett resigned: 'finding that the
extremely exacting nature of her work in Wexford makes so great a
demand on her time and strength that she cannot continue to perform the duties belonging to the position of President of the society
and has unfortunately felt it necessary to resign her office.'[16]

Without referring to the episode, Rudd[17] recalled that Lett was
a vivid person whom difficulties never daunted, but were there
only to be overcome, whilst Fingall was gracious and kept the committee together. Around the same time it is minuted that Lett was
not happy that individual members had the same voting rights as a
branch. She recommended that in future branches should be in the
majority on the Executive.

Reading through the early minutes of UI, it is interesting to note
the contrasting styles of presidency. Anita Lett's name appears continually with suggestions, ideas for challenging existing structures,
ideas which 'rock the boat', while for Lady Fingall very little appears,
except to record that she was late for meetings or left early — in
general her reign seems to have been without controversy.

The minutes also stressed the importance of encouraging effective communication between the central Executive and the regional
branches of UI, and ensuring that the benefits of membership
would be confined to paid-up members. In many ways these women
were confident in their ability to effect change and to create new
mediating structures through which practical advances could be
made. Rarely did they mention the novelty of their purpose, or
indulge in theoretical reflections on their place in society. Rural
Ireland for them was a business, despite the lofty references to
rural civilisation being made all around them. In the words of
Pilkington, 'Patriotism for women is a thing of deeds, not words.'

The UI had a particularly busy year in 1912. In May, a regular organiser was engaged, and in June the first General Meeting was held. This meeting included a discussion on the deficiency of the milk supply in rural districts, and a resolution was passed urging the twenty-one UI branches to see that children in their districts were supplied with milk throughout the year. Milk Supply Depots were started in several centres to deal with the scarcity of milk.

A paper was read by the President on the short supply of water to labourers' cottages, and this was followed by one on 'Dinners for school children' by the Hon. Mary Lawless. By June, a scheme was drawn up by a special sub-committee whereby a hot drink of cocoa would be supplied to children at their dinner. This scheme was successfully adopted by two branches and others were to take up the scheme before winter.

In August, with the aid of a generous donation, a voluntary organiser was appointed to devote her time to the 'crying needs of Connemara'. A poultry society was organised there but had to be abandoned as it was considered that people should have further education in co-operative principles before undertaking an enterprise that could have financial risk. In order to help the industries started by various branches, the committee took a stall at the Athlone Industrial Exhibition, which was a great success.

VILLAGE NURSES, INSTRUCTRESSES AND DEMONSTRATION HOUSES

One of the first concerns of UI was the question of rural nursing schemes. The inadequacy of existing health care schemes in rural districts was highlighted by Mrs Alex Rudd, a founder member: 'The people of Wexford were very industrious but there was very little money and the cottages were very old. When illness came, or accidents occurred, it was difficult to be nursed at home, and poorhouses and hospitals were very sad places. We then decided to have village nurses.'[18]

At the AGM in April 1911, President Lett outlined two schemes to train a local nurse in England. One scheme was to last twelve months and would cost £100, while the second scheme was of seven months duration and cost £39 8s 10d. Bree branch opted for the shorter scheme and Margaret Cowman of Ballybrennan was selected as a trainee.

It is interesting to recall her account of what happened.[19] She was given a sheet of paper with the name of the training home in

Edmonton, England, £30 in cash and the date she should be there. For a young girl of twenty who had never been away from home, the journey to England was both exciting and frightening. But as she recalled in later life, 'you obeyed your betters in those days'. The journey was hard and long, taking two days by boat and train. Margaret, obviously alone, was befriended by two gentlemen who knew of the Lett and Beatty families (related to the President of UI). They brought her meals and pointed her in the right direction when leaving her. She completed her course and returned to work in Bree. She soon became a familiar sight as she did her rounds on her bicycle, piling up mileage that is frightening by today's softer standards. Later on, by motor car, she continued to nurse in the district until she retired at the age of 72 after a life of service to the community and to the UI.

The nurse's training scheme made considerable progress. The UI report of 1916–17 states that there were specially trained nurses in places as far apart as Bree, Ballycarney, Lucan, Dunsany, Togher, Bruff, Shanagolden, Carrickbyrne, Castlecomer, Inishmore, Aran Islands and Kilworth. These nurses acted in a dual capacity, for their cottages were decorated by the local branches of UI and were then open to all members as 'demonstration houses', to show what could be done with simple materials, used with ingenuity, to improve homes. Demonstrations in hygiene and health care were given as part of the UI's programme on education. Another 'demonstration house' was a gate-lodge in which Mrs Hubert Lewis was installed as instructress in domestic economy which she taught not only to UI members at classes held in her house, but also to schoolchildren. Nor were the boys forgotten, for to them she gave instruction in the making of simple furniture from available materials — even the homely orange-box.[20]

At the December 1913 meeting the Chairman stressed the value of milk, and mentioned that the slow take-off of their milk depots was due to an attitude problem. People needed to be educated on the valuable properties contained in milk and the need for children to have milk all-year round — once the need was understood, the demand could be more effectively organised. Tea had to a great extent taken the place of milk on account of the greater facilities for buying. People should be taught that tea is actually poisonous for infants and young children, and very injurious to adults if taken in excessive strength or quantity. She appealed to all to investigate the need for milk in their own districts.

At the same meeting it was agreed that all branches should start a school garden or plot and that instructresses must be advised to give their cookery classes on open-turf fires in the cottages instead of on stoves. UI instructresses were to be directed to teach only plain dressmaking without finery, and good plain sewing. Also they themselves were recommended to wear home-spuns, ordinary strong boots and shoes and plain hats and to avoid all elaborate fashions when on duty. Other topics discussed were 'cocoa in schools', 'Toggenburg as the best breed of goats', and 'demonstration cottages'. At this one meeting, they dealt with issues of economics, environment and health — thus fulfilling their desire to be patriotic in a practical way.

The scarcity of cow's milk led the UI to seek other solutions, and members decided that goat's milk would be an ideal substitute, being tubercular-free in a country where tuberculosis was prevalent. The UI set up a goat farm on about ten acres of land rented from the home of a member, Sarah Deane of Foulksmills, Co. Wexford. It was run by a UI committee who imported a billy goat from England at the cost of £7 and the kid goats were distributed all over Wexford to individuals and schools. For many years, Sarah Deane bred and reared the Toggenburg breed of goats, and the animals were widely distributed under the UI network.

From the beginning, great importance was placed on the power of branches to bring forward their own resolutions and thus highlight issues which they deemed urgent, in the expectation that the Executive would act on them. Their resolutions tended to be of a practical nature, though quite diverse, and reflected the issues of concern in Irish society at any particular time. Some of the earlier resolutions in August 1910 were for clean second-hand clothes to be distributed, thus avoiding the spread of disease among the poor. Another resolution recommended that meals should be provided for schoolchildren, while another asked that nanny goats should receive the same treatment on trams as did the rams — that they be carried in a halter instead of a crate. Another resolution was:

> That the Executive Committee shall discuss the question of imbecile girls in the country, who through not being kept under proper supervision, are in danger of becoming or have become the victims of unscrupulous men, and thereby increase the population of Ireland with children, predestined (in all probability) to be idiots, lunatics or criminals, or who at best cannot be useful citizens.

A discussion took place on the subject and the UI wrote to the National Association for the Welfare of the Feeble Minded in England, to inquire about the working of the 1913 act in that country.

Again in 1913 another resolution was put forward proposing 'that in the cause of Temperance we ask the DATI (Department of Agriculture and Technical Instruction) to recommend to the county committees of agriculture that the government Premium Stud Horses and Bulls, and the Stud Turkey Cocks and Poultry Stations, shall not in future be allotted to any person owning licensed premises: these animals and birds living in the ownership of publicans places temptation to drink in the way of young farm hands.'

At the 1914 meeting it was noted that one of the effects of the War was an outburst of drunkenness among the women as well as the men and as the women of every household ought to economise, the Executive advised adhering to the branch rule of no intoxicants at meetings thus enabling the members to economise. The resolution in the same year calling for free meals for children of Dublin slums was rejected because it was estimated to be beyond UI's rural brief. This decision was overturned some years later when the UI supplied thousands of meals to Dublin children starting in 1918.

A NON-PARTY-POLITICAL AND NON-SECTARIAN POLICY

UI, by its terms of reference, was and non-sectarian and non-party political. At certain periods some members had difficulties with this, but in retrospect it became the cementing force for an organisation which embraces all women across all divides, enabling it to become the oldest and largest women's group in Ireland, and second in Europe to the Finnish Martha Movement founded in 1889. From the start the UI was strongly national.

It was born into a period when the spirit of self-help was unusually powerful in Ireland; when farmers were multiplying dairy and agricultural societies; when the Gaelic League was creating branches, the Industrial Development Associations were promoting industries, and the intellectuals were creating a great dramatic and literary movement. The impulse in all these movements was towards direct action, and a number of patriotic and energetic women were eager to share in them — with the underlying motive of service to their country.

So it was with the UI. For countrywomen, service to their country means service in their local community. UI felt that some matters were beyond their brief. An invitation to speak at a meeting of the

Irish Women's Reform League in 1913 was turned down because the UI knew that women's suffrage would be advocated from the chair — 'we must keep clear of anything controversial' was the President's reminder.

Organising milk depots was one thing, but emblazoning the name 'The UI' across the entrance was dangerous because 'it might arouse opposition'. Members felt they could not retain the Gaelic title of their paper since this inhibited sales. Articles on UI activities could not be sent to any paper 'but only those with the least political bias'. In 1913, an Executive member resigned 'as she objected to the Union Jack having been flown alone at the Bellevue Fete.' (Bellevue was the home of Lady Power, President of Bree branch.) UI was not responsible for any of the arrangements at the Fete but would do its best to see that nothing of the sort should happen again. At the same meeting after an amusing discussion, it was resolved that all officials of UI should wear dress of Irish manufacture at meetings when possible, and they should not support the sweatshops of Birmingham and Manchester.

UI DURING WORLD WAR I AND THE IRISH CIVIL WAR

The years between 1914 and 1922 were dramatic years for the UI. Although the organisation was non-party political and non-sectarian it could not but be affected by the cataclysmic events of that period. World War I and the 'Troubles' affected both the membership of UI and its activities.

Initially, World War I was popular in Ireland. Thousands of young men, both unionists and nationalists, joined the army. Altogether, about 200,000 Irishmen fought in World War I, of whom 60,000 lost their lives.

The war brought prosperity to Irish farmers. As the German U-boat blockade cut Britain off from other food sources, the demand for Irish beef, butter, and eggs rose. This pushed up the prices farmers received. Some exploited their good fortune by selling poor quality produce at the highest prices and their profiteering damaged the reputation of Irish produce after the war. Landless labourers and small farmers did less well in the war. The big farmers who employed labourers were unwilling to raise their wages in line with rising prices. And farmers with small holdings lacked the capital to take advantage of rising demand.

In typical fashion, UI responded to the crisis in a practical way. In August 1914, a branch of the Red Cross was formed in Co. Wexford under the auspices of the UI. Funds were collected for an ambulance which was sent to a hospital for Irish soldiers serving in France, run entirely by Irish doctors and nurses. After the war the ambulance was returned and sold in Enniscorthy and the proceeds were returned to the UI funds.

The growth of the organisation was halted by the First World War. In the war years women were needed on the land to make up for the short supply of male labour. Many members of the Executive were drawn into war work. In December 1914, the President's address referred to the present grave crisis caused by the war and how it gave women the opportunity of doing their share. UI requested the secretary of the Board of Trade in London to order the withdrawal of barley from brewers. At the same time some UI members had a scheme for growing wheat, as the available flour was very bad and they were glad to have their own wheat and get it milled for themselves. It was also proposed that branches procure open-air shelters which could be hired to TB patients returning from hospital. All available land should be converted into vegetable plots in order to increase food production, with the surplus available to sell to other countries. Every household should economise, using home bacon instead of American, pickling eggs for winter use and churning Sunday milk instead of sending it to the creameries, as it would supply the home with butter and butter-milk. Splagnum Moss should be used as war dressing, and the blackberry brigades were dispatched among the branches to make jam for wounded soldiers.

In 1914, the members had complained of their society being 'ridiculed as being composed of Englishwomen and Scotswomen', but the Executive insisted they did not need an Irish Vice-President to affirm their patriotic credentials.[21] The large Protestant establishment in the country, the ruling landlord and professional classes, now began to decline. The biggest drop occurred between the 1911 census and the 1920 census, as the British withdrew from garrison towns, young Protestants died during the war, and Protestant unionists moved to the North. These changes took place against a background of land reform, extension of the franchise and political independence.

In an account of the early years of the UI, E.A. Bishop states that, 'The work of the society has been described as being "like the incoming tide; advancing and retreating in waves but flowing steadily on".'[22]

The 1914–18 war was the first serious reverse. Many Executive members were swept into war work; organisers were dismissed due to lack of funds and many newly formed branches faded out. Only one organiser, Miss Nan O'Brien (Michael Collins' aunt) remained at work the whole time. She kept alive the ideals and work of the young society, so that in 1918 there followed a short period of progress and expansion. Individual members of the UI contributed to the various projects organised by the society: for example, Mrs Green gave £50 for school dinners on condition that the receiving school should ask the blessing in Irish before each meal, and Mrs Childers gave £125 to be administered by the UI on Denzil Lane food depot. Grants were received from the Carnegie United Kingdom Trust and from the Development Commission, while the Village Nurses Fund received help from surpluses left over from the war charities.

Employment opportunities improved in the country and by 1916 a police report said 'the mass of the people are sound and loyal'. But beneath the surface, things were stirring. A section of the Irish Volunteers under Eoin Mac Neill had refused to follow Redmond's lead. They wanted to have a rebellion while the war was on — 'England's difficulty was Ireland's opportunity'.

In London in 1914, historian Alice Stopford Green, who had an active sympathy with the Irish demand for a separate national identity, formed a small committee which was instrumental in collecting the £1,500 needed to buy arms for Irish Volunteers. One of those active on the London committee was Mary Spring Rice (one of the founder members of the UI), a daughter of Lord Monteagle and — such was the paradoxical nature of the times — a first cousin of the British Ambassador in Washington. She suggested that the best way to bring the weapons purchased in Germany home to Ireland was to sail them back in private, and therefore unobtrusive, yachts.[23]

This plan was successful. The *Asgard* (Erskine Childers' yacht) arrived at Howth on 26 July 1914 and was met by the Volunteers. The guns and ammunition were speedily unloaded and distributed.[24] The success of the gun running exploit reverberated through the country so that recruiting, which had become sluggish, recovered to such an extent that by September 1914, the force numbered 180,000.[25]

At Easter 1916 the minute book of the UI continued to record details of egg depots, cheese-making methods and development grants. The only reaction to the Rising was Mrs Lett's resolution 'that none of the UI organisers or instructresses should be permitted to join any association, social or political', a proposal they did not see fit to act on. (The minutes only state that it was proposed!)

The Easter Rising of 1916 started on a Monday and finished on Saturday with 550 dead, over 2,000 wounded, and £2.5 million of damage. Attitudes towards the rising varied: 'Unionists saw the rising as a treacherous attack on the empire in its hour of need. Among Nationalists, feelings were mixed. Some were angry at the death and destruction. As volunteer prisoners were being marched through Dublin, some people threw mud on them. Others were more ambivalent. They disliked the violence but were proud that the rebels had held out for a week against such overwhelming odds. They might have been wrong and foolish but they had also been brave.'[26]

After the Rising, the military rounded up the suspects. 1,800 were sent to prison in England, 170 were found guilty by court martial and 90 sentenced to death. As one execution followed another, public opinion swung round to support the rebels, resulting in a decline in popularity of Home Rulers and victory for Sinn Féin. This manifested itself in the 1918 elections where Sinn Féin took 73 seats to 6 for Home Rule (the proportional representation system of voting was not used). Whilst nationalists had changed dramatically since 1914, Ulster unionists had not, and were as determined as ever to remain in the UK and to demand separation from the rest of Ireland. The state of Ireland dates its existence from the first meeting of Dáil Éireann on 21 January 1919 – with Countess Markievicz as Minister for Labour becoming the first female cabinet minister in Britain. Few in Britain took Sinn Féin's claim to be a government seriously but Lloyd George was concerned with both the growing level of violence in Ireland and the 1914 Home Rule Act which was due to come into force. His priorities in 1919 were to suppress the IRA and deal with Ulster unionists.

In September 1919 the Dáil was declared illegal and the Government of Ireland Act was introduced in the House of Commons. (The provisions of the new act included two parliaments for Ireland, one in the North and one in the South). In 1920, martial law was declared and curfew imposed. Guerilla tactics became widespread and by December, the Government of Ireland Act became law.

Elections saw victory for unionists in the North and republican candidates in the South — leading to the Anglo-Irish truce in July 1921. There followed lengthy negotiations resulting in the Dáil voting in favour of the Treaty on 7 January 1922 — to be followed by civil war lasting until April 1923, the effects of which still linger:

> Bitterness between families, communities and state; political issues became polarised between those who supported and those who had opposed the Treaty at a time when social and economic issues needed more attention, and the Civil War hardened the resolve of Ulster Unionists to remain outside the Irish Free State.[27]

Just over six years after the Rising, the civil war left the same catastrophic results: hundreds dead, thousands in prison and millions of pounds of damage, but this time the Irish had no 'enemy' but one another, leaving a legacy of deep bitterness for future generations.

The War of Independence had a more direct bearing on UI women than did the civil war, given their standing in society. In 1919 an Executive member deplored 'the unwarrantable attack on a member of her household' by Sinn Féin soldiers searching for UVF arms. The minutes also recorded that the arms had in fact been moved from the house the previous month.

In October 1920, a letter was received from Lady Shaw, a member of the UI Executive, stating that as she had been raided she intended to give up all public work including her position on the Executive of UI. The committee accepted Lady Shaw's resignation with regret. At the same meeting a resolution was passed 'that the precedent with regard to the AGM of 1916 be followed and that it now be postponed until the year 1921', that precedent being that the 1916 AGM had been abandoned on account of the Rising and the Executive had then published a statement declaring that as the legal year in which the Annual Meeting of the Society should have been held expired at the end of April, it was decided it should not be held again until the following year.

Soon the wave receded again for in 1922 the civil war 'went over all the activities of the Society of the UI like a steamroller'.[28] A few valiant branches carried on but practically all work was in abeyance until in 1923, to quote AE, 'The Society of UI emerged like an emaciated kitten among a herd of elephants. Fortunately the life of that little body survived, though the means of sustenance had almost come to an end.'[29]

In her presidential address to the AGM in May 1922, Lady Fingall had shown that the kitten was still alive for she said that she 'hoped to be able to speak confidently of the future, and to assure them that their Society, whose activities during the last troubled years had been almost at a standstill. had recovered from its state of suspended animation and was ready to take its share in the re-making of Ireland. Their hopes had lost some of the lustre that they wore some months ago but they were not altogether quenched, and though their prospects at the moment were clouded with anxiety as to their country's future, they were not going to sit down and cry about it. If all that they had helped to build up in rural Ireland were swept away, they would start to build anew the moment they got the chance — and if the ground were not clear for building, they would at least begin to plan.'

The annual report of the UI for 1922 stated that the number of branches had remained 'nominally the same as last year, a total of 49. In many the work had been in abeyance, but a new lease of life was hoped for.'

By 1923 when the civil war ended, Ireland was in a desperate condition. Years of war had destroyed railways and bridges, factories and creameries, shops and houses. Claims for damages amounted to £10,000,000. Over 130,000 men were out of work. A bitter civil war had just ended and about 25% of the population refused to recognise the new government.[30]

TREATMENT OF EMPLOYEES

The UI were considerate and generous employers. Despite the continuous pressure of lack of funds, they always tried to act fairly to their employees and agreed to the need for three months' notice before termination of employment. As early as 1915 the UI arranged that its organisers should be insured under the Employer's Liability Act, and the question of payment of employees during illness was dealt with by the agreement that the salaries of employees during illness should be made up to the full amount including the amount of state insurance for the first week. After this period the matter was to come up before the Finance Committee. The UI, described as 'Promoters of Rural Industries', were insured with the North British and Mercantile Insurance Company Workmen's Compensation Assurance. Their policy covered three employees whose annual salary totalled £365.

When Miss Whitty was elected Secretary of the Society in July 1915, at a salary of £100 per annum, it was decided to pay second class travelling expenses between Bray and Dublin. Salaries for office staff seem to be higher than the norm for that time, and travel expenses were rare for employees.

In 1914, a Ms O'Donnell worked as organiser with UI and also as Poor Law Guardian. The committee asked her not to offer herself for re-election, and she agreed. This occurred despite a resolution passed in March 1914, 'That the UI co-operate with the Irish Women's Local Government Association and other bodies to promote the election of women Poor Law Guardians'. In Ms O'Donnell's case, it was the dual mandate which caused a problem.

In December 1916, the Executive Committee forwarded a resolution that the vacancy on the National Education Board should be filled by a woman.

IRELAND AFTER INDEPENDENCE

After decades of bloodshed and political upheaval, Ireland settled down to become a conservative, inward-looking rural society.[31]

All laws for the Free State were made by the Oireachtas which consisted of two houses — the Senate and the Dáil — the institutions of which were built along British lines. For instance, they left the organisation of a civil service to men who had learned their trade while serving in the British system. This had advantages in that it provided stability and a reservoir of experience and knowledge on which inexperienced politicians could draw. On the other hand, a civil service trained in old ways contributed to the conservatism which was such a notable feature of the new state, at least until a new generation emerged in the 1950s. This same conservatism applied in the legal system.

By 1923 the task of establishing law and order and of reviving the economy had begun in. At that period, farming was the country's main industry. From a total labour force of 1.3 million, 670,000 worked in agriculture, and agricultural produce made up 84 per cent of exports. But Irish farming suffered from severe structural problems. The majority of farms were small, and small farmers could not afford to invest in new technology. In addition farmers were reluctant to hand over the farm to their sons who often had to wait until they were well into their thirties or forties before taking over. In the 1920s, over 25 per cent of farmers were over sixty. Old men were unlikely to try new approaches to farming.

The sole outlet for Irish produce was the British market, but after the war Britain imported freely from other countries causing prices to fall. Government decided that good performance in the farming sector would help the whole economy, so the Minister for Agriculture concentrated on improving quality and making money available for farm improvements.

> His 1923 Land Act ordered the compulsory purchase of all land still held by landlords. By 1937, the social revolution begun in 1870 was complete. All Irish farmers now owned their farms. Purchase did not solve the other land problems, however, especially the basic problems of farms that were too small to be economically viable and farmers who were too poor to invest. The 1923 Act abolished the CDB which had been trying to increase farm size. Its functions were taken over by the Land Commission which was much less active.[32]

Nationalists had hoped that independence would bring an end to the decline in population which had lasted since the famine. This had not been achieved, however. Poor economic performance kept Irish people from marrying young, and forced them to emigrate in large numbers. In the 1920s the average Irish man married at the age of 33 and the average Irish woman at 29. Late marriages reduced family size, even without the use of contraceptives. In addition, a substantial number of Irish people never married at all. In the 1950s, 25% of the population was single. Emigration also continued after independence.[33]

The Catholic Church, as a pressure group, was able to influence politicians to introduce education bills. In practice, much of the legislation passed by the Irish Free State government in its early years bore a distinct relationship to Church views — 1923 Censorship of Films Act, 1924 Intoxicating Liquor Act, in 1925 divorce was forbidden and the 1929 Censorship of Publications Act also resembled Church policy.

The cultural ethos of the 1920s was one of exclusiveness. There were public demonstrations in favour of the introduction of a censorship board and trains carrying foreign newspapers were stopped and their cargoes burned. The campaign for the introduction of censorship witnessed its victory in 1929 when the Irish censorship board was set up. There is no doubt that this did much to perpetuate the cultural poverty of the country — writers felt hopelessly cut off from their audiences and the populace at large was deprived of the fresh air of the modernist movement in the arts outside Ireland.

WOMEN IN INDEPENDENT IRELAND

The emphasis on the national question between 1916 and 1923 led to the subordination of women's issues and 'ensured that the position of Irishwomen remained subservient, a situation compounded by the deepening of the Catholic ethos of the state.'[34] The authoritarianism of Irish society was reinforced in the Irish Free State, and there was no indication that the majority of Irishwomen opposed such a tendency. Many women who had been involved in the Troubles were forced out of political involvement by financial and domestic considerations. The old pattern of limited career possibilities reasserted itself in independent Ireland where, since men found it hard to get jobs, women were seen as rivals in the male struggle to support the family unit. In the 1920s, only about 20,000 women were members of trade unions and half of these were members of the INTO, with another 25% in the Irish Women Workers' Union. There were, however, some successful strikes by women in the 1920s, such as those of laundry workers and rosary bead makers. In 1929, female nurses in the mental hospitals at Portrane and Grangegorman secured increased wages.[35]

UI IN INDEPENDENT IRELAND

Another fresh start was made by the UI; a small office was taken over from another society and a secretary-organiser was installed. She did valuable work among a very diminished number of branches. Then the wave receded yet again, for in 1926 due to lack of funds the office had to be closed down for six months and the secretary-organiser, Miss Maude Slattery, went abroad to do relief work in Europe. The report to the Plunkett Foundation Trustees in 1926 showed that there were twenty branches of the UI in the country, with eight in Wexford, at Bree, Camolin, Carrigbyrne, Curracloe, Davidstown, Enniscorthy, Oylegate and Tombrack. Ballyragget branch was in Kilkenny, with Abbeyleix, Ballybrittas, Castletown and Rathdowney in Queens' County, Fethard in Tipperary, Skreen, Dromard and Drumore West in Sligo, Dunsany and Togher in Louth, and Cappagh in Waterford. There were also applications for new branches in Louth, Tipperary, Meath, Limerick and Dublin.

It was during the 1920s that the importance of having individual enthusiasts, prepared to devote their whole lives to the cause of women in rural Ireland could be appreciated. Lucy Franks, a former President of Castletown branch of the UI and a future President of the ICA, was one such woman, and much of the credit for the survival of the society during those barren years must go to her. A niece of the women's rights campaigner, Charlotte Despard, Franks had seen her own house burnt down during the civil war, and had travelled abroad where she picked up skills in various handcrafts. On her return she was drawn to the ideals of the UI once again. Muriel Gahan recalled that, 'To set out to bring life to an all but lifeless movement by learning how to make baskets sounds improbable and perhaps ridiculous, but this, in fact was what Lucy Franks did in 1926.'[36]

When the office had to be closed down she stepped into the breach and continued to work to keep the branches together. Miss Ross, then treasurer, was appointed to keep the accounts and to attend to correspondence, and the services of a part-time typist were obtained.

The branches were kept alive by the energy and enthusiasm of the members who sought various ways to revive their association. There were still some UI village nurses who, with a year's training in England, came to live and work from their own homes. Two milk depots were maintained by the local UI committees, at Fethard, Co. Tipperary and at Abbeyleix, Co. Laois. Also in Laois, Castletown had by now erected a hall. In Wexford, the goat farm under Miss Dean was still viable, and weaving continued at Bree branch. Gortlomain branch in Co. Clare had an embroidery industry whilst at Beltra, Co. Sligo the branch taught spinning, cheese and marmalade making. The basket-making classes were well attended and kept alive the team spirit. Lucy Franks took a stall at the Royal Dublin Society's Spring Show in 1927 to sell handcrafts and the baskets produced by the branches, and sales realised £50. This venture gave a great stimulus to members and the following year a 'school of basket-making' was started in Co. Wexford by Anita Lett and Mrs Roark. A Mr Crampton, of Messrs Dryads Ltd. of London, was brought over to teach for a fortnight.

In 1929, Gorey and Screen branches were started, and the branch at Fethard reopened. At that year's RDS Spring Show, sales at the UI stall amounted to £95. Four new branches started in Limerick, Sligo, Wexford and Tipperary, and the following year

£102 was realised at the UI stall in the RDS. A model cottage was shown, furnished by members and as a result, a great many orders were taken for the simple furnishings exhibited. In the same year Beltra branch in Co. Sligo had two lectures — on the Book of Kells and Irish traditional music. This branch also held a show in September and had a stall at Sligo county show. Nursing lectures on hygiene and home nursing were given by Miss Kavanagh, Inspector for Queen's Institute of District Nurses, at five centres. Other lectures given were 'The League of Nations' and 'Local History' and a delegate was sent to the Rural Women's Conference held in London.

In 1928 the UI Executive Committee was able to meet again, and set about organising short courses of instruction in simple crafts for new branches and to pay expenses of lecturers to branches. Lucy Franks was appointed honorary secretary and organiser and did much to revive the society, bringing fresh hope and new life to the branches which she visited constantly.

3
SUMMER SCHOOLS AND COUNTRY WORKERS

Two milestones in the history of UI occurred in the late 1920s — the first summer schools and the formation of Country Workers.

SUMMER SCHOOLS

In 1929, thanks to the energy and inspiration of Olivia Hughes, of Fethard, Co. Tipperary, an experiment was undertaken which was to have far-reaching results. That summer she invited any craft-workers who could come from the branches of UI to meet together on the slopes of Slievenamon (the highest peak of the Comeragh Mountains, whose name translates as 'The mountain of the women') to exchange ideas and skills and to study poetry, drama and singing.

Lucy Franks (Franksie) recorded her version of the first of the summer schools:[1]

> This year we made our first effort to hold a Summer Camp school. No one in the country had ever tried camping, so it was looked on as rather a mad scheme, especially when the members were told they would have to bring their own beds or bring a bag of sacking to be filled with hay. However, the camp leaders were undaunted — they got for a few pounds rent, two wooden huts well-built and spacious, furnished with some strong tables and chairs but little else. The situation was delightful, some 1,200 feet up the slopes of Slievenamon Mountain overlooking the plain in Co. Tipperary which ends in the Golden Vale. About eighteen girls came and three or four voluntary teachers in craft work. Each girl had to help with the camp work and the mornings after that were occupied with craft work — basket making in cane and rush, rush seating chairs, cane seating, rush mat

making, leather work — in the evening, community singing and Irish dancing. We practised the steps of 'the walls of Limerick, the bridge of Athlone and the waves of Tory'. We had lectures on local geology from an Oxford BA, Miss Patten on 'Irish place names' and Irish poetry from Mr Hughes. Members who could afford it paid 30/- for the session while those who could not, paid 10/-. Good meals and plentiful were provided, many local well wishers from farms in the district contributing gifts of eggs, soda bread and cakes. We want to make a bigger effort next year because the visible improvement in health and in work and the enjoyment of the girls make the effort more than worthwhile. Owing to the wonderful management of the camp leaders, the expenses worked out at about 15/- per head.

We could hold two or three camp schools in some of the empty mansions which abound in the country. We feel sure this movement would grow immensely — lack of funds hamper our efforts. We cannot pay for lecturers, nor give grants for village halls or rooms where our members can meet. We have a very small capital which yields under £100 per annum. So far our government has been unable to give us a grant, as they have more important matters to attend to, before the organising of countrywomen can be seen to.

This year, we sent a delegate to the Rural Women's Conference in London, held under the National Council of Women. Apathy is frequently displayed by the women themselves, until they begin to see that there is some object in bringing them together for monthly meetings, that is, when we can provide demonstrations or people who can give a talk on some interesting subject. In travelling round the country I hear the same story in nearly every country village, especially in the West — there is nothing for the girls in the winter, they know very little of any sort of hand-work, their only desire is to join their relatives, who have found a different kind of life in the States. Owing to the lack of funds for organising purposes, our Society is only struggling to keep going — we have 16 branches in country districts and about 500 members and subscribers.

From that informal gathering on that lovely mountain in 1929 have grown the annual summer schools, culminating in 1953 in the now imposing structure of An Grianán, Co Louth — Ireland's first adult residential college. Even the war years, when practically all transport was at a standstill, did not stop the summer schools.

(There were at first only two trains a week on the main lines and then for a while no passenger trains at all). True, the movement limped where it used to stride, but still it went on, always gathering strength until it received recognition from the government as an educational body. It was important that this education be a social as well as a practical endeavour.

The site for the first summer school, 1,200 feet up the slopes of Slievenamon mountain, was owned by Dr O'Connell of Fethard Co. Tipperary, father of two stalwart UI members — Phyllis and Helen O'Connell. At first the summer schools were held in a general air of picnic, in an empty house with improvised furniture where each member brought her camp bed or straw palliasse, but as the numbers grew steadily year by year, and the difficulties of transport and of catering under emergency conditions grew ever greater it became necessary to take over a school or college equipped for such numbers. Even then the number of those wishing to attend reached such proportions that two schools had to be run each year and the number of delegates from each guild limited to one, though an effort was made to fit in more delegates from the very newest guilds.

Most of the staffing of the schools was done voluntarily and it would not have been possible to run them so efficiently, at a cost so low that not even the poorest guild was debarred from sending a delegate, but for the loyal co-operation of all concerned. The work of the house was divided into shifts and the participants were drafted into a corresponding number of groups, so that each group had only one set of duties daily, moving forward one each day so that no group got the same duties twice running. Each group was under the care of a group leader, whose duty it was to see that each member knew her daily task and the time and place of all classes, outings and lectures. She was expected to encourage the timid and cheer the despondent (and subdue the exuberant). Upon the way she carried out her responsibilities depended the smooth working of the group system, which has been found most efficient and has been adopted by many guilds for their own work.

The mornings at summer school were devoted to classes which have included such diverse subjects as the Irish language; arithmetic, with special reference to accounts; needlework, embroidery, dressmaking and knitting; basket making; house decoration; spinning, dyeing and weaving; rug-making; sheepskin curing; glove making; toy making and simple carpentry; cooking and laundry work and colour and design. The physical side was catered for by health talks, keep-fit exercises, and games.

The afternoons were left free for expeditions and the evenings devoted to music and singing, Irish dancing; drama and verse-speaking; lectures and films; debates and discussion groups and to holding model guild meetings.

In the last few years before acquiring An Grianán, the summer college had been inaugurated — in effect a short University course which proved increasingly popular. Members attending the summer schools do so as delegates from their guilds and are expected to learn all that they possibly can and take it back to their guilds. Participants attended the summer college as private individuals, however, at their own expense. Though all the teaching and organisation of schools and college was done voluntarily, tribute must be paid to the great volume of help that was always forthcoming from local people wherever they were held — and as this was normally in a different place each year there was great variety in the approach to all subjects.

The association received no funding to carry out this important project, though many Dept. of Education teachers gave courses in their own free time and it would be impossible to assess the value of such generous co-operation. There were always local experts on such subjects as music, local history and antiquities, folklore, drama, Irish dancing etc. who placed their services at the disposal of the association. The difficulty was not to get enough help but to find time to fit in all the activities which presented themselves — each of value and of interest.

The summer schools from 1929 to 1953 were held every year in different parts of the country until the acquisition of An Grianán in 1954 through the generous sponsorship of the Kellogg Foundation of America. The name of the college had been chosen many years before, when the ICA's hope of acquiring a place of its own was just a dream. An Grianán is truly the 'Sunny Place' — a friendly place, a gift to the Irish nation, where women and an increasing number of men from all walks of life meet with a common purpose — the pursuit of knowledge. An Grianán has its roots in the early summer schools — and while relatives at home 'thought that the scheme of a mountain camp was mad', the seed sown at that first summer school grew through successive summers of music, drama, poetry, the crafts, health, vitality and oceans of fun, until it blossomed into the lovely flower that is An Grianán today — the jewel in the ICA crown. There, in a rural setting bordering the sea, ICA continues to provide for all comers the opportunity to learn a craft, perfect a skill, appreciate keep-fit, make music and make friends. It is difficult to evaluate the contribution these annual summer schools made to the overall development of the ICA, but without doubt they were the springboard for the acquisition of An Grianán. One has only to look back through the minute books at the accounts of these schools — the painstaking work, before, during and after — and marvel at the dedication of these pioneering women to which the ICA owes so much. One example is the report in the *Farmers' Gazette*:

The UI Summer School — an enjoyable time at Bentley

The weather was very kind to us during our fortnight at Curracloe, Co. Wexford. Only two showery mornings and the rest of the time real sunshine. Fifty UI members stayed at Bentley — 16 for the whole fortnight, 22 for a week, and 12 for weekends. Luckily, the house is magically elastic, and beds overflowed into tents, garages, and courtyards.

Mrs Wilson and Miss Mitchell, Bentley's owners, showed us every kindness. Miss Mitchell ruled the kitchen and made us the largest brown loaves I have ever seen. But the kitchen by no means exhausted her talents. Playing reels for the Irish dancers, dancing herself, teaching swimming, playing netball, singing alto — Miss Mitchell always seemed to have time and energy for anything that was going. We all hope very much that we shall have her at next year's summer school.

Miss Nell Ryan, the only lady on the Wexford County Council, paid us a visit and spoke most interestingly on the local government of the county, the activities and duties of the County Council and the rights of the individual, whether taxpayer or otherwise.

Miss Kavanagh, Inspector of Jubilee Nurses throughout Ireland, stayed at Bentley for three days. We all enjoyed her lectures enormously. Miss Kavanagh has an almost uncanny knack of imparting knowledge and of making whatever she describes absorbingly interesting. Some of us longed for an invalid in our midst that we might put our newly-acquired knowledge into practice but we all remained in uninterestingly good health.

Mr Acton Gibbon came over from Waterford to speak to us on Local History. He had drawn out an excellent map of the district and with its help gave us a fascinating account of past days.

The Gorey branch came over one day and presented some particularly good *tableaux vivants* from Irish history. Miss Brickenden gave an account of the characters as they appeared. We must congratulate her on the costumes and the colour and grouping of each tableau, which were most artistic and effective.

One evening the Ballyneskar Mummers gave us a mumming exhibition. We were all much struck by the perfect time and steps of their dancing. They have won numerous mumming competitions and their standard is undoubtedly very high. The paved courtyard where they danced gave a most picturesque setting to their performance. Afterwards some of the UI members danced an eight-handed reel and we all joined in for the Haymakers Jig.

The Irish cloaks and brooches of Irish design are a great addition to Irish dances and it is to be hoped that some members in every branch will learn how to make them.

On our last Friday we gave a second performance of Laurence Housman's 'Sister Clare' in the barn so kindly lent by Mr Burke. The casting was slightly different as the original 'Brother Juniper' had left us.

Mrs Burden, who came over from England for one night to tell us something of the lives of rural women in her country, British Columbia, was with us the same evening. She had brought over some slides, showing us scenes from Western Canada and thanks to Mr Woodroofe, who lent us his lantern, we were able to enjoy these after the entertainment. This was Mrs Burden's first visit to Ireland and we all hope it will not be her last.

Our mornings were occupied by craft work. Members had lessons in metal and rush work, basket-making from bent which grew on the shore, embroidery, dressmaking, millinery and stool seating. Altogether we had a very happy time. and were all discussing plans, before we left, for next year's Summer School.[2]

The summer schools were held all over Ireland, depending on suitable venues:

1929   Slievenamon, Co. Tipperary
1930   Cappard, Co. Laois
1931   Curracloe, Co. Wexford
1932   Cappagh House, Co. Waterford
1933   Termonfechin, Co. Louth

1934   Duffcarrig, Co. Wexford

1935   Castlefreake, Co. Cork

1936   Coolmaine Castle, Co. Kerry

1937   Castlefreake, Co. Cork

1938   Rosturk Castle, Co. Mayo

1939   Charleville, Enniskerry, Co. Wicklow

1940   Cancelled as the house booked in Co. Sligo was sold, and unsettled times made alternative arrangements impossible

1941   Avoca, Co. Wicklow

1942   St Valerie, Co. Wicklow

1943   Aravon, Bray, Co. Wicklow

1944   Aravon, Bray, Co. Wicklow

1945   Coláiste Sharman, Ramsfort, Gorey (owned by the Gaelic League)

1946   Garryvoe Irish College, Cork

1947   Grammar School, Galway

1948   Grammar School, Drogheda

1949   Grammar School, Sligo

1950   Crosshaven, Co. Cork

1951   Coláiste Sharman, Gorey

1952   St Augustine's Priory, Dungarvan

1953   St Eunan's, Letterkenny (attendance was down due to an outbreak of polio)

1954   An Grianán, Termonfechin, Co. Louth

If the initiation of the summer schools was one of the milestones of the UI in the late 1920s, the foundation of Country Workers was the second.

COUNTRY WORKERS

From 1910 onwards, the UI had organised exhibitions and demonstrations of country crafts during shows at the RDS. A search in the Mayo mountains to find a weaver for the 1930 Spring Show revealed several weavers who had little way of selling their homespun. The UI sought to give further help to isolated craftworkers in the West and also to help their own members improve their production of home produce and crafts. The result was the opening of the Country Shop in St Stephen's Green, Dublin (with a restaurant to finance it) and the formation of Country Workers Ltd, a non-profit company to direct its activities.

Country Workers Ltd had three stated objectives:

1. to help people in the small farm areas in the West by encouraging and supporting home industries such as handspinning, weaving and hand knitting;

2. to encourage craftworkers throughout the country and to promote country crafts and country produce generally with special emphasis on developing their co-operative organisations;

3. to promote and assist the work of the UI.

The founder directors of Country Workers were Lucy Franks, Olivia Hughes, Vida Lentaigne of Termonfechin, Co. Louth and Muriel Gahan of Dublin. Muriel Gahan was Managing Director at a salary of 30/— per week, and was responsible for the craft and produce development programme. The one non-UI founder director was Paddy Somerville Large of Bray, Co. Wicklow. He shortly afterwards married Grace Orpen, who, as Grace Somerville Large, became one of the association's most dedicated members.

COUNTRY SHOP

The Country Shop opened in December 1930 at 23 St Stephen's Green, Dublin and closed its doors in 1978, having served ICA and the people of Ireland admirably. It became the nerve centre for traditional crafts as well as a haven for rural people visiting Dublin. The Country Shop is remembered for its open fire, its hot buttered toast and fresh scones, potato cakes and fresh crumpets. 'Downstairs was the place for a winter's afternoon, but on a spring morning the seats by the window, with pale sunshine slanting in over the primroses and crocuses in the window boxes, were the best place in the city to sit and drink coffee.'[3]

Mary O'Driscoll, ICA member from Wexford (who worked for a time at An Grianán and became an Executive member when she moved to Cork on marriage), remembers picking snowdrops at An Grianán for the Country Shop tables. It was Lucy Franks who came up with the idea of running a restaurant and through it providing an outlet to display the crafts — an idea that accounted for the success of Country Workers Ltd. As well as housing Country Workers from 1946 to 1975, the building housed ICA from 1937 to 1964. It was also home to the Irish Homespun Society from its inception in

1935 until 1965 — indeed the premises soon became the Dublin 'centre of operations' for rural Ireland.

None of the founders of Country Workers had any romantic ideas about rural Ireland — all were aware of how harsh country life could be. They also saw in urban areas that life was becoming increasingly mechanised, and that the demand for craftworkers' goods was diminishing. They recognised that with the death of the traditional crafts, a whole way of life in the country was threatened. More pressingly, they saw poverty, and saw an untapped source of income in the shape of crafts. They saw that only new markets for the crafts would sustain craftworkers' livelihoods.

The miniature thatched cottage sign swinging in the breeze outside 23 St Stephen's Green became a much-loved landmark for Dubliners and country folk alike. Very soon the Country Shop established itself as a first class restaurant and a showcase for all that is good in Irish country crafts. From the first, any profit made in the restaurant was used to help the country craftworkers by means of grants, instruction, prize schemes and the like. Profit on craft sales went back to the workers as an annual Christmas bonus.

EXHIBITION OF CRAFTS

The first exhibition of crafts by Country Workers was held in the Country Shop in October 1933, including work done by different branches of UI, with almost all the exhibits made from home-produced material such as willows, rushes, wool, pottery or rich clay. Its success can be gauged by the account in the *Farmers' Gazette*:[4]

Exhibition at the Country Shop

This interesting and delightful exhibition, which was held last week, seemed like a chapter in Irish industrial history. On the immediate left there was a group collected from Aran, the girdle originally woven before looms were invented and made the same way today; the skin-shoes, the beautiful and elaborate knitting from handspun wool, and the 'ciseáns' of bent grass; on the right a fine example of modern art in a beautifully finished and inlaid half moon table of Irish oak from the Leixlip wood workers.

From Aran we passed to Avoca tweeds, where there were also some samples of the natural dyes from which these beautiful colours come, and then to tweeds from Kerry, Mayo and Donegal, all with different characteristics and their own special dyes. Beside them were the patchwork quilts from Oylegate, Monasterevan and Fethard, showing great taste and distinction.

The rush work and basket work was there in great variety — from the Industrial Bungalow at Enniscorthy and also from Fethard and Termonfechin. There were some beautiful sycamore potato bowls from Tyrone, and some of the wooden salt boxes that hang on the walls in country cottages made by a blind carpenter in Tipperary. A varied and excellent exhibit came from Termonfechin, which included gloves, willow baskets, footballs, knitting, bottled fruits and vegetables and jams. There were some beautifully cured skins from Castletown, and leather work from Hinchoge in Carrickmines and Shillelagh.

Toys, Rugs

There was a variety of country produce, including fruit drinks, candied peel, sweets, bottled fruits and some magnificent cheeses. They seem to specialise in toys in Co. Wexford, and they were sent up from Gorey, the UI branch at Bannow, and Miss Collins's industry. There were also some from Cork and the Avoca Industries showed some very attractive soft woolly ones.

The rugs were very interesting, for besides the beautiful coloured ones from Mayo, there were hooked rugs from Fethard, dyed with natural dyes, from onion, ling and elderberry. The designs by Miss M. Jellett were restful and dignified.

Country Cures

An unusual exhibit was that of a group of country cures sent from Mayo by a country woman who had used them all her life; these are traditional cures and well-known in the country tradition to the present day for their practical qualities.

We should like to have seen more iron work. The bread iron from Donegal, tongs from Wicklow, and hinges from Tipperary were very good specimens of their kind and more might be done in that way.

The Clare embroidery and some beautiful specimens of lace occupied one corner and another specially attractive group were a collection of sweet smelling herbs from 'an old world garden' at Dundrum.

Gloves and Shoes

There were súgán chairs from Kerry, Tipperary and Clare, each showing their characteristic shape; they were comfortable and well made and all different, and beside these were the highly finished and very modern ones made at Monksgrange, Enniscorthy. The lambs' wool quilts from Gortlomain, Gorey and Tara Hill and gloves and shoes

from Fethard, showed a rapid development of this industry, and
sheep's wool rugs looked very warm and comfortable.

Pottery was shown from several places — Practical jars and jugs from
Coalisland and Youghal, stone ware from Shillelagh, more ornamental
things from Carrigaline, and some very artistic exhibits of 'Knapton' pottery made by Miss Dill Wiliams at her studio in Dun Laoghaire.

Natural Dyes

Perhaps the most outstanding group of all was a row of small wooden bowls,
each holding a root and a few leaves of the most commonly used dyes —
onion, ling. birchbark, lichen, elderberry, walnut, blackberry, and others.

Miss Gahan is to be congratulated most warmly on her skilful
arrangement of the varied industries, and the short descriptive notes
accompanying each exhibit added greatly to their interest.

The following exhibits were judged by Mr Hughes of the Irish Cottage
Industries, Dawson St, Dublin and awarded stars of merit:

-   Knitting: Mrs Ward, Kincasslagh, Co. Donegal; Mrs. Faherty, Aran
    Island, Co. Galway
-   Homespuns: Mrs Chambers, Shrahmore, Co. Mayo
-   Homespun Rugs: Patrick Madden, Ballymoy, Co. Mayo
-   Handweaving: Miss Wynne, Avoca, Co. Wicklow
-   Hooked Wool Rug: UI, Fethard, Co. Tipperary
-   Lace (Carrickmacross): Miss McQuillan, Crossmaglen, Co. Armagh;
    (Limerick): Clare Embroidery Class, Ballyala, Ennis
-   Crochet: Knitting and Crochet Industry, Westport, Co. Mayo
-   Sprigging: Mrs Barton, Donegal
-   Mountmellick Work: Mrs Carter, Castletown UI, Leix
-   Quilts (Patchwork): Mrs McKeown, Oylegate UI, Co. Wexford; also
    winner of 2nd prize in the UI Branch exhibit presented by Mr Hughes
    of the Cottage Industries; (Patchwork): Mrs Fortune, Oylegate UI,
    Co. Wexford; (Embroidered): Mrs Pollard, Tipperary; (Applique and
    Homespun): Miss Lougheed, Dromore West, Co. Mayo
-   Baskets (Willow): Termonfechin UI, Co. Louth: (Rush): Fethard UI,
    Co. Tipperary
-   Gloves: Termonfechin UI, winners of a special prize given by the
    Country Shop for best UI exhibit
-   Uses of Sheep's Wool and Skins: Homecured Sheepskin Shoes:
    Fethard UI, Co. Tipperary

- Carpentry (Súgán Chair): F. O'Brien, Ballyalla, Ennis; (Oak Chair): Richard Orpen, Monk's Grange Enniscorthy
- Model of Car: James Stamp, Oylegate, Co. Wexford
- Wooden Bowls: John Atwell. Dungannon, Co. Tyrone
- Carving: Mrs Walker, Portlaw, Co. Waterford
- Pottery: E.D.M. Williams, Knapton Rd., Dun Laoghaire; J. Crawford, Shillelagh, Co. Wicklow
- Toys: Gorey UI, Co. Wexford; Miss Lamb, Enniskeane, Co. Cork
- Ironwork: J. McGarvey, Dunfanaghy, Co. Donegal; Robert Taylor, Kilcandra, Co. Wicklow
- Cheese: Mrs Barrow, Milestown, Co. Louth
- Bottled Fruit and Jams: Mrs Walsh, Termonfechin, Co. Louth
- Vegetable Dyes: P. O'Connell, Fethard, Co. Tipperary
- Country Cures: Mrs Dominick Murray, Shrahmore, Co. Mayo
- Flowers and Herbs: G. Thompson, The Old World Garden, Dundrum

Irish Homespun Society

In 1935, the Irish Homespun Society, An Cumann Sníomhacháin, was set up to revive rural industry in a permanent and economically viable way, giving advice on design and colour.

Agnes O'Farrelly of University College, Dublin was at one period chairperson as were UI members, Muriel Gahan and Dulcibella (Daa) Barton, sister of Robert Childers Barton, who had been a signatory of the 1921 Anglo-Irish Treaty. Daa Barton was a member of the Gaelic League and an early member of the UI. The Irish Homespun Society worked closely with the Irish Folklore Commission, until it became inactive in 1959.

Later Craft Exhibitions

Success brings its own problems and it was soon realised that the Country Shop could not hold an exhibition every year like the 1933 one. Such an undertaking would be too disruptive. In addition, there had been no major UI exhibit at the RDS Spring Show since 1930. The revival of the exhibit at the Spring Show seemed the answer: only there could crafts be exposed to such a volume of visitors from all over Ireland.

4
1930s AND THE BIRTH OF ICA

The 1930s brought a resurgence and increased membership within UI, due mostly to the establishment of the summer schools and Country Workers. At the same time, Ireland was hit by the great depression of 1930.

This depression meant exports fell by 10 per cent in 1931/32, and prices for agricultural produce declined even more rapidly. Emigration ceased and the flow of remittances from emigrants declined. The British government began to adopt protectionist policies. As a result of these developments, the Irish government introduced tariffs on bacon, butter and oats as well as on a range of industrial products in 1931.[1]

The scenario which the UI tried to address was a grim one. Homes in rural Ireland in the 1930s and 1940s did not have running water, electricity, or telephones. Roads were not tarred, there was little public lighting, and rural women led a harsh lifestyle — one of endless hauling of water, with the endless grind of cooking and washing inside, not to mention all the work women did outside, and then (by way of relaxing!) working by poor light in the evening.

UI IN 1930s

At this time, UI used temporary offices at the Employment Bureau for Women at 33 Molesworth St, before moving to the Civics Institute in South William St, which they left in the autumn of 1937 to move to a back room at 23 St Stephen's Green, home to Country Workers Ltd, and in 1944 changed to two front rooms where they remained until they purchased 58 Merrion Road in 1964.

The Executive was very conscious of the need for leadership in a struggling association, and never underestimated the importance and potential of the regular branch meeting for grassroots members. As Ferriter pointed out[2] a central theme throughout the ICA's history has been that of trying to preserve traditional, almost sacrosanct, family values whilst being open to new ideas. Regular guild meetings became an important social activity and linked very closely with members' homes. As one member put it:

> As homemakers and homekeepers, women are all the better for getting out of them occasionally and when they meet in the guild they are talking about it, planning for it, returning always with some new scheme for it, and with renewed interest.[3]

UI continued to inform members and publicise its work through its regular page in the *Farmers' Gazette*:[4]

Winter Programme Planning

To get full value out of the UI monthly meeting, it is worthwhile planning it in some detail beforehand. The branch is in a sense a hostess to itself, and an evening's entertainment takes as much planning and forethought as any other party where varied interests have to be catered for. At first sight, programme planning strikes a cold chill of terror in the heart of a UI Hon. Sec., who surely bears the burden of most of the planning and organising. How is it possible to ensure that the plan shall be carried out? How can one get outside help? And how to get a plan that will please all the members? All these thoughts resolve themselves into an effort to get a specimen programme together, and to try it and see how the members respond, and once started, ideas begin to come and one thing suggests another.

Monthly meetings generally last from two to three hours. Business should be the first item for twenty minutes, followed by a competition in which all members are expected to take part. Examples of these might take the form of cookery, best thrift article or home-made sweets or cakes, which can be either sold for the benefit of the branch or sampled by all at the tea which follows. Ten minutes for the first, 20 minutes for the tea, then a roll call, which may be instructive or amusing, every one should answer to this, or pay a penny to the funds. Travel talks are interesting for 10 or 20 minutes, and most people have friends who travel to distant parts of the country, if not further. Occasionally, a 6d market might be arranged, each member bringing something which cost them under 6d. to make, and they buy from each other, the proceeds being given for some special object.

The great advantage of pre-arranged programmes is that all the members come prepared to take their part.

Christmas Sales[5]
UIs in different parts of the country are busy preparing for their branch sales, which create not only a spirit of enterprise, but also bring local wellwishers together in desire to support home productions. Castletown and Abbeyleix are holding a combined sale in the UI hall, Castletown (in Upper Ossory) on Thurs, 7th.; while all the Co. Wexford branches have a sale and exhibition in St. Kirin's Hall, Wexford on Friday and Saturday, 15th. and 16th. inst.; Beltra (Co. Sligo) on Wed. 13th.

UI and Country Workers' guild Calendar
This calendar is just out in time to make a most charming Xmas gift. It is exactly what one wants in a calendar, very simple and very clear and the letterpress is beautifully chosen and arranged. The printing and general format is excellent. We hope that all branches and Irish countrywomen will support this interesting enterprise, and will send for their supplies immediately. They can be had from the UI office, 58 South William St. Dublin, or from Miss Brichenden, La Verna, Gorey, Co. Wexford, price 8d. uncoloured; 9d. coloured. Well worth the extra 1d. for a coloured one, we think! Postage 2d. extra.

At the 1931 AGM, Lucy Franks reported that the association was making progress and that there were eighteen active branches around the country. Seven of these were in Wexford — Bannow, Camolin, Curracloe, Gorey, Old Ross, Screen and Oylegate; three in Sligo — Beltra, Dromard and Inniscrone, two each in Tipperary — Fethard and Nenagh — and Queen's County — Abbeyleix and Castletown, with one each in Kilkenny (Ballyragget), Clare (Gortloman), Limerick (Knockarron) and Louth (Termonfechin). Two years later, at the 1933 AGM, Franks reported that despite the difficult year the existing branches had carried on steadily and new branches had been formed at Dunmore East, Co. Waterford, and Clonakilty and Courtmacsherry, Co. Cork.

BIRTH OF ICA
The UI was a non-political and non-sectarian organisation, yet as early as 1910 the political connotations of the name had been

recognised. Horace Plunkett stated that there was a possibility that some would see a hidden political agenda behind such a title. Again, in the 1916 minutes, an attempt to change the name failed, and between then and 1918 the issue was exhaustively discussed and caused endless rows. At the Spring Show stalls of 1929, the name 'UI and Country Workers guild' was used and a suggestion was made that the name should be kept permanently.

The Society's firm adherence to their rule of 'no politics' did not save them from coming under suspicion of being in some way attached to a new political association formed just then with almost the same name as their own. So, with infinite regret, it was decided that the old name 'The Society of United Irishwomen' must go and give place to the new 'Irish Countrywomen's Association'. At the 1934 AGM the following resolution was proposed by Lady Crofton, seconded by Lady Franks and carried unanimously: 'That owing to the present confusion of the name of the society with the political society now formed in Ireland, it is expedient that this society be dissolved and the requisite steps be forthwith taken to give effect to this resolution and to conform with the requirements of the Friendly Society Act of 1896.'

At the final meeting of UI, 16 January 1935, it was proposed by Lady Fingall, seconded by Mrs Gainfort and carried unanimously that: 'the sum of £829 3s 5d in the Nursing Fund be handed over to the Queen's Institute for District Nursing in Ireland and that the sum of £137 5s 8d to the credit of UI be paid to ICA' and at the 1935 AGM the transfer from the old UI to the new ICA was made, Lady Fingall being elected President, Miss Franks Hon. Sec. and Miss Edith Orr, assistant Hon. Sec. On the Instrument of Dissolution form necessary under the Friendly Societies Act, 1896, members had to sign showing their consent to the transactions. The membership of the association was then 691, and all but 135 of them actually signed.[6]

In the *Farmers' Gazette* of 13 April 1935, the heading ICA (Comluadar Ban Tuaithe) was seen for the first time and the following statement appeared:

The Society of UI, with which we have all been familiar for so many years has come to an end. The announcement may cause a shock to its adherents who have so loyally supported it through both its sunny and its rainy days.

And again Bishop asks:

Has all this work been in vain? Is failure the end of all these years of struggle and achievement? This is by no means so. On the contrary, it is a case of 'reculer pour mieux sauter' which may be freely translated as 'stepping back to go forward'. If the UI have ceased to be, it is only to make room for another Society, more adapted to the times, more developed and possibly freer in its mode of activity. ICA has really absorbed UI, so that it is the growth of one into the other rather than an end, and a continuation rather than a new beginning. Certain legal technicalities made it necessary to dissolve UI before establishing its successor, but much of the machinery and a large number of the old personnel passes on into the new society.

One great difference in the two constitutions is that the branches are now called guilds. A general decentralisation makes the guilds more independent and gives the countryside a prior importance to the Dublin group. This change has not been brought about without much consideration. General Meetings of UI were called and every point of the question fully discussed. Only then was the decision taken.

Though the older members will necessarily have feelings of regret for the name UI under which they have worked for so long, still they will surely give their energies and support to ICA where there is every hope it will do its large share towards building up rural life in Ireland.

So the new Association was born, though the traditional silver spoon was noticeably lacking and its absence would have to be made good by hard and continuous work.

ICA's First Annual Reports

In 1936–37, ICA had an office at 58 South William St, courtesy of Dublin Corporation. It still received no grant from government.

The annual report expressed pleasure that no large balance was reported, as it is ICA's policy not to lay by money once a safe margin for expenditure is assured. One guild was able to pay off a £29 debt during the year on its own hall whilst another guild laid down a hard tennis court. Committee work included children's parties, clothes for sale for the needy, nursing funds as well as demonstrations, craft classes, country dancing, talks, shows and stalls.

In 1938, the office was installed at 23 St Stephen's Green, courtesy of Country Workers. The ICA now had 61 guilds with a membership of over 2,000.

In 1939, regular guild meetings were of primary importance. 'There were also the different messages propagated through the now weekly ICA page in the *Farmers' Gazette* — it was essential that print overcame the restrictions of physical travel, that news from the different guilds be relayed, competitions be publicised and recipes and ideas for improved homemaking be swapped, as well as providing an outlet for the creativity of the more inspired members.'[7] It is interesting to note the variety of topics covered by the inter-guild competition for the winter of 1939, when six topics were chosen: 1. Thrift — article should not be more than 1/–, 2. Knitting — a pair of men's socks, 3. Vegetable Dying — six wool specimens dyed with natural dyes, 4. Folklore — the best collection about Christmas, 5. Handcraft — a pair of handmade slippers and 6. Cookery — a pot of marmalade.

In 1937, when there were seventy guilds, Carnegie United Kingdom Trust granted £500 to ICA to fund an organiser and an organising secretary. Miss Ella Walsh was the first paid organiser.

GUILD ACTIVITIES

The report of guild activities is very interesting when put in the context of the period — dressmaking, embroidery, plain sewing and the making of samplers, knitting, crochet, rug making, Italian quilting, Irish quilting, tufting, sheep's wool quilts and mattresses, glove-making, leatherwork, felt work, scarf making, hand loom weaving, slipper making, sandal making, rush work, basket making, sea grass stools and cane trays, cake making and icing, jams and marmalade, fruit bottling, cookery and a lecture demonstration by the Electricity Supply Board. (It was to take another ten years before rural electrification took place.) Lectures were given on a wide range of subjects, including first aid, invalid cookery and home nursing, the treatment of cuts and bruises, the prevention of tuberculosis, general hygiene and health talks and a lecture on diet, travel talks on Spain, Italy and other locations, lectures on poultry keeping, winter egg production, horticulture, fruit and vegetable growing and cooking, bulb growing, the planning of a herbaceous border, a lantern lecture on Irish antiquities, a lecture from the Abbey players, nature talks, talk on the Associated Countrywomen of the World and the ideals of the ICA.

Singing, Irish dancing, drama, and keep fit exercises formed part of the programme of some guilds, as well as excursions and picnics to places of local interest and beauty spots, also garden fetes and Christmas parties.

It was considered that no guild should count itself complete unless it undertook some work for others, and most guilds tried to fulfil this. The following are some of the ways in which guilds have helped others:

- Jumble sales and raffles for the parish
- Giving a children's party and treasure hunt
- Inviting another guild to a party
- Providing meals for school children
- Donations to central office
- Making clothes for distribution at Christmas, making layettes and holding needlework parties for a stall in aid of the Nursing Association
- Raising money to provide boots for poor children or making garments for distribution by the St Vincent de Paul Society
- Running a coffee van each month at a fair, organising a milk depot, providing meals for school children, working for the blind, carol singing and raffling a co-operative quilt to raise funds to help the local Jubilee Nurse
- Giving grants to the nursing fund, toys to the Orthopaedic Hospital, clothes to the Chinese Relief

ICA has always been aware of the importance of developing the social side of women's lives, and the improvement of homes or the making of handcrafts for profit were of secondary consideration.

The policy of ICA over the years was to teach countrywomen to tackle their own problems in a self-reliant way without depending too much on outside help. Members who attended conferences, in Ireland or abroad, had to submit their findings for circulation to all members. The same was true of all lectures and seminars — the object being to keep members informed and brighten rural life.

Muintir na Tíre, reformed in 1937, held a rural week summer school which ICA was invited to attend, and where ICA was also asked to give lectures. The minutes show that members were pleased to have another opportunity to make a case for rural women.

Lucy Franks represented the UI at the second ACWW conference in Stockholm in 1933, where she informed delegates of UI initiatives such as the Country Shop and the Summer Schools, as well as reporting on the social work of UI and that of the Women's National Health Association of Ireland. Indeed it was at this conference that the name ACWW was chosen and Lady Aberdeen was appointed honorary president. For a world conference of ACWW in London in 1938, ICA organised a céilí, and a team of national dancers travelled to take part in entertaining the delegates. Delegates were invited to become 'Foundation Friends' and the 'Pennies for Friendship' scheme was launched, inviting women in different organisations to contribute one penny each to the inter-national body. (ICA guilds are still very active in this worthwhile scheme although the 'pennies' have long been replaced with larger currency). The participation of UI and later ICA in ACWW was a great help in its development.

In the 1930s UI also began its links with the Joint Committee of Women's Societies and Social Workers. The committee was set up in 1935, after the Corrigan Report on sexual offences was pre-sented to government. This report suggested raising the age of consent to eighteen years, equal treatment in law for a woman found soliciting and her client, provision of a women's police force and jury service for women on the same basis as men. UI members also sought to tackle the social ills of city life as Dublin suffered serious deprivation and poverty. One member, Senator Kathleen Browne, accused the government of providing 'less protection to our young girls than the do the governments of Great Britain and Northern Ireland'.[8] The Joint Committee of Women's Societies and Social Workers continued to represent fourteen organisations on matters affecting women, young persons and children until 1993.

Among the new guilds opened in 1938 was one in Cappagh Hospital, Finglas, Co. Dublin, well known for its work in treating bone TB in young people. Practically every county in Ireland was represented among the patients. Most of these girls would return home after a period and each would act as propagandist for the ICA in her own district. In spite of their disabilities the patients were thrilled to be members of ICA and great things were expected of them.

Town Associates

Cork and Dublin Town Associates continued to grow, with the object of helping country guilds and acting as their godmothers. On these Town Associates fell the responsibility for providing lecturers and demonstrators, organising and running the stall at the RDS Spring Show for the display and sale of guild handcrafts, organising and running the monthly 'inter-guild competitions' which did so much to stimulate a healthy spirit of competition and to raise standards. The subjects for these competitions were chosen by the guilds themselves, through their delegates at the summer school, and covered a very diverse list of cultural and practical subjects. The members of the Town Associates were also responsible for the entertainment of visiting guild members and for finding hospitality for them when they attended meetings or were visiting hospital etc. They also organised Study Circles from time to time to provide an opportunity to learn more about certain subjects allied to the work of the ICA. In addition they ran a library of plays and had among their numbers experts in drama who were available to give help to guilds needing assistance in the production of plays. The Town Associates provided a valuable training ground in the work of the ICA and were a source of inspiration and help to the guilds in their area.

IRELAND IN 1937 — A NEW CONSTITUTION FOR A CHANGING COUNTRY

By the mid-1930s it was clear that the 1922 Constitution was no longer adequate, and the 1937 Constitution was voted in by 685,105 votes to 527,945, with over 30 per cent of the electorate abstaining. 'The 1937 Constitution was very much the work of de Valera, though the influence of the Catholic hierarchy was everywhere evident.'[9]

Through it de Valera tried to reconcile a number of opposing views:

> He made it fulfil nationalist aspirations by claiming to apply to the whole island but kept it realistic in limiting its practical application to the 26 counties. He made it republican in having a President as head of state but tried to avoid annoying the British or the unionists by not using that word, and he made it liberal and democratic in protecting certain freedoms and conservatively Catholic in its treatment of divorce, women and various social issues.[10]

Few groups in Irish society opposed the document, except women's groups who complained that Article 41 relegated women

Above: Diamond Jubilee Meitheal. ICA members re-enact the first ICA meeting of 1910.

Below: Past Presidents. *Back (L to R):* Nora Burton, Oonagh Corbett. *Front (L to R):* Josephine Carroll, Alice Ryan, Bea Trench.

Above: Miss A. Ryan and Mrs J. Norman at a pottery class with tutor Hester Levinge (*right*).

Left: Mother and Child Week. Children enjoy an art class while their mothers attend courses.

Opposite Page
Above: Co. Donegal members at a weaving class.

Below: Poultry farming, 1961. *L to R:* May Keely, Eileen Leahy, May Madden and G. Tubridy.

Above: Cookery course at An Grianán, 1970. Miss Kilduff (*left*) shares cookery tips with ICA members Mrs Una Sackman and Mrs Maura Stankard, Galway.

Below: ICA members in the 1990s enjoy a traditional meal hosted by the Chinese Embassy.

Above: The first residential course at An Grianán was held from 21 to 26 June 1954. Irish Traditional Music and Dance lessons were given by Dr Donal O'Sullivan and Treasa Bean Uí Currin, ICA, Ring, Co. Waterford. Members are pictured here on the lawn outside An Grianán.

Below: ICA members in attendance at the 1949 summer school in Galway.

Above: The Christmas Workshop group at An Grianán, 1970. Includes Mrs K. Hogan and Mrs J. Norman (tutors) and Sister Lelia from Thailand.

Below: Albanian singers entertain members at a recent ICA function.

Above: Students of the Horticulture course receive diplomas, December 1973. With the National President of the ICA, Mrs Josephine Carroll, the Principal of the College, Mr Kevin O'Carroll, and Mr W. O'Toole, Senior Inspector, Department of Agriculture, are (*back row, L to R*): Katie Corrigan, Julie Daly, Susan Deery, Mary Poinard, Mary Galligan, Eleanor Costello; (*front row, L to R*): Grainne Prior, Noreen Canavan.

Below: Lily Barrett, President of Tipperary Federation, unveils a plaque to mark the United Irish summer school at Sliabh na mBan in 1929.

Above: Mrs Kit Ahern, National President, ICA (1961–4) pictured at Shannon Airport (with bouquet) prior to a four-month worldwide tour. She was seen off by the Mayor of Limerick, Mrs Condell (fourth from left) and members of the ICA Guilds from Limerick and Kerry.

Right: ICA members on a trip to China in 1994.

to the kitchen sink. Hannah Sheehy Skeffington was one who did not agree with the constitution as her niece recalled:

> In 1937, I learned a little of her past feminism when she became steeped in the protest against de Valera's new Constitution. No more window smashing or hunger-striking, but active lobbying of TDs, pertinent letters to the papers, protest meetings, and a postcard canvas. The final rally in the Round Room of the Mansion House ended with prolonged acclamations for her rousing appeal to form a women's political party.[11]

All the women's protests were in vain as de Valera refused to take their fears on board, refusing even to meet them.

Much as Fianna Fáil and Cumann na nGaedheal may have differed on other issues, in their dealings with the hierarchy both parties reflected the values and opinions of the Church. While Cosgrave refused to make divorce legal, de Valera made it unconstitutional in 1937. While Cosgrave banned the sale of literature publicising contraceptives, de Valera's Criminal Law Amendment Bill banned the sale of contraceptives themselves. When the war broke out in Europe in 1939 the Church was in full support of the government's policy of neutrality.

In retrospect it seems strange that there was so little protest at much of the legislation passed between 1922 and 1939. It may be that emigration acted as a safety-valve and drained off those who were most likely to disturb the status quo and campaign for change. The Protestant minority was subdued in its response to many of the developments in the Free State, though Protestants did express in a determined fashion their resentment at the imposition of compulsory Irish in schools.

Much of the legislation passed in the 1930s reinforced the prevailing conservative view of the role of women in Irish society. In 1932 married women were banned from teaching in National schools, and this was later extended to the Civil Service where women had to surrender their jobs when they married.

The prospects of promotion for women were slim as it was assumed they would marry. Women were also paid less than men. This state of affairs endured until Ireland's entry to the EEC in 1973.

The government did introduce some social reform measures in the 1930s. In 1932, old-age pensions for the blind were increased. 1933 saw legislation on unemployment assistance, and in 1935 pensions were provided for widows and orphans.

COMMISSION ON VOCATIONAL ORGANISATION

In 1939 the government set up the Commission on Vocational Organisation. It heard evidence from a large number of organisations — professional bodies, trade unions and voluntary groups. It was a reluctant reaction to the demands of parish enthusiasts for a more decentralised system of Irish governance. By the end of the 1930s many women needed a voice in policymaking as it affected them. Women demanded that the state take some responsibility for childcare, or recognise the work of the woman of the house in some way. In addition, the voluntary social work carried out by many women who did not work for wages outside the home was not recognised by government. This commission gave some of these organisations a chance to state their views.[12] Amongst the groups who made submissions were the National Council for Women, the Joint Committee of Women's Societies and Social Workers, the Catholic Federation of Women Secondary School Teachers, and the ICA.

The ICA set up a sub-group to draw up a memorandum of its history, present activities and future needs. In December 1939, ICA applied for a hearing on the Vocational Commission, both by memorandum and by witnesses, and their reasons were three-fold:

1. ICA was the only association of countrywomen and was the largest body of women's opinion in Ireland.

2. The association was engaged in what it regarded as the most important work at that time in the country — homemaking and agriculture.

3. Governments of other countries realised the importance of countrywomen's movements (ICA was aware of this through membership of ACWW) but the Irish government had not yet realised it.

The Commission replied enclosing its terms of reference and requesting forty copies of a memorandum of such evidence. Despite being a voluntary organisation spread over 26 counties with no funding, ICA put a great deal of hard work into this submission and the oral hearing. They argued that countrywomen needed to be represented vocationally in a separate category both from farmers — thought of as male — and from other women working in the home, because they were both producers and consumers and it was impossible to distinguish their remunerative work from their home and life maintenance work.[13] The chairman, Bishop Michael Browne, was hostile to the women's definitions and demands, an attitude most probably stemming from a contemporary fear of women in public life.[14]

The ICA took some solace that it was not alone in receiving such treatment, as the same kind of obvious unfriendliness was shown to the other women's organisations. When the report of the Commission on Vocational Organisation appeared in 1944, there was no permanent place for 'home-makers' on the proposed National Vocational Assembly, although there was a provision for their co-option. Sean Lemass as Minster for Industry and Commerce confirmed that the government took a wholly negative view of the report and the Assembly never came into being, but the Commission's perspective on women's household work showed their evaluation of its importance and crucially, the very faint consultative voice they were prepared to allow its representatives.[15]

By 1939 when World War II broke out and Ireland declared its neutrality, ICA had an increased membership — 78 guilds in 22 of the 26 counties — and a stronger mandate. It was ever confident of achieving the objective of 'Better living' for rural women mainly through education and upgrading the members' skills in various handcrafts, but it was important that there should also be a social element. However, the association was struggling financially — the government was unable or unwilling to help, because 'they have far more important matters to attend to before the organising of countrywomen can be seen to.[16]

5
STRUCTURE OF ICA

The UI spread from its foundation in 1910, with its first branch in Bree, Co. Wexford. Soon there were other branches in Wexford as well as in Clare, Tipperary, Donegal, Laois and Cork. All these were governed by a centralised office in Dublin, until 1935. With the change of name to ICA, branches became guilds with authority for self-regulating. The structure devised at that time remains basically intact to the present day.

The revised constitution of the ICA, which was adopted at the AGM on 4 April 1990, states:

> 1. The name of the Association is Bantracht na Tuaithe or, in English, The Irish Countrywomen's Association (ICA).
>
> 2. Aims and Objectives: The objects of the Association are to bring women together in fellowship and through co-operative effort to develop and improve the standard of rural and urban life in Ireland, having due regard for our Irish culture, and to encourage the use of the Irish language in the affairs of Bantracht na Tuaithe. [*This Irish-language clause was added at a later AGM — Ed.*]

ICA PRESIDENTS

The ICA, as a voluntary organisation, has been very fortunate in the calibre of women elected President. Each had her own brand of presidency and different style and talents, and these combined to ensure that, overall, women gained — becoming better informed to make up their own minds, and therefore feeling better about themselves and wanting better and brighter homes, better lifestyles and better access to education and opportunities.

Various styles of President worked differently — some traditional, others radical, some interested in conservation and culture, others in business and enterprise. Yet each had only three years to achieve her goals. This often proved inadequate leaving the incoming President with the unfinished business of her predecessor, and as often happened, she did not necessarily hold the same ideas and opinions. Despite this, it is to each President's credit that the ICA, as a voluntary association, became such a powerful force in Irish society.

UI AND ICA PRESIDENTS 1910–2000

1910–1912	Anita Lett, Wexford
1912–1942	Lady Fingall, Meath
1942–1952	Lucy Franks, Laois
1952–1955	Alice Ryan, Tipperary
1955–1958	Olivia Hughes, Tipperary
1958–1961	Dorothy Smith, Cavan
1961–1964	Kit Ahern, Kerry
1964–1967	Nora Burton, Cork
1967–1970	Peggy Farrell, Roscommon
1970–1972	Oonagh Corbett, Wexford
1972–1974	Josephine Carroll, Monaghan
1974–1976	Bea Trench, Meath
1976–1979	Patsy Lawlor, Kildare
1979–1982	Camilla Hannon, Meath
1982–1985	Mamo McDonald, Monaghan
1985–1988	Ina Broughall, Carlow
1988–1991	Kitty Harlin, Meath
1991–1994	Monica Prendiville, Kerry
1994–1997	Brídín Twist, Clare
1997–2000	Eva Coyle, Donegal
2000–	Breda Raggett, Kilkenny

ICA STRUCTURE

STRUCTURE	REPRESENTATION	MEETINGS
COUNCIL	Executive Committee One voting delegate and non-voting members from each guild	3 times a year
EXECUTIVE COMMITTEE	27 Federation Presidents Eight elected members Honorary officers Five buan cairde	as arranged
FEDERATION	Elected officers Guild delegates Specialist officers County Development Advisers	Quarterly
GUILD	Elected officers Guild members	Monthly

COUNCIL: Council is the governing body of the ICA. It meets three times each year. Every guild in the country is entitled to send one voting delegate, though meetings are also open to all ICA members who wish to attend. The work of carrying out the instructions of Council is entrusted to the Executive.

EXECUTIVE: The administration of the ICA's affairs, subject to the control and direction of the Council, is carried out by the Executive Committee. It consists of the ICA President, the honorary secretary, the honorary treasurer, the five Vice-Presidents, the Buan Cairde, the Presidents of the 27 Federations and eight elected ICA members — two from each province. All elections are by secret ballot and no one office may be held for more than three years. The Executive Committee conducts the day-to-day business of the ICA but must be, in the words of the constitution, '... subject in all things to the control and direction of the Council whose orders it shall obey'.

FEDERATION: Where there are four or more guilds in a county, a county Federation may be formed, helping to strengthen the guilds in that county and to decentralise the work. The early Federations were Wexford in 1932 followed by Cork in 1936 and later Tipperary in 1941, with other counties very soon following their example. They proved a great support to the guilds, through more frequent county meetings, easier transport leading to greater mutual support, less dependence on any central system which in time should be necessary only as a link, unifying sturdy and self-reliant local groups. Federations became vitally important to guilds in developing local initiatives, a sense of responsibility and co-operation with county services of every kind. They have knowledge and understanding of local conditions not possible in a more centralised body, and in time this networking and exchange of views became one of the most valuable aspects of the association.

In the 1940s and 1950s if there were insufficient guilds in any one county, neighbouring county Federations were formed until each was strong enough to stand alone. By 1953, every county in Ireland had an ICA guild. Federation meetings are held quarterly and are open to all guild members in the county. Each guild appoints one member to be its voting delegate.

GUILD: The guild is the unit or basis of the ICA around which the whole structure of the movement has grown. The guild annually elects a President and committee. A guild may be formed in any place, rural or urban and membership is open to all women over sixteen years — there are no barriers of race, creed, class or political persuasion. All shades of opinion are represented by the more than 18,000 members who co-operate in a voluntary, non-sectarian and non-party political way to achieve their objectives. There are approximately 1,000 ICA guilds all over Ireland with a Federation in each of the 26 counties of Ireland, the exception being Tipperary which has two (a throwback to the Grand Jury System).

The formation of guilds has changed very little down through the years. In 1950, Esther Bishop wrote:

> One of the most valuable functions of the Association is in the training of women for leadership, and that this is coming to be recognised is made clear by the ever-growing number of its members who are being elected to public bodies all over the country. We hope that they are only the vanguard and that they will soon be joined by many others. That the need for women in public life was recognised by thinkers long ago is shown by the following quotation from an essay by AE in which he says: 'Women's voices were never heard in the councils of the Irish; therefore life has decayed in Ireland'.

Work of the guilds
This work naturally varies from district to district, so that any short survey is bound to be incomplete and generalised.

Most new guilds begin by concentrating largely on hand crafts, but after they pass the teething stage they demand more outlet for their energies than is supplied by hand crafts or by entertainment, and many of them find in social work an outlet for their gifts and their imaginations. Public questions create much interest and the extent to which these occupy the minds of the guilds is shown by the list of resolutions sent up to Council meeting during one year. These resolutions concerned school meals; the law of inheritance and succession; the supply of iodised salt to the districts in South Tipperary where goitre is very prevalent; the restoration of drawing as an obligatory subject in primary schools.

The practical work of each guild covers such subjects as poultry rearing, on the subject of which lectures and demonstrations are eagerly sought; lectures and demonstrations in gardening and bee-keeping, in first-aid and child welfare; in cookery, jam making and the preserving of fruit and vegetables; classes in handcrafts of every description, including dressmaking, weaving, dyeing and spinning. Cultural subjects are very popular and such things as Irish traditional dancing, music and drama are fostered.

As well as the ordinary work of the guild, each one is expected to undertake some social work outside it at least once a year and this takes very many forms and includes charitable work such as visiting the blind, collecting eggs for and dispatching them to the sick in hospitals, providing a fund for boots for needy children, etc. It also includes social work of such a varied nature as helping to maintain the district nurse; assisting at agricultural shows; and parish entertainment; running clean milk depots; running a coffee stall at a fair; running Christmas markets and acting as Branches of the County Library.[1]

FUNDING

All ICA members work in a voluntary capacity but the association employs a full-time General Secretary and staff at the central office in Dublin, a National Development Officer, a Counsellor, a Director and staff at the Adult Education College, and a Principal and staff at the Horticultural College. The ICA is chiefly financed through membership fees, and in recognition of its contribution to national life, government grants are also provided by the Departments of Agriculture and Education. Financial institutions, business and vocational bodies also give generous sponsorship to many ICA projects and to courses at An Grianán.

However, it is from abroad that the finance has come for the major ICA developments — firstly from the UK Carnegie Trust, then the Counterpart Fund-Marshall Aid, and over the last fifty years the Kellogg Foundation, USA, has been ICA's greatest ally.

FACILITIES

Through guild meetings, attending Council meetings and courses at An Grianán, members have the opportunity to acquire the knowledge and skills they choose. Courses are run in arts and crafts, public speaking, home economics and gardening. Members may also study historical, scientific, literary and cultural subjects as well as taking part in dancing, musical and dramatic activities. The international agenda is of vital importance to the average ICA member, and can include seminars, information workshops and even visits to foreign countries, in addition to hosting foreign visitors on numerous occasions.

Through the ICA, women all over Ireland are in constant touch with the government at national and local level, and the views and advice of the association are regularly sought by government departments. ICA representatives sit on many national committees (although women are poorly represented on most statutory bodies, however, considering they make up 51 per cent of the population.)

Facilities to set up home and small businesses, both individual and co-operative, with emphasis on a high standard of craftsmanship, is another important aspect of ICA activity.

6
THE 'EMERGENCY' AND ITS AFTERMATH

ICA DURING WORLD WAR II

At the start of the second world war, the ICA from its office in the Country Shop was struggling to secure funding, and its programmes were very much taken up with the practicalities of home-making and home-living as it related to the everyday existence of rural women. The ICA was concerned with preserving the best of Irish traditional culture but also being open to new ideas.

Conditions had not improved very much for women in rural Ireland since independence, and the ICA never underestimated the importance of the regular guild meetings as social events for members. Ferriter refers to the importance of guilds when he discusses the change of the society's name:

> The change in structure brought about by the name change in 1935 meant that branches were changed to self-managing and self-financing guilds, and the governance of the ICA was taken from a small executive to a national council of guilds, each with a vote, with meetings to be held quarterly.[1]

This is the structure that still remains. In 1940 these regular guild meetings were unrivalled in giving rural women the confidence, knowledge and practice to lobby effectively and to work assuredly with other rural organisations.

Lucy Franks speaking in Cork in September 1939 and referring to the political situation, urged 'guilds to prepare themselves, to join Red Cross, organise to make the best of everything we have got in the country, to economise in every department of the home and to grow more food'.

The 1940/41 annual report is peppered with reports of food shortages due to the war — yet in spite of all the difficulties ICA continued to flourish. In fact the crisis showed the great need for such an association, which allows the countrywomen of Ireland to be organised and ready to meet any emergency. Guilds were urged to grow more food and to make the best and most economical use of resources. Most rural families were self-supporting, but guilds were well aware of the plight of their fellow women, such as for example Marlborough St Parish in Dublin with its population of many thousands, most of them poor people living in tenements without a square yard of soil on which to grow food. ICA members realised that they must do their share of national food production by producing more and buying less imported goods.

In 1942, the Irish Housewives Association (IHA) was formed to campaign for fair prices for producer and consumer, and equitable distribution of all goods including food. Some years later they incorporated the Irish Women's Citizens Association into their membership and in 1966 initiated the Consumers Association of Ireland. 'ICA provided a room at the Country Shop for free, or at a nominal fee, when IHA needed a venue for public meetings and was struggling for financial survival. Down the years we have considered ICA as a sister organisation and we have supported each other on various issues.'[2]

In 1942 Lady Fingall was replaced by Lucy Franks as President. The ICA was concerned with producing enough surplus of the right kind for the continuing health of the nation. New methods of preserving fruit and vegetables for winter consumption were outlined. Derelict ground was taken over and cultivated co-operatively. Poultry and pig stocks were down due to the lack of feedstuffs. Evening meetings of guilds were curtailed because of lack of lighting, and often held only where members could make candles, such as in Abbeydorney, for example. Despite the lack of amenities, members were encouraged to be good economical cooks and clean and tidy housekeepers. Rural houses should be whitewashed, and inexpensive flowers and trees and shrubs grown to brighten the lives of both inhabitants and passers-by. Guilds were urged to keep the best traditions of their districts alive — its history, folklore and crafts have a rightful place in the guild's programme. Finding halls for meetings was a problem, and the social life of guilds got a jolt when tea rationing was introduced, but they continued to sing and dance and took a great interest in the radio broadcasts from the summer school when different counties told how they were coping with the Emergency and the shortage of household supplies. Hints and activities were circulated, one example of constructive thrift being the pattern for a circular skirt made by Alice Ryan at that year's school which was posted to all guilds.

Also in 1942, ICA planned a policy to get women elected at local elections, and drafted a set of questions for their members to ask politicians.

In 1943, the growth of the association continued, reaching 84 guilds in 22 counties with over 2,500 members. Phyllis O'Connell of Fethard, Co. Tipperary was appointed chief organiser, helped by funding of £750 from Country Workers to be matched by £250 from ICA over two years. New trustees of the ICA were Grace Somerville-Large, Alice Ryan and Josephine MacNeill.

The interests of members had widened noticeably. 'Provision of meals for school children, prevention of tuberculosis, improved conditions in rural schools and a healthy and adequate milk supply are all subjects of vital interests to all women but until recently there has been a marked apathy and lack of any feeling of responsibility by the majority of women in both town and country towards these most urgent needs. Now the countrywomen are interested and once roused they will not rest until they get something done.'

In 1942, the National Planning Council requested the ICA's views on farm improvements and facilities for rural recreation, in connection with the exhibition planned for 1943. The ICA complied by preparing a list of questions for guilds, and the National Planning Council acknowledged their contribution but noted that the proposed exhibition had been postponed. Some months later they again asked the ICA for information and criticism on such subjects as planning the farm kitchen, the grouping of rural houses, and schemes of rural water supply and electricity. The ICA had over the years voiced its disapproval of the methods of building labourers' cottages, with Anita Lett criticising the cottages in 1912, since the majority were built facing away from sunlight, far from a water supply and many of them were isolated. The association believed that with a little thought the housing could have been so different, and a group of four houses could have justified sinking a well. The ICA Executive was anxious that its views should be given by the ICA delegate to the National Planning Conference in 1944.

The period up to 1945 was one of economic depression partly due to World War II. The war masked the weakness of the government's policy of self-sufficiency in agriculture and protectionism in industry, which by the mid 1940s was causing an economic crisis.

As a great advocate of a united Ireland, de Valera was able to maintain a policy of neutrality during the war precisely because of partition, since Britain would have had to seize the treaty ports if it did not have bases in Ulster. The positive effects of neutrality were that it saved the country from the devastation of warfare, a new sense of national self-sufficiency and confidence was created, and the wide-spread support for the policy of neutrality did much to heal the wounds of the civil war. However, it also had negative effects, including economic stagnation, an increase in emigration as those who may have been more critical of life in the 1940s left the country, and the conservatism of those who remained behind was strengthened. In addition, neutrality cut Ireland off from the mainstream of European affairs with a resultant cultural impoverishment, and neutrality increased the gap between North and South in Ireland.[3]

The ICA annual report claimed that its members formed a united body of women, trained and ready for emergency, who are competent housewives, gardeners, craftswomen, receptive to new ideas, neighbourly, calm in a crisis, good businesswomen, able to sing and dance and to know and love Irish poetry and literature, able to enjoy the simple things of life, lovers of the countryside — lovers of Ireland.

Being an island country and not having a mercantile shipping fleet of its own, many goods (such as tea, fresh fruit, animal feed and dried fruit) were brought by British ships to England and redistributed in Ireland. With each passing year the rations became smaller. Shortages were immediately tackled by ICA who looked for substitutes to bolster the food ration. There are guild accounts of making wax baths from fat of fish and meat and setting wicks in them to provide home-made candles. The use of a haybox was demonstrated as an economic means of cooking, and carrots and parsnips flavoured with vanilla essence were recommended as a substitute for dried fruit in Christmas pudding. Needless to say, petrol was severely rationed and kept for essential services. (A letter in the archives dated 27 September 1946, from the Minister for Industry and Commerce grants the ICA a supplementary allowance of ten units). It is interesting to note that politicians placed responsibility for the quality of rural life in the hands of rural people, yet did not give them resources to achieve this. For example, the Department of Supplies refused to supply kerosene to warm ICA meetings, and the Department of Finance still resisted requests for a grant.

To this period of acute scarcities can be attributed the growth of small guilds within a radius of three to four miles, where members could walk to meetings and walk home in groups. Many of these guilds lasted only for the duration of the war and eventually closed, having served their purpose, with life slowly returning to normality. Bicycles were also used in the Emergency but these too were rare commodities. One record mentions Phyllis O'Connell, the first organiser, cycling from Fethard to Emly, a distance of some 35 miles.[4]

In 1945 the Irish form of the ICA name was changed to Bantracht na Tuatha and in 1949 'My Land' by Thomas Davis was adopted as the ICA anthem.

REPORTS AND SUBMISSIONS

In 1943, ICA made a submission to the Youth Unemployment Commission. 'Mrs Byrne reported that they were received by His Grace the Archbishop of Dublin and that Mr MacInerney had said that the ICA had furnished the best report and that it contained wonderful ideas if they could be achieved. They were very much interested in Miss O'Connell's organising work. His Grace congratulated them and wants to see them again to hear some more about ICA.' In 1948, the ICA made another submission to the Emigration Commission, delegates this time being Esther Bishop and Josephine MacNeill. Its memorandum mentioned the value of a countrywomen's organisation:

> In addition to the value to its members of a society such as ICA, is the value to the State of a strong countrywomen's organisation in voicing the wishes and the needs of a large section of its people. In Ireland, women in agriculture form the largest body of women in industry in the country (census returns). It is on the countrywoman that the well-being of the family depends and the whole structure of our rural life is built on that of the family. It is the desire of the ICA to see the countrywomen taking their full share of responsibility for building up a prosperous, happy Ireland.[5]

Amongst the remedies suggested to curb emigration were an alteration of the educational system to include rural needs, since the current system was based on urban needs with rural children preparing for examinations to find work away from the countryside, the provision of piped water, light and sanitation, long-term loans at low interest for the modernisation of family farms, the creation of pools of agricultural machinery available for hire, and the decentralisation of industry.

With reference to women's employment, the submission noted that domestic service in Ireland entailed a loss of social standing, but maintained that any work, however menial, might be undertaken in England without any such loss. Also, one was required to pay a premium to undertake nurse's training in Ireland while this did not apply in England.

However, all these submissions failed to yield results despite the hard work involved, with ICA constantly underpinning the need for education and training. Despite not being fruitful, the Executive felt that it laid the groundwork for what was to come and they were convinced that through training women in rural affairs they could do more than government and local authorities to bring the knowledge they had gained to the people concerned. This was a period of increased membership which meant more women were discussing their own problems and identifying their needs — chiefly concerned with food, housing, education and health — and using their socially disadvantaged position to learn to lobby effectively for the first time. It was not until the 1950s that the government responded in a positive way, offering ICA Matching Funds for organisers.

In the 1940s, ICA members took an increasing interest in community affairs, in local government, public health, and housing. In order to learn about existing services and study how they might be improved, a study circle met in central office to hear talks by experts on these various subjects. Summaries of the talks and also those given at the summer school were published in the weekly Notes, and guilds were asked to discuss them and to organise talks on these and similar subjects locally when possible. It was felt that many boards and committees would benefit by having women members, but that ICA's point of view and advice would be valuable only when its members were well informed. The confidence it lacked would come with increasing knowledge and the feeling of support given by an ever-widening group.

As the association grew and contacts widened, pleasant relations continued between ICA and the local Committees of Agriculture, Vocational Education, Young Farmers Clubs, Parish committees, Red Cross, Saor na Leanbh, the Irish Folklore Commission, Gaelic League, Comhdháil Náisiúnta na Gaeilge, Local

Shows, Libraries, officers of Public Health and County Managers. ICA hoped that the years of restricted activity due to World War II might prove to have been years of conservation and development, from which it might emerge stronger and better fitted to serve the women of Ireland, since government and local authorities were renowned as being slow to progress. When the war started, ICA had 74 guilds but after the war this number had increased to 171 guilds, despite five years of abnormal conditions, difficulty with travel, rural isolation, and lack of lighting for evening meetings in many country districts. By 1948, 6,000 members made up 207 guilds in 24 counties (Offaly and Monaghan being the two counties where ICA was absent).

Despite the increase in membership, ICA still had only one organiser, Phyllis O'Connell, since Country Workers Ltd was ICA's only external funder.

CRAFT EXHIBITIONS

Each Spring Show from 1936 to 1945, by invitation, the Homespun Society held an exhibition of country crafts with demonstrations by craftworkers in the Members' hall of the Royal Dublin Society, (with the exception of 1941 and 1944 when the Show was cancelled). The RDS gave full co-operation, and a grant of £160 to meet the cost of staging traditional crafts of every kind — spinners and weavers working at their looms and wheels, basket-makers, blacksmiths, chairmakers, stone carvers and much more. In 1946, the Society was invited to stage an exhibition at the Horse Show instead of the Spring Show and in the Pembroke Hall instead of the Members' Hall. This was a daunting task for a voluntary group since the Pembroke Hall is much larger. The Homespun Society organised many smaller exhibitions later, but none at the RDS whose invitation for the following year was regretfully refused. After the 1946 exhibition it was felt that the time had come to organise production in the country rather than hold exhibitions in the city. The Homespun Society remained in the background as an educational committee concerned with craftsmanship until it closed in 1965. It handed over its other work to Country Markets which, in 1947, it formed jointly with ICA.

Chrissie O'Gorman, an ICA member from Dualla, Co. Tipperary, carried out a meticulously documented county-by-county survey of the crafts of Ireland from March 1943 to November 1947. In 1946 a crafts organiser, Miranda Scally, was employed by Country Workers.

Other ICA members involved were Máirín McDonald, Joyce Nicholson and Daa Barton.

Country Markets

As early as 1942 there had been random summer market schemes in order to get a cash reward for women for their produce. After months of debate on the problem of making craft production economical and viable, a remedy in the form of establishing a co-operative for craftworkers was decided. Permission was given by the ICA Council to its Executive to join with the Homespun Society in an independent registered society, open to all men and women, affiliated to IAOS in 1946. Its aim was to help Ireland's small producers and traditional craftworkers organise the co-operative marketing of their farm, garden and home produce and crafts. ICA is represented on the Committee of Management and individual ICA members make up a large part of the membership of Country Markets Ltd.

The society is a co-operative for crafts and produce separate from ICA and the Homespun Society but incorporating that part of the work of both which can best be dealt with co-operatively. Its motto is 'the best at a fair price and money straight to the producers'. One of its initial objectives was to market eggs as Olivia Hughes of Fethard remarked, 'I feel we will stand or fall by our dealings in eggs, as eggs are the countrywoman's currency.' Even in the 1950s, one third of country market sales comprised eggs and poultry.

In January 1947, the first 'Country Market' was initiated at Fethard, Co. Tipperary. Its founder and chief co-operator was Olivia Hughes. There are now over seventy local produce markets nationwide, in almost every instance started by ICA members, supported by them and by other women. With their growing success more men are joining in.

The Post-War Period

The year 1947 brought weeks of snow, ice-bound roads, bitter cold and deep anxiety about the crops. All had a devastating effect on ICA meetings; attendance went down, plans had to be cancelled, and fund-raising functions failed. Yet despite this, work went on. Transport became easier when the chief organiser, Phyllis O'Connell, was provided with an anonymous gift of a van allowing her to visit guilds more frequently. (The anonymous donor later proved to be Bea Hamilton of Dublin.) The shortages of the war years were easing and more materials of all kinds were available. For some guilds, rural electrification had arrived and this also had an encouraging effect on meetings. Members were quick to avail of these helpful factors, and in most cases the importance of meetings and the increase in membership was due to members' own energy and initiative. In 1947, the subject of greatest popularity among the guilds was poultry rearing, with an interest also in go-ray skirts, and handcrafts were also important with the emphasis on raising standards.

A proposed ICA shop at Rineanna was rejected as the articles were not up to standard. The ICA responded to this through Country Markets, setting up proficiency tests which were certified through 'Brannraí' – always aware of keeping standards high, using the best raw materials and remaining conscious of market forces.

This was a difficult time to be at the helm of the association but Lucy Franks proved capable of handling all problems. Agreement and co-operation between guilds was difficult to achieve. Lucy Franks remarked that, 'opposition is as valuable as approval, it is apathy that is dangerous!' and 'talk that does not end in any kind of action is to be suppressed altogether.' Yet despite the hardships, the ICA continued to flourish in these years. Guilds were acquiring halls of their own, which gave a great sense of achievement, women's voices were being heard, homes were brighter and access to education was on the agenda.

The minutes record the election of Ennis, Hynes and Mahon to public bodies and the appointment of Josephine MacNeill to the Advisory Committee for Cultural Relations.

IDEALISED RURAL IRELAND

In the 1920s and 1930s there was a general assumption that writers should reflect the image of an ideal Ireland which lay behind the Irish-Ireland movement. It was a rural image based on small but comfortable farmers who were the heirs of an ancient Gaelic world. Untouched by modern materialism, they lived contentedly on their farms, not needing the material wealth that people in industrial societies craved. The most famous expression of this ideal came in a broadcast de Valera gave on St Patrick's day, 1943: 'The Ireland that we dreamed of could be the home of a people who ... were satisfied with frugal comfort and devoted their leisure to things of the spirit, a land whose countryside would be bright with cosy homesteads, whose

fields and villages would be joyous with sounds of industry, the romp-
ing of sturdy children, the contests of athletic youths, the laughter of
comely maidens, whose firesides would be the forums of the wisdom of
serene old age.'[6]

However, the reality was somewhat bleaker — country people
often lived on poor small farms without running water or electricity, with little or no infrastructure, enduring the bitter loneliness
and frustration of a life of rural poverty dominated by the land, the
state and the church.

The structure of the ICA meant that through their guilds, members could get involved and take responsibility for their communities.
Guilds participated and gave leadership in various campaigns to
bring modern facilities to rural areas, as well as contributing to
national issues, through bringing forward resolutions and through
working as educators.

RESOLUTIONS

Resolutions are usually proposed by a guild; they then move on to
Federation level and, if supported there, they are passed on for
the approval of Council. Each resolution has to be supported by
supplementary documentation providing information on the subject in hand. After thorough research, if the guild still feels
strongly, the resolution is brought to Federation and the process
begins. Due to the democratic structure of ICA, the huge diversity
of its membership, and the change of personnel on committees,
quite often a very good resolution can be watered down or
rejected altogether.

ICA has played an important role in alerting public opinion to
issues that affect the quality of life in rural Ireland. It has helped to
change hardened attitudes, and even when resolutions have been
unsuccessful, the process of formulation has proven to be a very
worthwhile learning experience for members. Since the foundation
of the ICA, resolutions tended to be of a practical nature.

The South Tipperary Federation book, for instance, recalls a
discussion on the unfair treatment of widows and orphans by the
laws of Eire, leading to the resolution in 1946, 'That the ICA call
upon the government to introduce legislation analogous to the
Inheritance (Family Provision) Act, 1938 which covers the law of
inheritance in England and Wales.'[7]

And from the *History of Cork Federation 1936–94*:[8]

To indicate the diversity of issues raised by the members at the time, the following resolutions were submitted to the Federation by the guilds during the years 1951–56 and forwarded to National Council, from where these were submitted to the relevant government departments:

1. The laws of inheritance should be revised.
2. There was a need for a night telephone service in rural areas.
3. Clear and legible labelling should be affixed to all patent medical and veterinary products.
4. The setting up of a statutory class size for primary schools.
5. Position of Irish language in schools.

Subjects covered by resolutions from Wexford in 1954 included the refusal of the Dept. of Education to employ married women in national schools, the hardship imposed by the income tax laws on parents of children with mental disabilities, estate duty on the property of married couples, downgrading of county hospitals, community services for the aged, equal division of Dept. of Education scholarships between boys and girls.

Resolutions concerned with an obviously blatant injustice usually pass through the various channels without much debate to the relevant government department for action. Otherwise, resolutions are exhaustively discussed and hotly debated, and have often caused arguments. However, the right of a guild to bring forward a resolution is stoutly upheld. These resolutions illustrate the concerns and interests of the guild in relation to events that touch members and their communities.

BRANNRAÍ

Since the formation of Country Markets in 1947, ICA has put craftsmanship on an official level — the accreditation being 'brannraí', ICA's proficiency tests to maintain and raise standards. Country Markets was formed to encourage high-standard crafts and to be of economic help to the craftworkers. The award for craft tests was a brannra, symbolised by a badge in the design of a Donegal bread iron. To obtain a brannra at pass, good or excellent grade a candidate must submit three articles in a given craft. With five 'excellent' grades in five different crafts a demonstrator's bar is obtained, giving the candidate the right to demonstrate those crafts in public. With three demonstrators' bars, the candidate may proceed to the teachers' test. This comprises two written papers and a practical part where the candidate's teaching methods are judged by external judges.

The finest craftsmanship was always encouraged in the brannraí system, and by 1953 there were 37 categories of crafts listed, while not neglecting the production of home grown foods and their most advantageous use. The first brannra was awarded in 1950 and by 1952, 16 had been awarded. By 1956, 260 and by 1966, 434 as well as 412 production tests mostly in cookery and gardening. Members entered their crafts in county show competitions, resulting in crafts people getting recognition and helping the sale of their work. By 1962 handcraft schools were being held in county towns with overwhelming success, while the number of candidates for various tests continued to grow. In 1968 the logical extension of brannra tests and demonstrators bars came about with stringently judged teacher's tests which by now many members were qualified to take.

ELECTRIFICATION

In 1946 rural electrification was undertaken by the semi-state Electricity Supply Board (ESB). At that time, 98 per cent of urban homes had electricity whilst only 2 per cent of rural homes were equipped with it. The state pursued different policies in relation to electrification and to the installation of running water. In fact, electrification was important for male farmers, whilst running water was important for rural women. The government powered ahead with electrification while the installation of running water lagged behind — women's work and women's tasks were simply not that important! ICA worked energetically on both of these issues.

IRELAND IN THE LATE 1940S

Around this time there was a changed agenda in Irish politics — the electorate wanted to know how the economy was being planned, what action was proposed on the issues of unemployment and emigration, and what policies existed regarding social issues such as health, welfare and housing. (The Beveridge Report leading to the welfare state in Britain had an influence, as the many Irish emigrants discussing it influenced opinion in Ireland.)

After fifteen years of Fianna Fáil government, an inter-party government in 1947 brought about three years of social and economic implications. In 1948, a trade agreement with Britain was concluded, followed in 1949 by the Land Rehabilitation Programme to reclaim derelict land. There was also an increase in the provision of houses, which transformed rural areas. Noel Browne brought about the rapid eradication of TB through mass x-rays, new sanatoriums, modern treatment and vaccination. When he came into office 3,000 to 4,000 people died of TB each year. In 1947, 124 people per 100,000 had TB, but by 1951 only 75 per 100,000 suffered from the disease. The chief source of funding was the establishment of Irish Hospital Sweepstakes. In addition, at this period the Industrial Development Agency and Córas Tráchtála were established, making a significant contribution to the growth of economic planning.

In 1947, the Mother and Child scheme was proposed. It was opposed diligently by the Catholic Church and the Medical Council, leading to its abandonment, despite Ireland having the highest rate of infant and maternal mortality in Europe.

In 1948 the Declaration of the Republic coincided with the work of the Commission on Emigration, which reported a poor standard of living particularly in rural areas with a lack of provision for power, water and sanitation in houses and farms. The marriage rate in Ireland was one of the lowest in the world and female emigration high due to the lack of economic opportunity, limited marriage options, the inferior public and political status of women, plus the frustrations of what was a drab and harsh life.

ICA GUILDS

In 1949, the ICA continued to grow, now numbering 234 guilds. These were a great strength to the association, their officers acting as spokespeople when the needs of the guilds had to be brought before county officials, and guild meetings giving members an opportunity to discuss their problems. Guild membership cost 2/-, with 1/- of that going to central office. This means the ICA had very limited funds to do all that was needed, but due to the untiring voluntary effort of so many members, much was given to local charities and children. ICA guilds still rely entirely on their own financial resources. Guilds which involve themselves in their local communities flourish, whilst the recluse guild has to struggle to exist. In addition, remote guilds found it difficult to carry on in the 1940s, since their rural population was diminished through emigration and late marriages. These problems were recognised by the organiser who visited them more frequently and encouraged them in their efforts to brighten and sustain rural life.

Guilds tended to flourish if:

1. They had a place of their own or at least access to a good warm place.

2. They had a mixture of age and interests.

3. A proper AGM was held, with regular change of officers and committee, and spreading of responsibility for jobs amongst members.

4. Members were willing to undertake committee work, to make the necessary sacrifice of time and energy to ensure a success-ful planned year's programme.

5. Communications were forever mindful of the top-down and bottom-up approach.

6. The social aspect was cultivated, through hospitality and friend-liness combined with a spirit of good fellowship and loyalty, and members' support for their association.

The ICA has always recognised that it is only as good as the strength of its guilds. Guilds are the backbone of this democratic organisation. The tradition in guilds is one of women coming together to share talents and experiences. For the first seventy years of the twentieth century, ICA would have provided the only social outlet for the majority of Irish women. It offered fun and friendship, and challenged members to encourage one another and to build a better world for themselves and their families. Each decade has brought new challenges and new responses from the members. The guild programmes reflect members' interest in arts and crafts, Irish heritage, culture, language, drama, music, writing and most importantly the social half-hour which was the vital ingre-dient to bind people together. Learning new skills had a multiplier effect on communities, with increasing awareness of women as cus-todians of the future generation. This in turn led to people having a sense of pride in their achievements, having confidence, and dimin-ishing the feelings of isolation. Standards of living were raised, and guilds became involved in local issues such as health, education, conservation, and keeping the community informed of events around the country.

ICA in a Changing Society

The annual reports and minute books belie the popular view of ICA as an association concerned with crafts and cookery. We see that the ICA was continually trying to empower women, encouraging them to lobby local authorities to provide essential services, while also aware of the reasons for women's lack of involvement. The controlling structures of church and state, combined with women's continual dependence on others, meant that women were shy and lacked self-esteem and confidence. ICA was active and vibrant during the 1940s, as the increase in membership shows. This meant that its contribution to achieving its aims was significant. ICA achieved a number of crucial changes through its objections to discriminatory legislation — defending the right of all women, homemakers and paid workers, to equal citizenship in the Irish Free State, looking for social reform concerning inheritance law, running water and electricity, free school lunches and other issues. These reforms would enhance the lives of thousands of rural women.

ICA became the vital link between the suffrage movement at the turn of the last century and the women's movement of the 1970s, having members in both. No history of Irish women could be complete without the ICA and its achievements.

ICA was often misunderstood, partly because change was slow and it was difficult to break away from its early image. The media tended to mistrust the ascendancy class — evident as far back as 1940 when the ICA had to reassure the Commission on Vocational Organisation that the association was democratic and of the people. The lady of the manor, they joked, would be very welcome indeed if she placed her motor car at the disposal of the organisation but 'we get on well without her'.[9] It was significant that the question was asked. The ICA had to assure the same commission that their members did not mind the term 'countrywomen' — 'They were charmed to be called countrywomen'. Caitriona Clear argues that the ICA itself was for years misunderstood and treated dismissively by many people, among them feminists.

7
RURAL WATER, ELECTRICITY AND DEVELOPMENT
IN THE 1950s

Concern for women's issues in Ireland reached a very low point in the 1950s. Rising prices and low incomes, unemployment (with married women in paid employment making up only 5.5 per cent of the labour force), emigration and industrial unrest all gave rise to increased dissatisfaction in the countryside. The limits put on women's lives, especially those of married women, became more stringent due to increased mechanisation and emphasis on production. Women's lives became ever more centred around the kitchen and the home.[1]

It was in this context that the work of the ICA took on a greater urgency and importance in improving standards of living and health, modernising domestic living through campaigning for piped water and electricity, providing social and cultural outlets, educating and informing members through demonstrations and training courses for rural women. ICA activities were greatly enhanced by the opening of An Grianán in 1954, the first adult residential college in Ireland, funded by the Kellogg Foundation of America and offering a variety of courses ranging from arts and crafts to home advisory services, community development, community enterprise and leadership.

In 1993, Marianne Heron recalled the period:

Ireland in the 1950s was in the economic doldrums. Emigration soared, unemployment was high and the country bore little relation to de Valera's St Patrick's Day dream of 1943. Protectionism sheltered industry but it also meant that in the absence of competition consumer prices were high. The cost of living rose by 147 per cent between 1939 and 1956 whilst wages rose by only 25 per cent. Large numbers of workers were still not organised and women especially emigrated in their thousands in search of better economic prospects.[2]

Ireland was still predominantly a rural economy, with 40 per cent of the active workforce engaged in agriculture and 22 per cent engaged in other areas of production including industry.[3] The outbreak of the Korean War in 1950 and a devaluation of the pound sterling led to an economic crisis as import prices and the cost of raw materials soared. A negative economic and social climate was marked by high levels of emigration, and the International Labour Organisation Convention on Equal Pay was not ratified in Ireland.

The Social Welfare Act of 1952 was crucial in establishing the welfare state but it did not hinder the continuation of the unquestioned discrimination against women employees, and their exclusion from unemployment and other benefits. The Adoption Act was also introduced in the same year.

The 1953 Health Act put the first significant dent in the power of the Catholic Church to dictate national policy. 'Opposition to censorship continued and it was estimated that between 1950 and 1955 an average of 600 books per annum were censored.'[4] However, there were signs of change — in 1951 the Arts Council was set up, with ICA member Muriel Gahan as the only female founder member. There was also much enthusiasm for theatre.

From the war years up to the mid-1960s, the major developments that ICA was concerned with included rural electrification, rural water supply, the Grant Counterpart Fund-Marshall Aid, An Grianán, Macra na Tuaithe and Credit Unions. In these years there was a crisis in rural life in Ireland which successive government policies failed to solve: this was caused by the relationship between emigration, late marriages and the quality of rural life, with a specific gender dimension. More women emigrated from the countryside during this period than men, due mainly to lack of employment opportunities, or the rejection of the social constraints associated with traditional rural life, such as poor marriage prospects or having the choice of a husband determined by matchmakers or by parents, and also due to the widening gap in material standards between urban and rural life.

By 1946 the overwhelming majority of urban houses had access to electricity, while few rural homes had this service. In the same year almost 92 per cent of urban homes had access to piped water and 35 per cent had a fixed bath. By comparison, over 91 per cent of rural homes were forced to rely on a pump, a well, a stream or some other unspecified source for domestic water supplies and less than 4 per cent of rural homes had a bath.[5]

DEVELOPMENT OF ICA

In June 1950, ICA received a request from the Dept of Agriculture to co-operate with Margaret Hockin of FAO (Food and Agriculture Organisation) who was coming to Ireland to study women's work. She convinced Mr Dillon, Minister for Agriculture, that ICA's work was important and effective, and pointed out that the ICA was the only source of accurate information about country life and therefore had a contribution to make in improving rural housing etc. She stressed the need for training facilities and for adequate meeting places. Women were at last becoming visible to the male establishment. In a follow-up to this, Mr Dillon was invited to open the ICA's Country Fair on 8 November 1950, for which he earned the *Irish Times* headline: 'Mr Dillon will "stand or fall" by eggs.'[6] The fair was a fundraising event for the organisers' fund. The idea was to simulate a real country fair – coffee van included (an idea from Fethard guild) – and there was music and dancing at a makeshift crossroads as well as a crafts and art exhibition. Promotion of electrification and running water in the home was an important feature.

The Dept. of Education requested the help of ICA to complete a UNESCO questionnaire on adult education, evidence that at last the ICA was being taken seriously as an educator in its own right and as a specialist in its own field.

In 1951, the Dept. of Agriculture invited two ICA members, Diana Deane of Doneraile and Sheila Connolly of Dualla, to the USA for the Rural Youth Leaders Conference. Government also gave a pound for pound matching grant for the employment of organisers.

In 1952 the Good Work Exhibition took place with the best of ICA members' crafts and arts. The exhibition toured ten towns finishing in Waterford to coincide with An Tóstal. The motivation for the exhibition came from the idea that if people around the country could see the excellent work being done by members in various guilds it would be an inspiration to others and would help to raise the standard of craftsmanship. The exhibition covered a large scope of work, with twenty-six examples of leather work, fourteen wool exhibits including home-spuns that were dyed, carded spun and woven in Dunlewey, Donegal and the now well known Lumra rugs, thirty-five needlework items including embroidery of all kinds, lace and crochet, patchwork quilts and furnishings, and up to thirty specimens of handweaving. The country produce section had, among the usual eggs, jams, honey and preserves, mead, made from an old recipe by Olivia Hughes and some home-made cheese, speciality of Violet Crichton of Beltra guild, Co. Sligo. Toys and some pewter work came from Olive Rowe of Rinne guild (a pioneer in introducing women to carpentry and cabinet-making). Angela Kehoe's authentic folk dolls were displayed, Mrs Michael Freyer of Castlebar Town Associates made pottery, and Mrs Walker of Portlaw guild presented woodcarving and figurines.

In 1952, Lucy Franks initiated a competition for gardens on derelict sites for An Tóstal, which proved popular with the members. In the same year the first Buan Cairde (honorary life members) were appointed: Lucy Franks, Josephine MacNeill and Alice Ryan.

Membership now stood at 10,000 in 346 guilds and 13 town associates, making up 20 Federations. By 1953, ICA was represented in each of the twenty-six counties, and by the late 1950s each county had a Federation, so it was with confidence that the association launched its annual journal *Ár Leabhar Féin: Our Book*. This period of great advancement saw some of the Executive work being 'farmed out' to Federations: Louth took planning, Limerick took links with outside bodies, Donegal took culture, Galway took traditional music and Tipperary took publicity. This policy of sharing responsibility widened the network of skilled and informed members and it continues to the present day although in a different format. At the same time, guilds around the country were acquiring their own meeting halls. Mrs Ruttle of Clare was instrumental in obtaining a cottage for £200 for Gortlamain. Fethard guild raised £200 to convert a nissen hut whilst Delgany, Co. Wicklow were in the process of acquiring their own location. Executive minutes record that Skreen guild, Co. Sligo bought a car for the jubilee nurse and that Curracloe guild in Co. Wexford was run by one family.

The Kellogg Foundation invited Olivia Hughes, then ICA President, and Doreen Smith (formerly secretary of ICA and later first principal of An Grianán) on a four-month fellowship programme from July to November 1955. On their return, a conference on rural youth work was organised at An Grianán which led to ICA and Macra na Feirme revitalising Macra na Tuaithe in 1956. It had been formed in February 1952 but until then only then only seven clubs had been formed and the emphasis was on a programme for boys rather than girls.

ICA was also involved in the setting up of Credit Unions by nominating Nora Herlihy, a member of Dublin Town Associates, as its representative on the proposed Credit Union study group set up to re-establish co-operative banking in Ireland. From that came the first branch at Donore Avenue, Dublin, leading to its present position of at least 530 active branches. The portrait of the principal founder member, Nora Herlihy, is displayed in a prominent place in every Credit Union office, and the other co-founders, Seamus McEoin and Sean Forde, are honoured in the chains held by each of the twenty-five chapter chairmen within the Irish movement.

Around the same time, an ICA deputation to the Minister of Agriculture requested governing body membership of a proposed Irish Agricultural Institute, a home economics advisory department and an agricultural degree course specifically for women. 'But on learning that a proposed institute made no provision for the education of countrywomen, this pushed Olivia Hughes as ICA President to write to national papers in December 1955 — "The money for the founding of the institute is coming from the USA and I have no reason to believe it has been earmarked 'For Irishmen Only'.... The progress of agriculture is not built in a vacuum of specialists and scientific research. In the end it depends on the farmhouse and the people on the land.... It is not only men who need the help of research and education in rural Ireland".[7]

ICA was always keen to inform itself of projects of good practice, even if it involved foreign travel, and members availed of this quite often in the 1950s — first with the Dept. of Agriculture, then Kellogg Foundation and later through the Counterpart Fund.

The 1950s was an important decade for the ICA, the increase in membership due in no small measure to the paid organisers. The increasing scale of their activities led to new developments each year in co-operation with state and local services, including participation on housing, agricultural, library and vocational committees.

Presidents in the 1950s

Lucy Franks' term of office as ICA President was 1942 to 1952, when she was replaced by Alice Ryan of Emly, Co. Tipperary who was President from 1952–55. It was Lucy Franks who at the first summer school in 1929 pleaded, 'women to lead are badly needed, women of wide understanding and vision who know what country conditions are and not what one would like to imagine them to be.' Alice Ryan, speaking at the 1939 summer school said: 'We should change the man's saying "a woman's place is in the home" to "a woman's place is where she can best help her home".'

In 1955, another Tipperary member, Olivia Hughes of Fethard guild, became President. In a 1940s radio broadcast on summer schools, she said: 'it was the work and self-sacrifice and patriotism of unpaid enthusiasts that made ICA such an important women's organisation.'

This was a period of great advancement for the ICA, due in no small measure to the vision and hope of these three leaders who recognised the obvious need of rural people and their hunger for change — nowhere more acute than among women.

In 1958 Dorothy Smith was elected ICA President and held her first Council meeting in Cavan where Phyllis Faris was Federation President. Also that year Doreen Smith resigned as 'Maoirsheacht' of An Grianán and was replaced by Marie Lewis.

RURAL WATER AND ELECTRICITY

ICA recognised that if its objective of 'better living' was to be achieved, the two basic commodities to be addressed were water and electricity. We now take these essentials for granted until the rare occurrence of a power failure or interruption of water supply. In the 1950s, however, most activities in rural Ireland depended on daylight. A most essential chore was to have oil lamps and lanterns cleaned and ready for use, or a supply of candles in stock. Water had to be drawn from wells, and heating and cooking depended on solid fuel such as timber and turf. Harvesting turf was a very slow and heavy task in itself and depended on good weather. Many people cooked at the open hearth or on the range. There was much cleaning of ashes and chimneys attached to these methods. Generally clothes had to be washed by hand, and ironed using heavy irons which had to be first heated in the fire. On the farm, cows had to be milked by hand and it was difficult to maintain a good standard of hygiene in dairies without hot or cold running water or any form of refrigeration. Mary O'Brien, an esteemed Buan Cara from Athlone recalled the loneliness of living in the country and recalls with pleasure when electricity came to her area: 'It was lovely to look out at night and see the lights from your neighbour's homes shining like stars in the distance'.

By 1946 the overwhelming majority of urban houses had access to electricity, while few rural homes had this service. In the same year almost 92 per cent of urban homes had access to piped water and 35 per cent had a fixed bath. By comparison, over 91 per cent of rural homes were forced to rely on a pump, a well, a stream or some other unspecified source for domestic water supplies and less than 4 per cent of rural homes had a bath.[8]

The ICA Executive agreed that priority should be given to the vital needs of piped water and electricity in rural homes. ICA, in its attempt to achieve these amenities for rural Ireland, looked at the working of the government machine, from central government to county administrators and local authorities, and attempted to learn to manipulate these structures and their methods in a bid to lobby for change. Examining their own structures, the ICA saw that the regular meetings which its now self-financing and self-managing guilds convened were unrivalled in giving rural women the confidence, knowledge and practice to lobby effectively and to work assuredly with other organisations.

Rural electrification went ahead at a much faster pace than piped water, the reason for this being beyond the control of the ICA, who had put the same effort into both campaigns. Michael Shiels suggests in *Quiet Revolution* that the advent of rural electrification brought nearer the prospect of piped water and labour saving houses, and the ICA threw itself into a full scale campaign to promote these.[9] Piped water was regarded as a priority, since it would end the drudgery of hauling buckets from the well and it would transform sanitary facilities which even in the late 1940s were of an extremely basic nature. Shiels also suggests that 'the subsequent raising of the standard of Irish rural kitchens as pleasant and efficient places in which to live and work was due in great part to the ESB/ICA Kitchen in its various forms, mobile and static — reinforcing as it did in a most effective way the continuing educational efforts of the association'.

After the war, standards of housekeeping were higher because women were better informed and better educated. Incomes were also rising, and they had bigger and better houses, and improved standards of health, hygiene and domesticity. Moreover, many rural women had returned from abroad where they had worked as domestic servants and experienced better standards of living. However, higher standards of living needed generous quantities of water, and by 1950 most of the problems had been tackled by urban areas so that the gap widened between urban and rural living, just when women were more conscious of the importance of such amenities.

Higher standards of housekeeping posed a considerable strain on rural women, with an ordinary family requiring about nine gallons of water a day and an extra nine on washday. A speaker at one post-war ICA Council meeting compared the 'simple process of washing up after dinner in town and country'. For the countrywoman, without running water, this involved eight separate operations — filling and refilling a kettle, heating successive supplies of water, throwing out dirty water. A townswoman merely 'stands at her sink and turns on her hot and cold tap as required'.

> The countrywoman must first fill her kettle with water, which has to be brought in from outside — two stages in the process. Her kettle is likely to be a heavy iron kettle which she must proceed to lift onto the open fire — a third stage. When the water is hot, she lifts the kettle off the fire and pours it into the basin — a fourth stage. She begins to wash her dishes. Soon the water is greasy. She must throw it out and fill up her basin out of the kettle again — a fifth stage. She finishes washing her dishes and dries them. Now her basin is dirty and greasy. She must lift up her kettle again, pour in more hot water if there is any left, rinse her basin and put it away — a sixth stage. She must now refill her kettle with cold water. Otherwise, if she leaves it near the fire the bottom will be burned out of it — a seventh stage. Likely by this time her pail of cold water is empty and she must go outside the house to fill up again — the eighth stage. That is to say, that apart from the actual washing and drying of the dishes, there have been eight operations to carry out. For the townswoman, there is just one operation in the same process: she stands at her sink and turns on her hot and cold tap as required.

The cause of rural water seems to have been seen as a matter of concern only for women. The ICA's efforts to promote the benefits of running water were not universally welcome in the Irish countryside. Most vocal opposition came, somewhat ironically, from the National Farmers' Association (NFA) who were afraid rates would increase with the arrival of running water. The NFA picketed an ICA meeting in Waterford. As the NFA was a powerful lobby group, it managed to delay water schemes. Government acceded to the NFA's request to change from regional to group water schemes, thereby slowing the process.

ICA had begun its efforts for rural water at a Country Fair in the Autumn of 1950. Some years later, at the request of

James Dillon, Minister for Agriculture, ICA joined with the ESB in setting up an All Electric Kitchen as part of the Department of Agriculture's RDS Spring Show Exhibition. Its success led to a consultation the following year between the ESB and the ICA housing adviser (architect Eleanor Butler) on the provision of a modern labour-saving farm kitchen. This kitchen was equipped with piped water, electrical equipment and other kinds of modern equipment. In 1958 it took to the road and was known as 'the Mobile Farm Kitchen', travelling Ireland with a home adviser in charge. In the 1950s, the logical starting point for radical improvement in rural women's lives and working conditions was the kitchen — changing from an open turf fire and barrels for water to free-standing cookers and running water. Over a considerable period, ICA guilds, Muintir na Tíre, Macra na Feirme and other groups were visited in all parts of the country, before the kitchen finally went to An Grianán, where its equipment was transferred to one of the college's renovated yard buildings still known today as the Farm Kitchen.

Mary Daly suggests that just as leisure appliances such as radios and more recently televisions spread more rapidly among consumers than labour saving devices such as washing machines, so electricity — which was associated with leisure — spread more rapidly to rural households than piped water. The fact that leisure products were used by men, while household appliances were primarily of benefit to women, is an important consideration when viewing the different rates of progress.

Government gave high priority to rural electrification, as this was the responsibility of the semi-state ESB, but bringing water supply to rural areas was the responsibility of passive County Councils who did not avail of government department grants, and was not seen as important. In the 1950s, government concern for the survival of rural Ireland led to higher spending on roads, houses and other infrastructure, yet there was little concern with providing running water. Water was seen as being primarily of benefit to women. Hygiene was not a high priority, and therefore the onus for promoting the spread of running water in rural areas fell on the ICA. The success of rural electrification by the ESB was the result of the vigorous policies pursued. Nothing was left to chance and all areas were canvassed with the co-operation of all rural organisations. When the whole country was covered by the electricity service, ESB then became interested in rural water as they saw a promising market for pumps and other equipment.

For a voluntary organisation like the ICA, under-funded and taken for granted, progress was slow but nonetheless it never took its eye off the objective of better living for all. Through its work with rural electrification, the ICA was receiving formal public credit for work it had been doing in private for much of the century. As a result, it now had the status and authority to lead, which it used in 1960 when the Joint Committee on Rural Water Supplies was formed to increase public understanding of the need for rural water supplies and the problems that have to be surmounted.

The members of the Joint Committee were: Mrs A. Barrington, ICA; Mr T. Breathnach, An Foras Talúntais; Mr P. Brennan, TD, Member of Wicklow County Council; Mrs J. Coady, ICA; Rev. J. Collins, CC, Manor Kilbride; Mr J. G. Coffey, Kilkenny County Engineer; Mr R. Deasy, NFA; Mr P. J. Dowling, ESB; Miss M. Ennis, ICA; Dr A. Eustace, CMO, Co. Meath; Muriel Gahan, ICA; Mr M. W. L. Graves, Stewarts and Lloyds of Ireland Ltd; Mr T.P. Mahony, Wavin Pipes Ltd.; Miss E. MacCurtain, Bord Fáilte Éireann; Mr N. Meghen, Limerick County Manager and Vice-President of Muintir na Tíre; Mrs N. Minihan, ICA; Miss P. O'Connell, ICA; Dr J.G. O'Flynn, Muintir na Tíre; Mr C. O'Neill, *Farmers' Gazette*; Mr L. Sheedy, *Irish Farmer's Journal*; Mrs D. Tomlin, ICA.

Neil Blaney, Minister for Local Government declared, 'Now that the cause has been taken up by the ICA, we may assuredly look forward to the breaking down by the farmers' wives and daughters of the farmers' traditional conservatism in this matter.'

Group water schemes became ICA's prime focus for discussion and action, with the shift from regional to group schemes. The onus was thus shifted from central government to local authorities, where women had to assume a more active role in canvassing neighbours, collecting down-payments, and raising consciousness of the value of such amenities. This slow access to running water shows government's apathy towards women's needs, and reveals much about the status of women in rural Ireland at that time.

In 1961, ICA organised a successful 'Turn of the Tap' exhibition in the Mansion House and a conference on rural water supply at An Grianán. ESB has remained an outstanding supporter of the ICA.

GOVERNMENT FUNDING AND ICA PROGRESS

James Dillon, Fine Gael Minister for Agriculture from 1948 to 1951, continually stressed the importance of voluntary organisations. ICA reacted by presenting him with a threefold plan covering organisers, a residential college and home advisory services. Only the first part of the plan was granted, that of pound for pound funding for organisers. This was the first breakthrough, getting government recognition through financial support for the work the ICA had been doing for forty years.

> Once the new organisers began work in October 1951, ICA expanded more rapidly and by 1952 there were sixty new guilds. Five full-time organisers — Phyllis O'Connell, Chief Organiser, Kathleen Gleeson, Cork, Ena O'Reilly, Cavan and Muriel Kehoe, Dublin were appointed, with Ann Roche of Waterford, Kathleen Donnelly of Wexford, Sheila Connolly of Dualla, Pauline Frawley of Galway, Diana Deane of Doneraile and Ena McKeever of Meath as part-time organisers — all had been scrupulously tested over the summer for the requisite qualities of enthusiasm, fun and initiative. ICA funded expenses and travel whilst government would cover salaries — but by July 1952 the association had to get overdraft facilities as the grant was not yet received! The minutes of Executive expressed members' fears at this position.
>
> The same Executive meeting stressed the involvement of members in local elections and planning policies. Members were asked to support the President of Kiltimagh guild, Mrs Clarke, who was standing for the Senate election [nominated by the ICA — Ed]. Many women whose names later became prominent in the movement joined ICA at this time: Áine Barrington, Joan Coady, Margaret Erraught, Phyllis Faris, Joan Norman and Noreen O'Boyle to name but a few.[10]

US Funds

Whilst the 1940s and 1950s were very hard times for Ireland on the whole, ICA doubled its efforts to counteract this, and the records show its determination to react positively and become more self-reliant. As a consequence, its membership went from strength to strength. Administratively, the ICA sought to become more professional, having learnt from both the rural water and rural electrification campaigns. Occasionally, there were rumblings of discontent from rural guilds who bemoaned the lack of effective communication between central office and the regions. Funding, or the lack of it, had caused disputes in the past but it was thought to be of more crucial importance to prioritise the lobbying of outside bodies than to polarise internal tensions. Rarely did the ICA speak or write overtly about discrimination against women at this period if they felt it existed."

Despite repeated memoranda from the ICA, the Dept. of Agriculture refused to include it on the Agricultural Productive Council. ICA's response was not to protest vigorously about gender discrimination, but to work assiduously behind the scenes to gather more information on the subject in hand and to become more knowledgeable on the specifics of agricultural policy, pouncing on events which hindered the equity of rural modernisation as it affected women. This professional determination was rewarded in 1956, the year in which the Irish government found itself a recipient of European Counterpart Fund-Marshall Aid, to be used partly for the promotion and extension of facilities in rural Ireland, through the co-operation of the US Dept. of Agriculture. The ICA's cultivation of its American contacts (notably Kellogg Foundation) was paying dividends, and at very short notice ICA was asked to submit a detailed proposal for the use of some of the funds. As an organisation, it was in an unrivalled position to assess the needs and priorities of a rural Ireland being courted for modernisation. Even more impressive was the dexterity with which the committee set up for the purpose under the chairmanship of Esther Bishop, was able to submit a weighty proposal in just one month. The success of their application — yielding £10,000 over four years — enabled ICA to appoint four specialist advisers who toured the country handing on their expertise to guild members — architect Eleanor Butler, home economics adviser Margaret Crowley, interior design adviser Valerie Bond, and production and marketing adviser Ann Roche.

Architect Eleanor Butler was selected to go to Europe to study progress in the area of rural housing. She toured Holland, Denmark and Norway. On returning home she lectured throughout Ireland on proper house planning with special emphasis on the kitchen.

Ann Roche of Waterford was sent to Cornwall, Denmark and the Scilly Isles to study horticulture and marketing. On her return she toured Ireland under the auspices of Country Markets and sowed the seed for the many Country Markets that now sell surplus garden and home produce and traditional crafts.

Margaret Crowley, a domestic economy instructress from Cork, was chosen to go to the USA to study rural home economics at Kentucky University on a Kellogg Foundation Fellowship, and also at the US Department of Agriculture in Washington. On coming home, she also toured rural Ireland preaching the need for a fully fledged home economics service.

Valerie Bond was not recruited until the 1960s as an interior designer.

At Executive level, the Counterpart Fund committee called for a great degree of transparency and accountability from their appointees, demanding regular and detailed reports and updates from the well-travelled specialists, insisting on the continuity of the plan's aims, and evidence of its emphasis on practical home improvement. ICA saw the operation as being instrumental in furthering its standing with the Dept. of Agriculture. In 1959, the ICA, chiefly through the work of Kathleen Delap, organised a Rural Family Conference on the advice of Dr Margaret Hockin, Director of Home Economics, FAO. The themes were women in rural life, the family and the farm. This gathering of rural expertise including government members, county administrators and academics was used as a stepping stone towards achieving one of the central aims of the ICA in 1963 — the provision of an official home economics advisory service for rural areas.

FARM GUEST HOUSE SCHEME

The ICA played a major role in encouraging the rural guest house scheme from the 1950s onwards. In 1957 the first course in Farm Guest House management was held at An Grianán. ICA saw this as another way for its members to supplement their incomes, and to this end the association appointed a roaming specialist to advise on every facet of rural guest house keeping, plus a roaming home decorating adviser. Today, hundreds of women are supplementing farm incomes by keeping guests. Not only is this a remunerative sideline for the farm family income but it also has a great educational value, both for the urban family coming into contact with the rudiments of country living, and for the rural family getting an insight into the outlook and lifestyle of the urban dweller.[12] ICA facilitated this scheme by introducing short courses in Farm Guest House management at An Grianán.

Up to now, the ICA had often shown a reluctance to criticise the government. The Agricultural Research Institute had done little to help women. New schemes and advancement programmes for rural areas were designed by and for men. Women were still not being consulted on the basis of their number, nor was their contribution to the agricultural economy being fairly quantified in monetary terms.

ICA recognised that countrywomen played an instrumental part in increasing the farm income, thus causing Olivia Hughes, ICA President 1955–58 to write: 'These are some thoughts which may be helpful about home economics. I have been a farmer's wife since 1918 and kept farm accounts for years. I have visited every county in the republic during the three years I was President of the association, I have been a member of the UI and ICA since 1924. In 1955 I travelled for four months in the USA studying adult education in rural areas. The countrywoman's chief need is for money which she can call her own!' Hughes went on to criticise government's obfuscation in dealing with the chief need of rural women through immunising themselves in departments with sectional interests. These departments, she insisted, had done little to foster better living in the rural community.[13]

IRELAND IN THE 1950s

The Irish economy stagnated throughout the fifties as successive governments had not tackled the basic economic problems of falling agricultural exports and industries too small and uncompetitive to export their produce.

Legislation concerning women included the 1957 Married Woman's Status Act, giving married women control of their own property, and in 1958 the ban on women in the Garda Síochána was lifted, although women were admitted at lower pay and had to retire on marriage. (This ban was lifted for women primary teachers only because of a shortage of teachers). The Brennan Commission of enquiry into the Civil Service where 9,000 women worked at the lowest grade, reflected how deep-seated the negative view of women at work was, particularly within 'Official Ireland'.

The economic disaster at last forced politicians and civil servants to re-examine traditional policies. Change was helped by the arrival on the scene of younger people, unaffected by the policies of the 1930s and more in tune with the way the world had developed since World War II. The first public sign of a new approach came in November 1958, when the First Programme for Economic Development was published, based on a five-year plan drawn up by T.K. Whitaker, secretary of the Dept. of Finance. Its implementation caused an economic up-turn and produced very rapid changes in Irish society.

Rising prices, unemployment, emigration and industrial unrest gave rise to increased dissatisfaction and it was in this context that the work of the ICA took on a greater urgency and importance in improving standards of living and health, modernising domestic living through campaigning for piped water and electricity, providing social and cultural outlets, educating and informing its members through training courses and demonstrations for rural women. The activities of the association were greatly enhanced by the opening of An Grianán in 1954 — the first adult residential college in Ireland, funded by the Kellogg Foundation of America, offering courses ranging from arts and crafts to home advisory services, community development, community enterprise and leadership.

8
AN GRIANÁN

ORIGINS IN ICA's SUMMER SCHOOLS

The birth of An Grianán, Adult Education College, Co. Louth may have been in 1954 but it owes its origin to the association's summer schools.

Since the UI held its first summer school at Slievenamon in 1929, hundreds of women have used the opportunity to escape from the daily monotony of house and farm work — it would have been the only holiday many of these women had, and they would have been aware that they were the privileged ones — some of their fellow members never had the opportunity to attend a summer school. Skills and crafts were taught to members who might not otherwise have the chance to gain this knowledge. Every guild had the right to send one delegate each year. The work of the summer school was to help the guilds help themselves. There were sessions on guild management and the duties of officers, talks by experts on subjects such as women on County Councils, the services available under the various government schemes, health in the home, and nature study. The practical aspect was not neglected, with craftwork demonstrations and other lessons that could be usefully extended into home life.

Each school lasted for eleven days, the participants having eight actual working days, and one Sunday for leisure. Everyone at the house, whether student or teacher, took part in the activities and helped with the household duties. Members were divided into groups of eight or nine, each group being responsible for one household job each day. This innovative system fostered co-operation and friendship in the small groups.

No barriers existed in the organisation of the schools. A report on the fifteenth summer school says: 'Inclusiveness is the first mark of the ICA and is visible immediately at this annual gathering. The forthright speech of Ulster mingled with the lilt of the South and the soft voices of the West. There was a healthy rivalry between counties and a determination to make each guild as good as the next.'¹ This spirit of co-operation influenced the entire organisation of the summer schools. An example of this was the movement of summer schools from county to county, from Slievenamon to Bray to Castlefreake and many other areas. This added convenience, meaning that if it was too far for a woman to travel one year, perhaps the next year a school would be held in her own locality.

Attendance at summer schools was a liberating experience for women, who had less freedom at that time than they do now. And possibly part of the current freedom springs from the bold steps eighteen women first took on the chilly slopes of Slievenamon in 1929. When Lucy Franks envisioned the first of ICA's summer schools, she was adamant that younger women in the country needed practical skills and a better vision of the future because 'at present their only desire is to join their relatives who have found a different kind of life in the States' and it was later her wish that ICA acquire a permanent residential college where this could take place.

With the vision of setting up a permanent residential college for ICA members, a sub-group was created under the chairmanship of Cerise Parker and attached to Dublin Town Associates whose President Ann Blythe is credited with calling the college 'An Grianán' (long before a property had been secured). The problems facing this sub-group were two-fold:

1. Decision about premises and the cost. Out of a possible thirty premises they chose the Tearmann Hotel, Termonfechin, Co. Louth. The invoice from Good and Ganly dated 11/12/1953 totalled £30,950 made up of £24,750 for the hotel plus furniture and fittings, and 10 acres of additional land @£100 per acre, making a total of 53.5 acres, including auctioneers fees @2.5 per cent. Fee for the solicitor came to £647 13s and stamp duty on the property was £399 10s. Shortly after this transaction, the association realised that the cattle needed more access to water and therefore more land was purchased, bringing the total acreage close to eighty acres.

2. Funding. ICA was successful with its application to the Kellogg Foundation of the USA.

Role of Kellogg Foundation

A chance meeting occurred when Dr Morris of Kellogg visited Ireland. Sheila Findlater was on the sub-committee for a college, and her brother, Alex, introduced Dr Morris to Muriel Gahan, who extolled the ICA's need for a residential college. The Executive minutes of December 1953 thank Muriel Gahan for being the right person in the right place at the right moment. Dr Morris was prepared to buy and equip a college. The ICA received £48,000 including £5,000 per year for five years, after which time running costs would be the ICA's responsibility. In November 1953 an interim payment was made on the Tearmann Hotel.

The ICA now had to acquire a professional status and to conform to legal obligations. The Country Women's Trust (a company limited by guarantee) was set up in 1954 but it took until 1956 before all the legal procedures were completed. The Country Women's Trust (CWT) is merely a trustee to hold the assets of the association and the original trustees were Olivia Hughes, Ann Blythe, Sara Ryan, Dorothy Smith, Muriel Gahan and Kathleen Delap. Among these only Kathleen Delap ('our national treasure' as she is wont to be called) is still alive — she shares the same birthyear as the association which is an omen in itself.

AN GRIANÁN

The Kellogg Foundation of America had sufficient trust and confidence in the ICA in 1954 to provide funding to secure a college for the health, education and welfare of the people of Ireland, as its director, Dr R. Mawby said:

> Of all the many constructive programs of the ICA, we are most familiar with the activities at An Grianán. The W.K. Kellogg Foundation of USA was set up in 1930 by the late Mr William Keith Kellogg, who devoted to it 95% of the fortune which he had accumulated as a manufacturer of processed breakfast cereals. Fifty per cent of the annual profit of the Kellogg business goes to maintain the fund. The ICA were the recipients of the Kellogg Foundation's first Irish grant. The Foundation has been associated with the adult education and horticultural training programmes since their inception, from the negotiations and purchase of the property in late 1953 and early 1954 to the planning for refurbishment and additions to the main buildings scheduled for 1979 and 1980. The establishment and operation of the adult education programme at An Grianán represented the fulfilment of a dream held by officers and supporters of the ICA over many years. Mr Kellogg when establishing his foundation observed that the greatest good for the

greatest number can only come through the education of the child, the parent and community in general — your college and its programmes are a manifestation of the same philosophy.

An Grianán was the first ever residential adult education college for women in Ireland. In 1954, adult education was a thought in the minds of forward looking people. The ICA, then a small organisation, first gave concrete expression to that thought. This has been a success story achieved through hard work, much planning and forethought, and the wholehearted support of all the members.

The early days of An Grianán were a great success due to the infectious enthusiasm of ICA members whose foresight and capacity for hard work gave the whole venture a bright and promising future, and due to the trust placed in the ICA by the W.K. Kellogg Foundation.

The first course at An Grianán was held in the summer of 1954, with the President of Ireland, Sean T. O'Kelly, doing the honours and Dr Donal O'Sullivan, director of Irish folk music and song at UCD and Trinity College giving the course.

The courses became the embodiment of the ideals of the ICA as laid down in its constitution — 'to develop and improve the conditions of rural life in Ireland by means of educating countrywomen in arts and crafts, agricultural science, domestic science, social studies, music and the fine arts.'

A look through the museum at An Grianán gives a good insight into how successful the college has been. Crafts such as embroidery, rushwork, wood-turning and lumra are all representative of the many pieces created by the thousands of members across the land. In addition, within the ICA, craftswomen are honoured by the brannraí system which rewards and encourages their artistry.

The ICA is rightly proud of giving members the talents, expertise and above all the self-confidence to assert themselves as members of modern Irish society.

MEMORIES OF PHYLLIS O'CONNELL, ICA CHIEF ORGANISER

At the UI meeting in Fethard sometime in the '30s [1933 — Ed.] the secretary read the notice of the annual summer school. It was to be held at Newtown House, Termonfechin, Co. Louth, then the residence of Mrs Lenteigne (a UI member). The property later changed hands and became the Tearmann Hotel, Termonfechin. At the time none of this meant much to me but as I had never been north of Dublin I decided to go. We had lots of fun both home-made and contributed by kind neighbours. As well as doing toymaking classes and cheesemaking we danced and sang and played tennis and netball and of course, swam and sunbathed. Over the years members have given freely and in so many ways, the benefit of their thoughts, time and skills and have built up something of lasting value. Perhaps they could be likened to the wise virgins of scripture; when the offer came from the Kellogg Foundation their lamps were ready, trimmed and filled.[2]

GLIMPSES OF THE EARLY DAYS — A MOSAIC OF MEMORIES

This was the title of a report given by Marie Lewis (one time Administrator of An Grianán and later General Secretary of the ICA) and in it she captured the very essence of what An Grianán has come to mean to the members:

I first saw An Grianán in Autumn and in sunshine. The name in burnished copper lettering encircled the curved stonework leading to double wrought-iron gates. A sweep of gravelled avenue, patterned with shadows from overhanging ancient trees, curled through lush parkland. In the close-cut lawn facing the house a cherry tree in flaming colours stood in a circle of coloured crisp leaves. It was love at first sight.

Imprinted on memory are all the beautiful sights and sounds that formed part of my life within those abounding eighty acres — the magnificent copper beech tree and variegated sycamore on the twisty, narrow sea-path; the rustling beech hedge edging the pathway; the thousands of snowdrops in the dark shrubbery which surrounded the walled garden; the myriads of primroses that starred the banks in the little wood by the Mass-path, where fronds of fern, bluebells, and wild parsley grew; the scented lime trees; the massed rhododendrons; the sound of the sea on the still night air; the hum of bees from the hives near the cherry tree; the excited cackling of laying hens; the rattle of buckets from the dairy; the friendly bark of the dog.

It was 1956 when I arrived at An Grianán, and though the pace of life was much slower then, this great movement in adult education was already gathering momentum under the inspired direction of its dedicated committees. Many improvements had taken place in the house and outbuildings and the Kellogg Hall had just been officially opened. The outer and inner halls, the library and office backing it, had already taken on character with rushwork, lumra rugs, paintings, books, sheepskins, and patchwork. Otherwise the house had not yet shaken off the hotel-like atmosphere. The repetition of colour schemes in the bedrooms was uninspiring.

The lovely proportions of the drawing-room were diminished by a multitude of small round glass-topped tables. The dining room with its long refectory style seating arrangement and porridge/rust colour scheme was saved from dullness by the sparkle of crisp white table linen, fresh flowers and gleaming silverware.

In the courtyard the small cottage used as a centre for the teenage housekeeping courses, was bounded by a nondescript hedge. The tiled workroom beside the archway was furnished with sewing machines, tables and chairs. Adjoining this was the L-shaped weaving room, with a lovely collection of looms, sadly needing workers. Upstairs were cubicles and small bedrooms. On the south-facing block was a cobbled-floor coach house used as a garage for the green Hillman van which proudly bore the An Grianán crest. Beside it was the stable with half-doors where the donkey was housed. In the centre of the roof above this block was a fine old metal bell. On the third side of the quadrangle was the hen house and dairy, and through the archway was the farmyard with lean-to hayshed, calf house and stalls for four cows. The kitchen yard had an assortment of small buildings used for garage, fuel shed, store room, chick-rearing room, apple store and potting shed. The walled garden had a large and a small greenhouse. Forsythia and lilacs were close by the gate. A peach tree flourished against the wall. An endless variety of fruit supplied the house requirements throughout the year.

Within this setting was a staff of efficient, cheerful people who cleaned and polished, washed and scrubbed, cooked and baked, milked and churned, sowed and harvested, planned and typed. The atmosphere was happy and relaxed.

In the years following, the house took on a new look with bright colour schemes and furnishings. Sponsors supplied equipment from saucepan sets to cookers. The cottage was renovated, a pottery shed equipped, newly laid out workrooms were added, new bedrooms replaced the old lofts, a farm kitchen museum took over from the hen house, a new poultry unit was erected, a piggery was built, a new potting shed was sited within the garden. The yards and avenue were tarmacadamed, dry-rot was eliminated, new electric wiring and sewerage system were laid on, tennis courts were resurfaced.

At a distance of twenty-one years, the problems and frustrations associated with An Grianán's growing pains are mercifully dimmed. But the sharply-etched cameos of time and place, where ideas were voiced and history made, will always stay:

— Mrs Olivia Hughes, strolling down the sea path near the copper beech, unfolding her dream of a Horticultural College for women.

— Miss Muriel Gahan outlining her plans as she purposefully walked across the courtyard to inspect the stables and loft, her inner eye already seeing the potters, weavers, fabric printers, rushworkers installed.

— Miss Joyce Nicholson in her super car and beribboned straw hat proudly ushering in her VIP passenger — the Kellogg man on his annual visit — with an excited whisper that he is interested in our farm development plan.

— Mrs Anne Blythe, serenely standing on an empty stage in the Kellogg Hall, shafts of sunlight framing her, while she discussed the possibility of the carpenter from the Abbey Theatre coming on loan to make stage fittings suitable for professional standards.

— Mrs Máirín Beaumont, balancing her teacup near the trolley in the Inner Hall, fervently expressing her wish that some courses at An Grianán be conducted through the medium of Irish.

— Mrs Signe Lloyd, carefully replacing hymnals in the drawing room press, confiding (in her charming Danish/Irish voice) her secret wish that evening prayers would be recited in common.

— Cheery Miss Nora Byrne with specs swinging from neck-chain, pacing the site near the tennis courts while a vision of the new poultry unit takes shape.

— Amiable Mrs Phyllis Faris touring the farmyard, her pensive look changing to one of satisfaction: 'why not have a piggery there?'

— Rose-cheeked financial wizard, Mrs Sarah Ryan, sitting alert in the drawing room at Executive Conference, tendrils of silvery hair escaping from wispy silver hair-net, clearing her throat preparatory to proposing an Endowment Fund for An Grianán's future needs.

— Dynamic Mrs Áine Barrington, her curly hair highlighted with slanting sun pouring through Kellogg Hall windows, outlining the advantages of a Committee of Management.

— Enthusiastic Mrs Joan Coady at a round table meeting in the office, advocating the publishing of *An Grianán News Quarterly*, then only a couple of stencilled pages — later to become a monthly.

— Gentle Mrs Maeve Curtis, advocate for communications, initiating her first disciples into basic principles by the drawing room fire. Her 'Who, What, Where, Why, When' an easily remembered message.

Now across the years I remember with pleasure the wonderful team of colleagues whose co-operation, support and friendship helped in the making of An Grianán. They rose magnificently to every occasion from coping with the annual Fete when hundreds of bus-loads came to support this Travel Aid effort, to organising the Annual Autumn Show to supplement An Ciste. They welcomed and fed the hundreds of visitors who came on their annual outings, they provided a day and night taxi service for members to trains and buses, in the days before the private car was the norm. They operated an emergency ambulance service when a premature birth was imminent, and on another occasion when a sudden serious illness in the small hours of the morning necessitated hospital treatment. They rounded-up straying cattle and turned out straying sheep who nibbled every green leaf and blade in the dark of the night. They assisted at the delivery of calves who usually chose to come at night. They used their individual talents to give talks or demonstrations at courses. They picked and preserved the surplus fruit and vegetables. They bunched and marketed flowers — from snowdrops and primroses to sweetpeas and chrysanthemums. They supplied the house with honey from their own beekeeping project. They baked and sold biscuits, apple tarts, mince pies and found a ready market for rolls of uncooked pastry. They operated a mail-order service for chrysanthemum cuttings. All these money-making efforts were carried out in their off-time, to help boost An Grianán's diminishing revenue. Two outstanding individual efforts were:

♦ making a 50lb five-tier cake for the ICA Golden Jubilee function at An Grianán,

♦ writing a memorable script for a pageant to commemorate the same occasion.

In those days An Grianán was like the local community centre. All the local clubs in the district made use of the college facilities for their meetings, concerts, plays, and socials. In turn, the members of these clubs helped out — some as members of the Agricultural Advisory

Committee, some as hostesses for guild outings, some with a hand during harvesting, or stewarding at the Fetes. Local enthusiasts enjoyed the facility of the tennis courts, local schoolgirls came every Monday for classes in cookery and dressmaking and for one three-month period the children came once weekly to join with members at the choral singing classes.

A mention of music reminds me of the Cork Youth Orchestra courses. There they are on the lawn — now the site of the Horticultural College — rehearsing in the sunshine. And on the same lawn but on another occasion, Mrs Grace Somerville-Large conducts a PT session for a group of not-too-young students attending a Primary Teachers course. Her sister, Mrs Cerise Parker, leading a Nature Study group would more likely be further afield — collecting shells on the mile of lovely strand or identifying flowers and plants that grew in the Sea Fields and sand dunes. I can still see the tiny faces of hearts-ease that grew in profusion in the sheltered sandy hollows. That same Sea Field provided us with one of our triumphs — the quality and yield of its first barley crop was a record in the county.

Now that the floodgates of memory are open, it is difficult to staunch the flow, for in so doing I cut off any mention of many well-loved personalities and many memorable milestones. But on my roll of honour are the other early stalwarts of committees — Miss Lucy Franks, Miss Alice Ryan, Mrs Ena McKeever, Mrs Bea Trench, Mrs Pat Duffy, Miss Sheila Findlater, Mrs Ellen Quane, Mrs Elizabeth Drew, Miss Mai Ennis, Miss Dorothy Fagan, Miss Margaret Long, Miss Ella and Miss Anne Walsh, Mrs Esther Bishop — the architects of the blue-print which gave An Grianán its solid foundations.[3]

ICA IN A CHANGING SOCIETY: 1960S

THE ICA AT FIFTY

The ICA celebrated its golden jubilee in 1960 and it had cause to celebrate, having just come out of a period that would prove to be one of the most important decades in its history — it had expanded its facilities for education of a practical and theoretical nature, it had succeeded in obtaining a government grant-in-aid, it successfully lobbied for funds from abroad, it employed full-time organisers to tour the country in order to increase membership, and it encouraged women's participation in rural trade, education and social activities.

By 1960 the ICA had 498 guilds and 15,000 members. The association continued to build on what had been achieved in the 1950s, a productive, lively and forward-looking decade. This was followed up with many momentous steps and years of great positive achievement — acquiring and running an adult residential college, purchasing its own office premises in Dublin and hosting a world conference of ACWW.

IRELAND IN THE 1960S

In the 1960s, changes began to occur in Ireland due to two factors: the Second Vatican Council led the Catholic Church to rethink its attitude in interfering with the statutory entitlements of Irish citizens, and Ireland applied to join the European Economic Community (EEC).

The economic upturn of the 1960s produced very rapid changes in Irish society as Irish people struggled to catch up with the standards of living developed elsewhere since the war.

Since the foundation of the Free State, the conservative population saw radio, films, public dance halls, etc. as a threat to traditional

values and partly controlled same by the 1929 Censorship Board to
censor books and periodicals. The South became a Catholic state
after 1922 due to the huge Catholic majority. Middle and working
class Protestants settled in to make the best of the situation. Many of
them emigrated. Partly because of this and partly because of the
Catholic Church's policy on mixed marriages, the Protestant portion
of the population had fallen by half by the 1960s. It was not until the
ecumenical movement of the 1960s that the Protestant community
felt secure enough with the South to play a fuller part in the state.[1]

The Catholic bishops' influence was very obvious, regarding
censorship of films and books, the ban on divorce, their stamp on
the 1937 Constitution, and the failure of the first airing of the
Mother and Child scheme.

> Noel Browne, Minister for Health, lost and the bishops won again,
> but by bringing the matter to the public's notice, he made both the
> Catholic bishops and the politicians a little more cautious in the
> future. In the 1960s a better-educated Catholic public and a more
> open Catholic Church had to find other ways of approaching difficult
> social and moral issues.[2]

The Second Vatican Council, 1962–65, encouraged a more
forthright discussion of religious and social matters than had previously been considered acceptable. Also the coming of television
to Ireland on New Year's eve, 1961 made the discussions of topics
ranging from mixed marriages to censorship and contraception an
unremarkable daily occurrence. Television was one of the most
important agents of change in the post-war period — it reduced the
respect for authority figures, as politicians or clergy appearing on
television had to defend their opinions.

All these influences made a rise in the standard of living possible,
and Irish society began to catch up on the outside world. Economic
prosperity meant more jobs and more money to spend. People
spent more on improving their houses. Levels of nutrition
improved and combined with better medical services to improve
public health.

ICA DEVELOPMENT PLAN

ICA launched a five-year development plan in 1962, designed in
particular to increase the participation of small western farms and

gaeltacht areas in the affairs of the association — areas which the ICA had failed to penetrate sufficiently. The three principal goals in this five-year development plan were expansion, co-operation and education. (The success of this plan was that guild numbers rose from 500 to 900). The plan concentrated on improved credit facilities and home improvement schemes. In 1963 Mr Lemass, An Taoiseach, met a deputation of Executive members and was given a broad outline of the programme. So great was his interest that he set up an inter-departmental committee to interview Executive representatives and question them on the programme. As a result, an additional government grant-in-aid was made to the ICA to enable the rural development projects to go ahead.

ACQUISITION OF OFFICES

With the expansion of the ICA came the need for adequate offices. Regretfully they had to leave 23 St. Stephen's Green where for so many years they had enjoyed the hospitality of Country Workers. 'A well-situated house in Ballsbridge, suitable for offices, was bought by auction' for the reasonable sum of £7,500 which the association paid off to the National Bank in College Green, Dublin in five years through the target of £5 per guild. Alterations were carried out and almost completed by the end of 1963. 'As from 1 January 1964, 58 Merrion Road, Ballsbridge (opposite the RDS) will be the central office of the ICA.'[3]

Kathleen Delap, Honorary Secretary at the time, recalls approaching the manager of the then National Bank, College Green, Dublin, for a loan and not knowing what he meant when he asked for collateral! She did not have any but ICA got the loan for £7,000 — the title deeds being equitable mortgage which they repaid in due course. Such was the naiveté and courage of the Executive of this voluntary organisation — which by now had achieved the establishment of a central office in Merrion Road, Dublin and an Adult Education College at An Grianán.

ICA GOLDEN JUBILEE

The ICA celebrated its fiftieth birthday on 15 May 1960 and its theme was 'Beautiful Ireland' in every sphere. 'Guild members were busy with garden schemes and the planting of ornamental trees and shrubs in public places, practising together in choirs and orchestras, writing up their memories of 'early days' and delving into old minute books and newspaper records, as well as painting and generally brightening up their guild premises and homes in preparation for Jubilee day.'

It was found that revision of the ICA's constitution was necessary at the 1960 AGM in order that ICA be recognised as a charity in the legal sense and thus be entitled to accept donations and to own halls or other buildings without being subject to income tax.

Bea Orpen (later to become ICA President) designed the presidential chain and Lucy Garratt made it. The centrepiece is an exquisitely-cut crystal drop presented by Lucy Franks with a chain made of crystal beads tipped and linked with silver. The strands are held by oak leaves in repoussé work, repeating the pattern around the crystal drop in the medallion.

SECOND FIFTY YEARS

When the Golden Jubilee celebrations in 1960 were over, the ICA began its second fifty years with renewed energy, strengthened by the accumulated wisdom of the past.

ICA continued its work to bring 'Better living' for all, with agitation for rural water schemes its major project at this time. By 1960, only 12 per cent of rural houses had a water supply. The 1956 census showed there were 1.4 million people in rural Ireland, meaning that 1,232,000 people did not have running water — still depending on a well, pump or stream! A one-day conference was held in 1960 at An Grianán from which a 'Campaign for rural water supplies committee' was set up, and ICA followed this up with an exhibition entitled 'Turn of the Tap' during their 1961 AGM. It took ICA a long time to convince governments of the need for rural water, since successive governments had misdirected funds into areas which would give an economic return. Eventually, however, it was a successful campaign.

The AGM of 1961 brought to an end the presidency of Dorothy Smith and the incoming President was Kit Ahern of Kerry.

In 1962, the Dept. of Agriculture announced a pilot scheme for Rural Home Economics Advisers in the Munster Institute, Cork. Great things were expected of this effort to set up a service which ICA had been long demanding as the right of rural women. Twelve trained advisers would return to their counties in 1963, and ICA urged its members to avail of their services and show that the demand is greater than the pilot scheme could supply.

In 1963 Marie Lewis, Director of An Grianán was sent by the ICA on a seven-month scholarship to the Hague, Holland and

Mrs P. Duffy, An Grianán Bursar, kept things running smoothly in her absence. The same year the Choral Festival held in the Mansion House in Dublin was a great success.

Lucy Franks, affectionately known to many members as 'Franksie' died on 13 July 1964. ICA's debt to her over the years in incalculable.

In 1965 the *Irish Countrywoman* was launched (incorporating *An Grianán Quarterly*), published in Cork with a circulation of 10,000 monthly. The same year, Mavis Baumann of Dungarvan donated a cup for national art which is still been competed for.

In 1967, the UN Commission on the Status of Women issued a directive to women's international non-governmental organisations to ask their affiliates to examine the status of women in their own countries. In Ireland in 1968 an ad-hoc committee was formed from ten women's groupings, including ICA, to investigate discriminations against women. They subsequently presented a detailed memorandum to government, calling among other things for the establishment of a commission on the status of women.

Peggy Farrell was into her last year of ICA presidency when she was appointed to the Senate and on 22 August 1969 she tendered her resignation to the ICA Executive. Opinions were divided as to whether a President could continue in office whilst serving for a political party — the constitution was ambiguous. When the letter of resignation was received, it was accepted and a decision taken to clarify the constitution for the future. The Executive then proceeded to elect a President (from among the Vice-Presidents) to serve until the AGM and Nora Burton was deemed elected. At the same Executive meeting congratulations were sent to former President Kit Ahern on her election to the Senate as she did not hold any office in the ICA at the time.

ACTIVITIES OF FEDERATIONS AND GUILDS

It is interesting to note what ordinary ICA members were involved in forty years ago — a glimpse of what they were up to can be judged both from the tasks 'farmed out' to Federations and the resolutions brought forward from Councils at that time. Kilkenny Federation took responsibility for radio, while Limerick looked after Literary debate and Dublin was charged with organising hospitality. Drama became the work of Wicklow Federation, with Cavan taking on the task of Savings, and Laois working on Macra na Tuaithe. Education and Agriculture were 'farmed out' to Wexford

and Meath respectively, while Galway looked after Exchange programmes and Offaly took on the task of Road safety. Kildare
Federation was busy with the Eleanora Gibbon competition, and
North Tipperary worked on Care of the aged. In Clare, Federation
members concentrated on Roadside gardens, with Sligo working on
Folklore and South Tipperary taking responsibility for Programme
planning. Child welfare, Press cuttings and Better buying became
the work of Federations in Westmeath, Kerry and Louth respec-
tively, while members in Cork took on the ICA publication, *The
Irish Countrywoman* (*An Grianán News Quarterly* was launched
in 1959). Buy Irish was delegated to Leitrim Federation, while
Carlow looked after Irish in the guilds, Waterford worked on
Inter-Federation competitions and Longford took on the task of
Rehabilitation.

The guilds through their resolutions continued to participate
and give leadership in various campaigns to bring modern facilities
to rural areas as well as contributing to national issues. One of the
most interesting resolutions was the one put forward by Waterford
in 1958 that a school be started in each county for the education of
mentally retarded children so that such children might retain contact with their homes. Another resolution from Cork asked that
ICA should take steps to initiate a system of home helps for the
country districts of Ireland. ICA prioritised the pollution problem,
the need for clean water, highlighted the indiscriminate dumping of
vehicles and effluent into rivers and called for offenders to be pros-
ecuted. A 1963 resolution from Meath proposed 'That the Dept. of
Education be asked to provide career guidance experts to advise
school leavers in the Primary, Vocational and Secondary schools'.

Resolutions passed at Councils concerned:

+ payments by local authorities to parents and foster parents,
+ rebate on rates for agricultural holdings for female as well as
  male workers.
+ scholarships to be set up in memory of deceased persons rather
  than memorials built,
+ classification of films for children,
+ dental care for children aged twelve to sixteen and a half years,
+ rates reduction on ancient mansions,
+ the rateable valuation of a dwelling should not be increased as a
  result of improvements due to installation of water and toilet
  facilities.

The resolution not passed at that time concerned the Irish language as an optional subject in state examinations for children who have had a considerable part of their education outside the state.

Longford's resolution for the 1965 ACWW Triennial conference: 'That all Constituent Societies and individual members of ACWW support the work of any group or organisation concerned with the prevention of pollution of our air and water and the contamination of land which endanger human life or wildlife or the life of domestic animals, and urge their governments to legislate in support of these objectives and to exercise strict control over all substances used in agriculture and industry which are harmful to such life and may have adverse effects on future generations.' These last two resolutions show how the association was ahead of its time — what a pity no one listened!

ICA AND THE IRISH LANGUAGE

During her presidency Kit Ahern always displayed a grá and enthusiasm for the Irish language which was why at every Federation she travelled to there was some Irish spoken. De Valera had advised the association: 'Stick to less contentious causes and to promote the use of Irish'.[4] The 1964 minutes record congratulations to Kit Ahern on her nomination by the Taoiseach to the Senate.

For the golden jubilee, the ICA badge had been reproduced with Gaelic lettering and 'My Land' had been translated by an Irish-speaking guild.

From its foundation in 1910, the association had always encouraged Irish culture and language — its objective even then while improving living standards in rural areas was to also have 'due regard for our Irish culture and to encourage the use of Irish in the affairs of Bantracht na Tuaithe'. In 1913, in line with the promotion of all things Irish, Anita Lett organised camogie games for UI members, causing AE to remark, 'Some of you have light-heartedly, in the growing sympathy of unity, revived the dances, songs and sports which are the right relaxation of labour.'[5] The association promoted all aspects of Irish culture down through the years through various competitions, and when the ACWW conference was held in London in the 1930s a group of ICA Irish dancers went over for a céilí. On this trip and the many other occasions that members went abroad they were always encouraged to wear Irish-made clothes. The annual report of 1943 makes reference to members singing and dancing, knowing and loving Irish poetry and literature. Also in the minutes for the 1950s, when a vacancy arose for a secretary the requirements specified were 'to have Irish and preferably not a male'. The ICA prayer before meetings was composed by Bridget Buckley of Cashel, 'Beannuigh sinn, a Thiarna, agus cuidigh linn an obair atá romhainn a dhéanamh chun do Ghlóire-se agus chun leas ár dtíre.'

In 1962, grant-aid was received to send a specialist organiser to gaeltacht areas. Nóra Ní Chlochartsaigh, a native speaking domestic economy instructress for Carna, Co. Galway, was appointed to do this pioneering work.

On one occasion, Brinaleck guild in Co. Donegal returned minutes as they were not in Irish, and conflict occurred in a guild in Galway gaeltacht where some members wanted meetings to be bilingual while others wanted meetings completely in Irish — proof that it is difficult to please all in an association as diverse as ICA.

Irish nights were organised yearly in all guilds; summer schools never failed to include Irish-oriented activities, and later when An Grianán courses were organised, Irish singing, dancing and literature were very much part of them. Then and later, special Irish courses for members were funded by Bord na Gaeilge.

The Timire Gaeilge is the Officer for the promotion of the Irish language in each Federation. She should encourage each guild to have a Timire Gaeilge, someone with an interest in the Irish language, culture and traditions and who will organise various events to promote these. She should encourage members to be bilingual at meetings and in correspondence. Where possible, she should help guilds to organise or attend classes in céilí and set dancing, drámaíocht, amhránaíocht, traditional music and úrlabhraíocht éifeachtach.

She should also encourage members to take Arts Awards tests 'trí Ghaeilge'. As long as there are good Timire the survival of the Irish language in ICA is in safe hands.

INTERNATIONAL ACTIVITIES AND ACWW CONFERENCE

Kit Ahern represented ICA at an ACWW conference in Melbourne, Australia where she spoke on the theme of 'People and Opportunities'. On this tour she also stopped off in Rome to attend a rural conference.

ICA agreed to host the Triennial Conference of Associated Country Women of the World (ACWW) in 1965, so in 1962 an

ad-hoc committee was set up under Kit Ahern with Joan Coady as
honorary secretary. Convenors were appointed for all aspects of
the conference and members were asked to contribute a
Conference Shilling. Everywhere, ICA members worked busily
creating handmade gifts to be sold at the conference — the proceeds to help defray weighty conference expenses. Willing
hostesses were sought to offer hospitality in their homes to people
who might wish to visit the birthplace of an Irish ancestor. The
Federation of Women's Institutes of Northern Ireland agreed to co-
operate on several aspects of the conference.

Nora Burton of Cork was ICA President in 1965 at the time of
the conference, held in the RDS, Dublin. At the time, this was the
largest and longest conference ever held in the country, involving
over three thousand visitors, with 1,500 of these coming from
twenty-seven countries. It was an enormous undertaking, and
expert skills were needed to organise a conference of this magni-
tude — all this from a voluntary association of women in Ireland in
the 1960s!

Anita Hickey of New Ross, grand-daughter of Anita Lett,
founder and first President of the association, did secretarial work
for the conference. It was a time of committees, sub-committees
and sub-sub-committees — and it worked. Fittingly, the theme of
the conference was 'Working Together'.

The conference lasted from 14 to 26 September and included
seven plenary sessions. At the opening ceremony the platform party
included President de Valera, An Taoiseach Sean Lemass, President
van Beekhoff of ACWW, the Minister for Education George Colley,
the deputy Minister for Agriculture P.J. Lalor, and the Lord Mayor
of Dublin. The ceremony began when the flags of the countries
where ACWW had member societies were borne into the hall by
young daughters of ICA members dressed in pinafore dresses of
white báinín over dark-blue printed blouses. All conference members wore the shamrock brooch given by the hostesses. Fascinating
decorative panels were displayed around the hall: these were
specially designed using a symbolic art form of figures resembling
the carved stone figures of the early Christian art period, depicting
various activities undertaken by women through the ages — agriculture, horticulture and the arts. On the balcony were many
outstanding examples of the traditional Irish patchwork quilts.

The Taoiseach, Sean Lemass, in his opening address paid tribute to the ICA for the great work they were doing to promote the

prosperity and well-being of rural families and he gratefully acknowledged the support given freely by the organisation to the promotion
of government schemes for the benefit of rural communities.

Apart from the work of the conference, delegates took time to
avail of ICA hospitality. There was a get-together party at the
Zoological Gardens, a horse show at the RDS followed by a céilí,
and a visit to the Gaiety Theatre for 'The Crucible' presented by
Tuam Theatre Guild. The Taoiseach hosted a state reception for
delegates, a fashion show was organised, and the conference entertainments culminated in a Slán Abhaile and céilí farewell party. All
of this was in addition to tours to places of interest, visits to guilds
and An Grianán resulting in many members establishing and forg-
ing links with women of like minds all over the world.

The achievements of these few years alone speaks volumes of
ICA's contribution to Irish society. Many momentous steps were
taken, with years of great positive achievement — acquiring and
running an adult residential college, purchasing their own office
premises in Dublin and hosting a world conference of ACWW. The
Executive of the time must be admired — whether through naïveté
or not, they certainly did not lack courage.

AN GRIANÁN DEVELOPS

Meanwhile the adult residential college continued to grow. New
courses were introduced for mothers with toddlers in 1961, and
cottage courses for young adults and teenagers to study home economics. In 1964 'Friends of An Grianán' was formed, and among
their first contributions were a lawn mower, upholstered chairs for
the Kellogg Hall, a projector and water heater for the still room.
Forty years later, they are still contributing.

To help defray costs, Federations 'adopted' bedrooms and the
diamond jubilee Meitheal work groups donated all articles made during the week to enhance An Grianán. One setback for the college
occurred in 1968 when it had to close during an epidemic of foot-
and-mouth disease.

HORTICULTURAL COLLEGE: ONE WOMAN'S DREAM

In the immediate years after the war, it was impossible to obtain
fresh vegetables, fruit and flowers in the shops and markets. Olivia
Hughes realised that if women were not involved in horticulture,
they being the backbone of gardening, there would not be any
flowers in our gardens to beautify the countryside and for tourists

to admire. She began to think about special education for women in horticulture. Horticulture instructors were few and far between. Another very important point is that instructors employed by County Councils were for rural areas only and were not supposed to work for towns and suburbs, although there were many gardens in new housing estates. Olivia Hughes' dream was that a girl living in a town would be able to obtain plenty of work on these new gardens once she had done a special course in horticulture.

At every Executive meeting of ICA, she brought up the subject of a horticulture course for girls the idea met a lot of opposition. Various points of view and worries were put forward — It was not right or considered the thing for girls to do gardening; 'Would we get students to come to the courses'? 'Where would they get jobs'? 'Who would employ them'? — all very real reasons to examine carefully. Gradually, through determination and research, a start was made.

On 21 October 1964, details of a Youth Garden Scheme envisaged by Olivia Hughes, were given to An Grianán Planning Meeting. The scheme was to be a trainee course for girls interested in making a career in horticulture; it would cover all aspects from practical gardening to fruit bottling, preserving and floral arrangements, to marketing the finished product. There would be a small weekly allowance for pocket money — around £1 a week to start, increasing to perhaps £3 a week at the end of the course. Qualified teachers would instruct and visits would be made to good gardens. John Fanning, Horticulturist, was to be consulted before plans were finalised. The proposed scheme was thoroughly approved by the Executive, who made the following recommendations:

1. That applicants should have about three years post-primary education;

2. That all Vocational and Secondary schools and Macra na Tuaithe groups should be notified;

3. A start would be made with a pilot scheme for say three trainees and an effort would be made to start not later than March 1965;

4. Perhaps some prominent seed firms could be encouraged to sponsor the course;

5. Perhaps an ICA member could be sent to Waterferry college in England, which specialised in similar courses, to study their methods.

Some members, including Olivia Hughes, did a survey of jobs available for girls who had completed a course in horticulture. Owners of large gardens, hotels, and nurseries were contacted. The answer was 'Yes' — there were plenty of job opportunities.

On 26 August 1965 a Horticultural Committee was formed to go into the whole question of a horticultural course for girls at An Grianán and it was decided that Mr Mawby of the Kellogg Foundation be told of ICA's ideas on the matter. Events gathered momentum and on 21 June 1967 the welcome news was given that the Kellogg Foundation had approved a grant for the Horticultural Training Scheme, subject to certain conditions. With the approval of both the Department of Agriculture and the Department of Education, plans were drawn up to make the school a commercial proposition.

The first course opened in Autumn 1968 with fifteen girls who lived in the cottage, and classes were held in the Lucy Franks Hall. The first Principal was Kevin O'Carroll and the first instructors were Rosemary McVitty and Rosemary Hyde.

As Olivia Hughes saw her dream becoming a reality, she expressed her hopes for the future:

> It is my hope that countrywomen will never cease to experiment and will never settle down into routine channels; that they will always choose adventure and education rather than routine; that they will make sacrifices for the sake of learning, and that, at An Grianán, they will have a chance of meeting all that is best and most beautiful in Ireland.

There is no doubt that it is to this dream of Mrs Olivia Hughes that ICA owes the Horticultural College at An Grianán.

REPORT ON THE COLLEGE OF HORTICULTURE BY PRINCIPAL CHRIS DOUGLAS

> The college provides a programme leading to Certificate and Diploma qualifications in Horticulture and in Sportsturf Management, as well as a two-year block release programme in green-keeping.
>
> Changes in the college's training programme in recent years have reflected the trends in horticulture over the same period and the trends in employment for our graduates. The course structures are now modular with core and elective modules, affording students the opportunity to choose study areas of their own preference.

The Certificate in Commercial Horticulture provides a broad-based training content, covering the horticultural related sciences and also gives students an appreciation of all areas of horticulture.

The Horticultural Diploma programme concentrates on those areas of development in horticulture where students have been most interested and that provide most employment opportunities, including nursery stock production, landscaping, and garden centre management.

The Sportsturf Management programme provides training for those interested in employment in the sportsturf industry, and particularly green-keeping. In addition, the block release green-keeping programme provides training for those already employed on golf courses.

Facilities at the college provide accommodation for sixty residential students, plus classroom, sports and other facilities for a total student population of up to ninety students. Practical facilities on campus include commercial production units for fruit crops, glasshouse crops and nursery stocks; a garden centre and coffee shop open to the public all year round, incorporating a number of demonstration and model gardens, and demonstration units for vegetables, sportsturf maintenance, beekeeping and landscape features.

All courses are certified and approved by Teagasc and co-funded by the European Social Fund.

PRESIDENTS AND PROGRESS

Peggy Farrell of Roscommon was elected ICA President in 1967. Under the chair of Patricia Duignan, President of Strokestown ICA guild, the 'Slieve Bawn Co-operative Handcraft Market Ltd.' was registered in December 1966 and Peggy Farrell was a founder member of this successful enterprise. An ICA organiser, Theresa Colhoun (née King) was seconded to it for one year to help with organising and day-to-day management.

Peggy Farrell was elected at a time when ICA membership reached 20,000 with 800 guilds. The organising team and specialist advisers numbered twelve. Each President builds on the foundations of her predecessor, and this was a period of expansion for the ICA. Being a business woman, she brought a businesslike approach to the ICA and by 1970 membership was 26,000 with 900 guilds. She claimed to have no time for ethos or concepts — 'just put your head down and get things done'. Meetings were cut to every two months, the overdraft at An Grianán came down and as funding for the Horticultural College was already in place, she saw it through. Once again, the Kellogg Foundation had come to ICA's assistance with $140,000 and at last the Dept. of Agriculture was prepared to recognise the college.

At the 1967 Council meeting, Peggy Farrell did not agree with supporting the National Farmers' Association march, as she felt ICA should not take part in this controversy. It was up to each individual to do what she wanted, and ICA should remain neutral. ICA's offer to mediate was not taken up.

The organisers could not be replaced due to lack of finance, and with the help of the treasurer Josephine Carroll, a human resources survey was carried out at guild level to ascertain the skills and talents available. In 1968 the VCO (voluntary county organiser) training scheme was started. This scheme encourages each Federation to recognise the available various talents of its members and provide training for them to develop and organise the guilds in their Federation.

Also in the same year, a survey of the ICA's organisational structure was undertaken by the Institute of Public Administration. The funding for engaging a consultant to do this came from the interest obtained from the Kellogg Foundation grant. The survey field work took place between 15 October and 14 December 1968. It concluded that the present organisation of the association was basically sound and communications were good. However, some degree of rationalisation of the administrative and organisational structure was necessary if the organisation was to make the best use of the resources available.

It reported that the ICA was expanding rapidly. The number of guilds had increased by 100 per cent from 420 in 1964 to 840 in 1968. Total membership was 24,000 and the total cash turnover was about £50,000. The advent of the horticultural project and the new training school for commercial horticulture, the expansion of An Grianán courses, the introduction of voluntary county organisers, etc., had imposed increasing burdens on the honorary officers and on their supporting staff. These increased burdens showed up the weakness in the structure for day-to-day management and organisation of the association. The continued success of the association would depend on its tackling and solving these problems. The report recommended an effective administrative underpinning for day-to-day management of the ICA's finances, staff, buildings etc. At present each section operated independently, resulting in duplication of effort, waste of resources and higher administrative costs. There was an urgent need for all concerned to view the ICA as a single entity leading to more effective functioning and better co-ordination of activities. If this were done, the ICA could have, for no more than its existing expenditure on staff, an administrative structure well-matched to its present needs. The lack of a full-time chief executive was the most striking defect found in the administrative structure of the association. The association had become too large, was spending too much money and was employing too many staff to let this situation continue to drift. The report also recommended holding on to a central office in Dublin, exploring regionalisation, and advised that there was space only for the horticultural project or the farm, but not both.

Regrettably, the farm at An Grianán had not been a viable commercial proposition. (The minutes state that while it is lovely to have fresh milk and eggs, one must consider the costs). This report sparked off a lengthy debate within the ICA and the minute books are peppered with suggestions and ideas, but the only major decision to emerge was that the farm was closed and staff made redundant. Other points were watered down or abandoned altogether, although Joan Coady did act as Chief Executive for a short time.

The year 1968 also saw the opening of the Lucy Franks Memorial Garden House at An Grianán with her nephew, Cecil Franks, officiating.

Also in 1968, ICA took corporate membership of An Taisce.

A CHANGING SOCIETY

In the 1960s, the women's movement developed, emigration decreased, the marriage rate increased and people began to marry younger. The 1964 Guardianship of Infants Act was passed, giving women guardianship rights equal to those of men. In 1965 the Succession Act abolished distinctions between inheritance rights for males and females. The right of widows to a just share of their husbands' estate was increased and clarified.

In Ireland generally, when the programmes for Economic Development were drawn up, the need for an educated and skilled workforce was recognised. An enquiry into the education system was set up and in 1965 its report, *Investment in Education*, was published. It painted a somewhat depressing picture of a system where almost no fundamental change had been carried out since the nineteenth century. The education system would have to change if Ireland were to become a modern industrial society, and this dramatic change came in 1966 when the Minster for Education, Donagh O'Malley, announced free second-level education. At this time, ICA highlighted the plight of widows on pensions since support for children stopped at sixteen though second-level education was for all.

This access to free second-level education and the increase in the numbers of homes with television, including UK stations, meant that issues were being discussed openly before a startled public. Issues such as birth control, drugs, premarital relations, pornography, and the place of the Church in the modern world had not previously been openly discussed. This made a nonsense of the censorship on books and films, and also shook up Irish domesticity. These diverse pressures and the economic and social changes transformed Ireland — the mood was now one of impatience, criticism and excitement, but this was soon checked by Northern Ireland's troubles and then rekindled by the challenge of entry to the EEC.

Young people in the 1960s were not inhibited, with widespread student unrest, revival of interest in politics and growing preoccupation with social injustice. The change in young people's attitudes to the past was due to their being better informed through studying Irish history and through television programmes — their view of the past was less romantic and less distorted by the prejudices and patriotic over-simplification of their predecessors. F.S.L. Lyons wrote, 'This change in attitude may be one of the great formative influences upon the future — this change is in understanding and not indifference.'[6]

A GROWING ASSOCIATION

The 1960s was a decade of great expansion for the ICA. Its membership almost doubled, helped by its five-year development plan. In 1960, there were 498 guilds and 15,000 members, but by 1970 this had increased to 900 guilds and 26,000 members. It acquired its central office in Dublin and saw the home advisers scheme become a reality. In the 1960s, 'the ICA guilds continued to police the morals of rural Ireland, proposed changes in agricultural rates, pension provisions, the education and welfare of their children, conditions of hospitals, tax rates and medical care, equity in employment law and transport concerns were also prioritised and in their warnings on the dangers of pollution to the country environment they were more far-sighted than many of their peer organisations'.[7]

It was the decade when ICA hosted a major international conference where the emphasis on social reform was significant. It expanded its facilities and its courses at its adult education college and it opened the first Horticultural College for girls — all in all a most satisfying and exciting decade.

10
THE WOMEN'S DECADE: 1970S

IMPROVEMENT IN WOMEN'S RIGHTS

The 1970s witnessed the greatest number of changes in the great-est number of areas since independence — due mostly to Ireland joining the EEC in January 1973. Without this move it is highly unlikely that equal pay and equal treatment legislation would have reached the statute books when they did — in fact it is possible that this might never have happened. 'Irish women have the EEC to thank for the removal of the marriage bar in employment in 1973, the introduction of maternity leave, greater opportuni-ties to train at a skilled trade, protection against dismissal on preg-nancy, the disappearance of advertisements specifying the sex of an applicant for a job and greater equality in the social welfare code.'[1]

In 1968 an ad-hoc committee had been formed to lobby for a national Commission on the Status of Women, and in December 1969 members were invited to a meeting with the Minister for Finance, Charlie Haughey, under whose auspices the commission was to be set up. The ad-hoc committee was represented at that meeting by Dr Boland of Women's International Zionist Organisation, Mrs Browne of Business and Professional Women, Kathleen Delap of the ICA, Dr Weekes of Dublin University Women Graduates Association, and Hilda Tweedy of IHA. It was a very favourable meeting with the Minister agreeing that the mem-bership of the commission should be shared equally between male and female and the chairperson would be chosen by the commit-tee. On 4 April 1970, the terms of reference of the Commission were published:

> To examine and report on the status of women in Irish society, to make
> recommendations on the steps necessary to ensure the participation of

women on equal terms with men in the political, social, cultural and
economic life of the country, and to indicate the implications generally — including the estimated costs — of such recommendations.[2]

There were thirteen appointments to the first Commission on
the Status of Women with Dr Tekle Beere as chairperson. Seven
appointees were women, including three ICA members — Kathleen
Delap, Alice McTiernan and Kathleen Gleeson.

ICA has been involved from the very beginning, in its work with
the ad-hoc committee in 1968 which laid the groundwork for many
of the legislative reforms and other measures which helped to bring
about change for the better in women's lives. The timing was right,
as by the 1960s ICA programmes of education and consciousness-
raising among rural women were changing entrenched attitudes and
there was a political awareness of the multiple discriminations
against women practised by the State.

The ICA, through resolutions brought forward from Council
over the years, was very aware that Irish society needed to be
changed. In 1969 one of the smallest Federations, Leitrim, showed
concern by calling for the implementation of equal pay, at a time
when women's wages were only 53 per cent of men's, and that
resolution was brought to government level where it received a mere
acknowledgement — it was obviously premature. The ICA then made
this the basis of its submission to the new Commission. The association had contributions under every heading in that report. Its
submission stressed the position of the woman in the home who was
without legal protection: she had no right over family property and
her work within the home counted for nothing in financial terms.
Unless the family home was under joint ownership, it could be sold
without a wife's knowledge or consent and she and her children
could be made homeless. She was denied dental and optical benefits. If she was deserted, she was not entitled to state support.
Unmarried mothers and their illegitimate children faced condem-
nation from society and were often impoverished and deprived.
Contraception was illegal. On marriage, women had to resign from
jobs in the civil service, semi-state bodies and in banking — the
major employers of women in the workforce. In law, women were
regarded as their husband's chattels.

The findings of this Commission on the Status of Women in
Ireland were published in 1972. This report is widely regarded as a
charter for women in the modern Irish state. The Women's

Representative Committee was set up in 1974 to oversee the implementation of the recommendations and by 1980, 36 of the 49
recommendations had been achieved — remarkable progress in one
decade!

Recommendations included widening employment opportunities
for girls by changing subject choices in schools, creating a more
proactive approach to appointments of women to posts by government together with professional groups, trade unions and employer
organisations. It was in the area of employment and equal pay,
however, that the Commission was strongest in its criticism and
hence made most recommendations.

The 1973 Social Welfare Act provided for a deserted wife's
allowance and an unmarried mother's allowance, the payment of
children's allowance to mothers, and payments to single women
over 58 years and to wives of prisoners. Also in 1973, the marriage
ban forcing married women to resign from civil service employment was lifted. In the same year the Council for the Status of
Women (CSW) was formed to monitor the Commission's report
and also to act as an umbrella body for all women's associations.
This report marked a watershed in the development of women's
rights and their admission to the political agenda. It was a defini-
tive document, forming the basis for government reform and giving
pressure groups a blueprint for change. From the ad-hoc stage to
the final report, events had been initiated by women not noted for
their radicalism, and yet their actions were to have a significant
impact over the following decade.

With ICA delegates on CSW, the association is deeply involved
in the long struggle for recognition for the council, and these delegates play an active part in its work, holding positions on its
Executive. CSW changed its name to National Council for Women
of Ireland (NCWI) in 1996.

Also in 1973, Senator Mary Robinson, (later to become
President of Ireland), introduced a Private Member's Bill in the
Senate to amend the 1935 Criminal Law Act, leading to the
Supreme Court in 1974 ruling in favour of Mrs Mary McGee and
allowing importation of contraceptives. Since 1974, women are not
excluded from Jury service. The 1976 Family Law Act provided for
maintenance of spouse and children, while the Family Home
Protection Act required both spouses to consent to sale of the
family home. This act went some way towards alleviating the situation by allowing a wife to get a barring order imposed on her

husband, thus preventing him from coming near the family home. However, the reality still remained that most battered wives simply put up with the abuse, seeing no practical alternative. The 1977 Employment Equality Act was passed and the Employment Equality Agency set up with Sylvia Meehan as Chairwoman. In the same year the first Rape Crisis Centre opened in Dublin. The Women's Political Association was founded in 1970 to support and encourage female participation in politics, and in 1972 Cherish was established to support unmarried mothers. At this time, Irish society was becoming more consumerist, affluent and permissive. A better educated generation questioned all forms of authority, whether parental, educational, church or state. The media began to play an increasingly important role in shaping viewpoints.

ICA DIAMOND JUBILEE

It was fitting that it was the Wexford Federation of ICA, where the association was founded, that produced the President for the diamond jubilee in 1970 in the person of Oonagh Corbett. She took as her theme the need for ICA members to set themselves goals, work courageously towards them and for each one to contribute to the association according to her particular ability. Much had been achieved in the sixty years of the association's existence — from St Aidan's Hall in Bree to a central office in Dublin, and two colleges at An Grianán, a membership of 26,000 spread over the twenty-six counties. The association was becoming confident that its effort for the furtherance of adult education was contributing to the well-being of the country and constituted a work of national importance.

The diamond jubilee national celebration commenced with the unveiling of a sundial at Bree, Co. Wexford on 21 May. Wexford Federation under the President, Mrs Rothwell, arranged the programme. Each Federation would arrange its own 60th anniversary celebrations. The theme for all would be 'Our Irish Heritage', and the objective for the year was to 'conserve and preserve', paying particular attention to crafts, artifacts, old buildings and monuments, with an active interest in clean water and the prevention of pollution of both air and water, culminating with the Meitheal which took place in September 1970, at An Grianán, and which had the following programme:

  + Selected groups under various headings to make and leave behind some rush baskets for table use, hand-made pottery for bedroom ashtrays, a decorative wall-hanging in creative embroidery, a panel or screen in collage, a collection of shells, grasses and flora for a Nature Museum, a local history guide book of the district, a collection of dried and pressed flowers mounted for wall hanging.

* Script writers to record the week's activities and camera enthusiasts to film the work, as well as dressmakers to make costumes of the period and actresses to 'stage' that first meeting of the association in 1910. Poetry, music and history were featured in the evenings.

To celebrate ICA's diamond jubilee, four field days were organised by Country Markets:

— Fethard opened by Theodora Fitzgibbon
— Kells opened by T.J. Maher of the National Farmers' Association
— Boyle opened by General Costello
— Ennis opened by Patrick Hillery, Minister for External Affairs, later to become President of Ireland.

Winifred Nolan scripted her lecture 'Our History 1910–1970' for the Meitheal; a film entitled *The ICA: 60 years a-growing* was produced and the ICA choir held a concert at the RDS on 25 November 1970 where 1,200 people attended at 6/– each.

Thirty black and white drawings by Nano Reid were commissioned by the Arts Council to be hung on the main stairs at An Grianán.

PRESIDENTS IN THE 1970S

Every president brings her own personal style to the Presidency and much also depends on the particular challenges she faces during her given term of office. During Peggy Farrell's Presidency difficult decisions had to be made and things had to get done. Peggy Farrell identified very much with the philosophy of Olivia Hughes, an earlier President — the achievement of economic independence for women, or 'money to call one's own'. She was succeeded by Oonagh Corbett who brought her own idealistic and aspirational style to the post. One particular quote from Oonagh Corbett reflects her ideology: 'the greatest luxury should be the home environment, and the wife or mother plays a vital role in establishing that'. It was during her tenure that a resolution from

Kildare Federation on contraception was ruled out as a sectarian issue at the 1971 AGM, however, a policy statement on Northern Ireland was issued: 'violence on all sides is condemned, and internment without trial is unjust and inhuman and a violation of human dignity'.

At the AGM of 1972 when ICA membership stood at 26,714, Josephine Carroll in her acceptance speech as President, declared: 'Now is the time I feel when we must ask ourselves what contribution can we, the women of Ireland both North and South, make towards securing a lasting peace in Ireland based on justice and the coming together of all creeds.' She was always referred to as 'the Hands-across-the-Border President' and it was apt that the President for these years should have been a Monaghan woman who was reared in the North. Throughout her presidency she sought to get women involved in the search for peace in the North. Through her speeches at Council meetings she made it clear that the most important thing was to get people united; she was concerned about bringing people together to stop the violence, getting them to be friends and to work out a solution. But the general body of the ICA at the time was reluctant to get too involved, being afraid of offending anybody. Over the years, the ICA had exchanged visits with the Women's Institutes in Northern Ireland, and when the ICA consulted WI it was found that they themselves were very hamstrung by the situation.

In the end the ICA's contribution was its involvement with the Women's Voluntary Emergency Services. This had been created in 1972 when evacuees from the north were arriving daily in the south and needed hospitality. Kathleen Delap was co-ordinator for that committee and the chair was taken by Lady Wicklow who had worked with ICA (under her name of Eleanor Butler) as an architect during the Counterpart project in the 1950s.

There was a growing awareness of the wider context of the role of women among ICA members, particularly in the light of Ireland's entry to the EEC. At the request of the government, in 1973, ICA submitted a paper on the various aspects of European unity. They felt that from a financial and trading point of view, to have an equal unit of currency for the whole union would lead to fairer transactions and therefore monetary union was absolutely essential. But they found that the question of defence would prove very difficult because countries within Europe were not united, citing Germany East and West, Ireland North and South.

Josephine Carroll's presidency occurred when the report of the first Commission on the Status of Women was published, and a questionnaire on recommendation number 48 of this report (in favour of family planning) was sent to the guilds, resulting in 288 guilds in favour and sixteen against. It was a time of change for women in society, and different interest groups were becoming more vocal. Josephine Carroll was very conscious of preventing the ICA being used by other groupings who needed the support of the largest women's organisation in Ireland. In her own words, 'They didn't really want us — they looked on us as a crowd of fuddy-duddy ould dears, you know'.[3] ICA came under attack from all sides and was considered to be no longer relevant, but the association was proud of its tradition and knew that changes come slowly. The Executive was critical of those who called on them to change and replace their structures, but never offered constructive solutions. Josephine Carroll was aware of a balancing act — on the one hand the Executive had to be forward thinking but on the other they were dealing with a very traditional membership.

Carroll was very disappointed by government's response to the different resolutions brought over the years, and particularly the resolution on underage drinking and drugs — when the ICA's deputation was told by the Minister that, 'Its not that bad at all; you only think it is.' That was the late 1960s! The way forward for the ICA, she felt, was to continue monitoring what was happening in government and elsewhere but to concentrate on producing more action than talk — 'ICA has a history of not being listened to.' And she continued, 'As far as the future is concerned, the ICA is prepared to be involved in anything which aids better living. We would like to see our members involved in social work, such as meals on wheels, community development or advice bureaux and would also like to see more members on urban and rural committees of county councils in order to put the woman's point of view forward. Over the years the ICA has been accused of taking a middle-of-the-road attitude towards certain controversial subjects.'

At the 1973 Summer Council meeting, Carroll stressed the importance of the Report of the Commission on the Status of Women and asked members to discuss the various questions raised, including women in employment, training and retraining of women for employment, the case of deserted wives and unmarried mothers as well as family planning and contraception, abortion and divorce. The views formed from assimilation of this information by the members was to be fed back to the Executive and would form the mandate for the President to speak on their behalf on these matters.

In October 1982, the Irish Council of Itinerant Settlements requested the co-operation of the ICA, and the association obliged by conducting a survey of itinerants' crafts and skills in each Federation. At the same time, the ICA prepared policy documents on care of the child, juvenile offenders, adoption, matrimonial disputes, desertion and property succession. Carroll felt that the ICA had three tasks: to add to the volume of knowledge arising from the skills of members, to set standards of good practice and behaviour, and to encourage the next generation to be better than the present one.

ICA DEVELOPMENTS

The Horticultural College was officially opened by the US ambassador on 20 May 1971.

Tipperary was in the news during these years. In 1972 Phyllis O'Connell, chief organiser retired and was made Buan Cara in 1976. In 1974, Lord and Lady Donoughmore were kidnapped and released unharmed — Lady Donoughmore was a long serving member of Knocklofty guild.[4]

Resolutions passed at Council in 1972 included one to 'Call on government in the interests of social justice not to impose VAT on food, and to abolish the means test for non-contributory old age pensions. Another from Leitrim asked that 'Ireland should nominate and select at least one woman representative on the Economic and Social Welfare Committee of the EEC'. It was to take nearly thirty years before that happened — Brídín Twist becoming the first woman on that committee in 1995.

Membership in 1973 was 28,749, with thirty-two students of horticulture. Once again the ICA appealed to the Kellogg Foundation and the government for funds to extend both the Horticultural and Adult Education colleges at An Grianán — rapid progress for colleges which had only been in existence for four years and twenty years respectively.

At the association's AGM in 1974, Bea Trench came in as President with her theme: 'ICA is an accepted part of Ireland and we should be concerned for the community in which we live and for our countryside as ours is "A world to share". However, this sharing brings waste and the pollution of our countryside, so we have a special responsibility regarding this problem and its re-cycling. In fact it calls for a new Department of the Environment.' Concluding, she felt that this was the largest AGM ever held, 'so what could we not do if we put our minds to it?'

This was a difficult period for the ICA although the membership was increasing. On the ideological side it continually had to justify and defend its existence and on the practical side it was concerned with the day-to-day running of its organisation. Its magazine was showing a loss, both An Grianán and the Horticultural College were on overdraft facilities, and central office had to borrow money for six months at 14 per cent. Even the idea that central office be moved to An Grianán was mooted. (In 1975 central office was valued at £45,000, so in ten years its value had increased six-fold). The financial report was poor in February 1975, and there were staff problems at both colleges. In the Adult Education College, Federations helped out by supplying hostesses, most of whom were friendly and helpful. However, some were too rigid and formidable resulting from time to time in difficult decisions having to be made. One instance of this occurred when a very efficient and hard-working employee who was a great craftswoman lacked the personality for dealing with people, (members still talk of her with fear in their voices). She was suspended with pay and asked to resign, but refused, and the Board had no option but to terminate her employment. An ICA member was then employed in a temporary capacity as administrator, and the minutes note that her presence was of immense value – 'there is now a very happy atmosphere' at the college.

HORTICULTURAL COLLEGE

The year 1975 was a bad one for the Horticultural College, with poor crops and poor weather plus the cost of fuel and oil very high. A special meeting on finance was called on 10 March 1975 to rectify matters, and plans were drawn up to put things on a more businesslike footing, including appointing a PRO to promote both the ICA and the two colleges, initiating a major fundraising effort, and setting up a three-year presidency.

The Horticultural College, a completely new venture for the ICA, was still in its infancy, and presented several teething problems and misunderstandings. On the one side there was a young staff dictating to the ICA and on the other side, a voluntary committee who had to change office under the constitution, resulting in a lack of continuity which creates difficulties for business.

The Adult Education College also suffered staffing problems. In the autumn of 1977 Ann Power was appointed administrator of the Adult Education College and Chris Douglas replaced Kevin O'Carroll as principal of the Horticultural College. Negotiations continued with the unions and the minutes record 'for the first time in seven years, the two establishments had really got together'.

Activities and Resolutions 1976–78

Even though the ICA may not have been very financially healthy, the activities of members were many and varied. In 1976, Limerick Federation did a study on the Land Structural Reform proposals. Another study addressed the discussion paper on the Law of Nullity in Ireland, and also on the Tourism Development Plan 1976–80.

Amongst the resolutions put forward in this period was one in 1977 calling on the government to immediately repeal 'the outdated legislation concerning "criminal conversation" provision whereby a husband could sue for damages any man with whom his wife had sexual intercourse,' i.e., for loss of services. Here the wife was still seen as the husband's chattel, although adultery was not a criminal offence for husband or wife. Dungarvan guild through Joan Bailey pursued this resolution for five years bringing it to a successful conclusion in 1982.

In September 1978, two very interesting resolutions were passed by Council: calling on the government to take action about the unpaid work of women in the home and about the updating of the Children's Act of 1908 as per the 1959 UN Declaration of Rights of the Child.

Some of the competitions which ran during 1976–77 included musical composition, painting, cookery, public speaking (Irish or English), Bord Fáilte garden competition, two competitions for ICA choirs — Oireachtas (Foras Éireann cup), and Sligo feis ceoil (Cottage Rake cup) — Maeve Curtis Memorial award (a reporter's award sponsored by the *Cork Examiner*) and finally the Merit Award scheme which was for guild projects that contribute to their community.

Eleanora Gibbon, an ICA member, was the person who introduced the Montessori method of teaching to Ireland. Her husband later donated a sum of money to the ICA in her memory. The Executive used this money to commission a Cork jeweller to design a special cup that was to be competed for by the Federations. The cup was for singing and dancing competitions as an alternative to crafts.

THE ISSUE OF PARTY POLITICS

At this period, membership stood at approximately 30,000 and there was increasing participation by members on public bodies and County Councils.

ICA has always exercised its rights as a nominating member to the cultural and education panel in the Senate and also sought the selection of the Taoiseach. Many members unsuccessfully contested the senate elections as independent candidates over the years, and all found to their cost (in time, energy, travel as well as finance), that up against the party machines their chances would always be slim.

The successful ICA members nominated to the senate by the Taoiseach were Kit Ahern, Peggy Farrell, and Camilla Hannon. Other ICA members who were elected senators include Eibhlin Mhic Choisdealbha (Edith Drury) of Tuam, Jenny Dowdall of Cork and Kathleen Browne of Wexford, with Patsy Lawlor of Kildare the most recent. The best illustration of the real attitudes of male politicians to women, however, is seen from the nominations, with each Taoiseach having the power to nominate eleven members at his discretion. Arguably this would allow a Taoiseach, worried about the absence of women from parliament, a practical means of helping to improve matters. Significantly, no Taoiseach ever made any marked use of the opportunity.

Mr de Valera had five opportunities of appointing eleven nominees. Out of a possible fifty-five, he appointed three women altogether — two of whom were sisters of heroes of the 1916 Rising and the third was a leading member of Cumann na mBan. Mr Costello had two opportunities to nominate eleven senators and appointed one woman once. Mr Lemass, who occasionally spoke about the need for more women in politics, also had two opportunities. He appointed three women, two of whom were sisters of heroes of the 1916 Rising. Mr Lynch had two opportunities — the first time he appointed one woman and the second time (1977) appointed three. Mr Cosgrave, under pressure from various women's organisations, did not appoint even one woman to the 1973–77 Senate.[5]

These figures give eloquent witness to the real feelings of those concerned about the importance of higher levels of representation for women, and also to the weakness of women as a pressure group in general.

ICA and Women in Public Life

Bea Trench, ICA President in 1974 said, 'We are slow to take our place in public life or even raise our voice when we have something worthwhile to say, and sadder still, when a woman does have the courage to go into public life, we do not always support her.'

The same problems continue to surface, though they are perhaps not as contentious, every time a member seeks election to the Senate or Dáil, or to become a Taoiseach's nominee — the latest being when Brídín Twist resigned in 1997 to contest a general election seat in Clare, with just one month left of her three-year term as President. (The Executive elected Sally Ward of Sligo as interim President until the AGM of 1997.)

The problem of losing valuable people to party politics was always a contentious issue — on the one hand the success of ICA was deeply rooted in its observance of its 'non-party political and non-sectarian' rule. The 'non-sectarian' requirement caused only little waves within the membership and then mostly by media presumptions, but it was the 'non-party politics' rule which reared its head in practically every decade since the foundation of the association, and in fact became a safety net for the organisation. This is understandable when one considers the time frame, with early twentieth-century Ireland being torn apart by the ravages of civil war, and the resulting wounds remaining — until more recent times — very raw. The association evolved throughout this period, and it was thus always going to be difficult to politicise the organisation when it was felt that the bulk of its work had been achieved precisely because of the fact that its roots were in a non-political co-operative culture.

Whilst the formal politicisation of the Irishwoman has taken nearly a full century, those conflicts within the ICA constituted a learning process. Women's associations founded in the 1970s do not have the history or the baggage of the ICA, founded in 1910. However, as Patsy Lawlor maintained, the society's role had been limited not by its constitution but by its own self-perception and by self-inflicted non-existent archaic rules. In a large democratic organisation, disputes and differences of opinion are to be expected and it is impossible to find a common pattern to fit the expected and it is impossible to find a common pattern to fit the ideas of 30,000 women.

> The dominant ethos in Irish society ensured that the odds were stacked against the ICA's official involvement in party politics, which was why their representatives often insisted that localism was the best form of patriotism and why they were more likely to elect each other at local rather than national level.[6]

ICA membership was at its peak at this period, when it would have been opportune to use its muscle but the ethos of politics was lacking, and the momentum seems to have been lost with the decline in its membership.

This raises the question of why women are so lacking in confidence when in fact they have special qualities badly needed in society. Judging by the resolutions brought by the ICA over the years, members are very much aware of their heritage, sensitive to the beauty of the country and concerned to preserve and conserve — striking a balance between economic development and preservation of natural beauty. Experience has shown that bringing resolutions, no matter how good, to government was not sufficient. The Executive needs to be more vigorous, and continually lobby public representatives until laws are changed.

Bea Trench, President from 1974–76, commented that 'the association was simply too quiet and did not give enough support to women in public life.' If there was resentful scorn from some quarters about the refusal to take a more political stance, there was a familiar reassurance from others. At the 1974 AGM, Erskine Childers, President of Ireland, told members: 'It is not the government of the day or the opposition of the day — it is the voluntary organisations that alter the destiny of the country'.

The attitudes of modern women towards work, family and lifestyle have changed radically: in examining ICA archives, one should not condemn the members for failing to achieve the objectives sought by contemporary women's groups — they fought for the issues which appeared relevant to their time. ICA always saw the family not as an isolated unit but as an integral part of the fabric of society, and reflecting contemporary socio-economic conditions. It is very easy to criticise and hope for change but much harder to come up with solutions regarding what is to be changed and how. Kathleen Delap, Buan Cara, wrote in the 1975 *Journal of the*

Institute of Public Administration, 'The Commission on the Status of Women's Report laid great emphasis on marriage as a partnership of shared duties — the husband taking a share in household duties when the wife is working outside the home.'[7] She went on to suggest another approach, both more conservative and at the same time more radical. On the conservative side, she suggested that a couple should think very hard before deciding to give someone else the task of bringing up their children, because that is what it means if the wife works outside the home. She did not mean that the wife should just stay around until the children go to school. Apart from the fact that school holidays are much longer and more frequent than the holidays given to most employees, a child of school-going age is as much in need — sometimes even more so — of a parent to come home to as is a toddler. The radical approach she suggested was:

> If both husband and wife want to continue working and are ambitious to make a success of their careers, should they not decide against having children at all? After all, why do we have children? Is it because it is the 'done thing' or because we want someone to look after us in our old age? Or is it because we love them and want to do the best for them? If the last reason is paramount, the best we can do includes being on hand whenever we are needed....

In the same article, Professor Michael Fogarty is quoted as saying, 'If you want to get to the top of your profession or calling, remain single.' Delap did not go as far as Professor Fogarty about celibacy, but thought that the couple who both want to work at the highest level of their intellects and abilities should think seriously about remaining childless.

These sentiments were expressed over twenty-five years ago, and childcare still remains a problem for Irish society.

Women in the 1970s were confronted with stresses to an extent unknown before; they were no longer prepared to accept unhappy conditions or unsatisfactory relationships. They no longer accepted the philosophy that for the sake of the family, they would put up with anything. They were demanding more, and questioning more the traditional attitudes and traditional roles within the family and society.

The Employment Equality Act in 1977 ended discrimination based on sex and marital status in the area of employment, including advertising and promotion. In order to oversee the implementation of this act and the Anti-Discrimination (Pay) Act of 1974, an

Employment Equality Agency was established with Sylvia Meehan as Chairwoman. In the same year the first Rape Crisis Centre opened in Dublin. A further piece of protective legislation was the Unfair Dismissal Act, 1977, which protected employees, including expectant mothers, from unfair dismissal.

Economically and socially, Ireland modernised and became more in tune with developments in Europe, yet women still had feelings of alienation from the official political process and decision-making. Looking at twenty-five statutory and non-statutory bodies, women were found to be serving on eleven — 50 women and 432 men — the 'glass ceiling' was very much in evidence. Women's work in the home remained undervalued. Irish society was now becoming more consumerist, affluent and permissive. A better-educated generation questioned all forms of authority — parental, educational, church and state. The media began to play an increasingly important role in shaping viewpoints.[8]

Societal attitudes towards women taking up employment outside the home, including married women, were beginning to change. This often swung to the opposite extreme where 'the woman who had only one career, that of parent, has found herself apologising, and wondering if she shouldn't be making arrangements to go back to work.'[9] However, there was little doubt that, these extremes aside, the centre ground of women's opinion still believed that the greatest career of all for women was marriage and the raising of a family.

EUROPEAN LINKS

In 1977 ICA became affiliated to COFACE — the Confederation of Family Organisations in the European Community. COFACE is responsible for putting policies on the family before the EU. It has four standing committees and the corresponding four ICA commit-tees reflect the briefs of these committees:

♦ Social Affairs and Health

♦ Education

♦ Agriculture and Rural Development

♦ Consumer Affairs

Four Vice-Presidents of ICA have responsibility for these and must keep abreast of what is happening in all the European states so as to be in a position to help and advise any guild should the need arise. Qualified people in the four areas are appointed to the relevant committees and their findings become the ICA's 'white paper' for submissions to government.

This link with the EU has proven to be of great benefit to the ICA despite the initial problems of translation of all documents from French to English, and the difficulties of travel from all corners of Ireland to a meeting in Brussels at very short notice – but all concerned learned to adapt very quickly or be left behind! Members have taken their places on various committees of COFACE over the years, culminating with Kitty Harlin (ICA President from 1988–1991) becoming its Director in 1993.

ICA IN THE 'WOMEN'S DECADE'

Patsy Lawlor was elected President in 1976 and her theme was the role of ICA in the community and the three-point plan: Health and Welfare, Leadership and Environment. This was to be achieved by a positive action in the community through voluntary effort, by widening the scope of guild activities and by broadening the vision to look beyond personal needs. She concluded her incoming address by throwing out a challenge to the members: 'As an association of 30,000 women affiliated to ACWW, are we the voice we should be? If we even started to whisper together, the decibels of noise would exceed the tolerance level, so why not try it?'

The year 1976 was a good time to become ICA President, according to Patsy Lawlor: 'We were into the woman's decade. AIM, CSW, and Rape Crisis Centre had been formed. Women were becoming more aware of their potential and men were recognising the potential – or perhaps the voting power – of women.' In such a climate, the ICA became a great forum for debate and lobbying. Issues such as divorce, contraception and rape were discussed and debated openly. In the 1970s the association did a survey on family planning, when contraception was still illegal in Ireland. The majority of replies from the guilds were in favour of having access to family planning. ICA was true to its objective of 'better living' by informing its members and then trusting in their integrity to make up their own minds. 'There is little point in ignoring such issues or indeed more recent ones like AIDS and the drink and drug problems of teenagers – they don't go away just because you don't talk about them.' The ICA had a major input in such areas as health, social welfare, justice and education through their resolutions brought up from guilds, and through the various submissions they made to relevant government departments, but they still had their

critics — even among the women's movement. As the modern feminist movement developed in the 1970s, the ICA was seen as
conservative and 'stuffy' and was continually challenged for not
doing anything for Irish women. Certainly the fact that they
unquestioningly supported the institution of the family brought
them into conflict with younger feminists.

CLOSURE OF COUNTRY SHOP

The 1970s saw the establishment of the Craft Council of Ireland
and the closure of the Country Shop and disbandment of Country
Workers Ltd. Their closing marked the end of an era but they had
served their purpose: they had preserved and developed the traditional crafts which were put on a sound footing. Craftworkers'
self-worth had been restored and they were recognised for their
creative gifts. With these closures, Country Markets moved in
January 1975 to rent-free accommodation at ICA's central office.

The Country Shop's closing marked the end of an era for many.
'Those who have been involved in Country Workers Ltd development programme in the past will continue to work for it as
members of one or more of the co-operating organisations with
which they have been so happily associating for up to 48 years —
RDS, ICA, Country Markets and the Crafts Council of Ireland. And
so the work goes on,' said Muriel Gahan. The newspapers were full
of laments. In *The Irish Times* 'Pro-Quidnunc' mourned its passing,
having gone there for the last time on 18 October 1978, the day
before the contents were sold at auction — 'Irishman's Diary went
to a wake yesterday for an old and greatly loved Dublin institution,
which went to every possible length to disguise the fact that the big
grey city lay outside its walls. Yesterday, the curious were allowed
in to poke and root in the sad debris of almost half a century of a
unique institution, a part of countless Dublin childhoods.'

LOOKING TO THE FUTURE

It was Patsy Lawlor who proposed changing the format of *The Irish
Countrywoman* to a glossy one produced by a commercial firm
under the name *Irish Woman*, and it made its first appearance
in July 1978. However, not all members were in agreement and
some objected. Lawlor's response was to make a plea to the members, 'Look on change as progress and not as a threat ... the time
has come for when the veneer of politeness should be shed'.
Unfortunately the change was not a success and there were

repeated calls that the ICA should have a journal for its survival in the future.

ICA was very aware of how essential it was in a voluntary group that the ordinary member should have a sense of identity with her association. The journal provided the advantage of allowing members to browse through it in the comfort of their own homes and become familiar with the day-to-day details of the association. For example, in the May 1977 journal alone, amongst other notices, there was an obituary for Sarah Ryan, for many years treasurer of ICA, report on Council meetings, lists of competitions to come and results of those already held and most important of all were the reports of guilds from around the country, from which members saw the activities of other guilds and could therefore learn from each other. In that journal under guild reports was one from Sevenhouses guild, Kilkenny:

> Our big ambition as a guild was realised when one of our members, Patty Anderson, was elected Federation President. Here she is carrying on a family tradition as the Anderson family has been connected with the ICA since Mrs Hilda Anderson joined the UI in Castletown, Queens Co., in 1911 where she had as fellow member the late Lucy Franks. Mrs Anderson is still, at the age of 87, an active member of Sevenhouses guild.

There is another first for Sevenhouses guild as one of their members Breda Raggett is ICA President for the year 2000 and the first Kilkenny woman to become President.

The failure of the glossy magazine to reach all members was disappointing to the Executive, but despite numerous requests in the minutes no replacement has been found. At the same time ICA membership dropped rapidly in the years 1974–78 – from 28,672 to 23,500, though this also coincided with the increase in membership fee from £1 to £3. Executive decided that a plan of action had to be undertaken to curb the decline of membership. Federations and guilds were asked to survey their members and assess their needs whilst Executive engaged the Market Research Bureau of Ireland in 1979 to carry out an evaluation of the organisation. The general objectives of this survey were to measure the corporate reputation of the ICA among women aged 22 to 50, and to identify the reasons why membership was not increasing and if possible, why membership had decreased. The conclusions drawn were as follows:

1. Among older members, the ICA was perceived as an organisation which did develop people through broad education and
   stimulation but among non-members and recent members this
   development was primarily associated with learning crafts. This
   difference in emphasis should be resolved if new members were
   to be encouraged to join and remain.

2. An organisation of the size and distribution of the ICA required
   strong leadership and guidance allied to a certain level of
   autonomy for guilds in the detailed planning of events. The
   activities of the guilds must move from their present repetitive
   nature to be more interesting, dynamic and relevant to the
   present.

3. The ICA must promote itself more strongly, to advertise and
   invite new members to join.

4. Awareness of An Grianán was high, but again it was more
   strongly associated with craft-learning than with the other types
   of courses offered. Only one-third of all females interviewed
   were aware that An Grianán was open to everybody.

5. The new magazine, *Irish Woman*, had the support of younger
   members.[10]

Very little in the conclusions of the MRBI survey was new. The
ICA had already undertaken this process with the IPA report of
1968, but since it is the quality of the personalities in a voluntary
organisation which determine the effectiveness of the actions, not all
the findings were carried through. However, those that were proved
beneficial, such as the organisation of group meetings when neighbouring guilds got together socially and exchanged ideas and skills.

Also in 1979, the Dept of Education sanctioned funding for two
new development officers with the promise of two more: Sylvia
Spring of Carlow and Deirdre McKinley of Donegal were appointed.

Coming to the end of the 1970s, the work of the association
became very intense: it was involved in securing funding for the
proposed extensions to both colleges — the Kellogg Foundation had
once again promised support if the Irish government would match
it. The amount now being sought was near to £1 million. The
Executive was worried that the association needed more development officers if it was to stem the loss of members, and in 1979 An
Grianán celebrated its 25th anniversary, coinciding with the election of a new President.

SILVER JUBILEE REPORT BY ANN POWER, ADMINISTRATOR

An Grianán 1979: has twenty-five years of existence produced any changes? I think the answer is yes and no.

Certainly there are obvious visual changes. Through the generosity of the Association of the 'Friends of An Grianán', Federations, guilds and individual donors, it has been possible to maintain a good standard of furnishing. A house of such beauty and gracious dimensions deserves to be beautifully furnished. The installation of central heating throughout the college some years ago has certainly added to the comfort.

So, whereas the appearance of the interior changes from time to time 'The Sunny Place' still radiates the same warm welcome and a friendly relaxed atmosphere. In an ever-changing troubled world, An Grianán is a haven where one becomes refreshed in mind and body. This is not to say that we are static or in a rut, nor does it mean that we are complacent. We are ever-conscious of the wisdom of preserving and perpetuating that which is good from the past, by keeping alive and fostering a love of our traditional arts and crafts. Our aims and ideas remain the same. While committed to preserving the good things of the past, we acknowledge the necessity of living in the present and meeting demands and of being aware that the future presents a challenge.

It is very evident from discussions which take place on a variety of subjects that our members today are very active in community affairs and are helping to form policies aimed at improving the quality of life for all. The volume of 'happy talk' in the dining room seldom varies, or if it does it never decreases.

The advent of a television set for leisure time viewing was deplored by some. It has not interfered with the traditional Grianán nights in the drawing room. The enjoyment of participants and listeners is always obvious and these nights of impromptu entertainment play just as important a part in the week's proceedings as the time spent in class.

More and more younger people are coming to An Grianán and no longer is a male student a nine-days wonder. An Grianán and its activities are becoming more widely known. Melissa from Chicago came last year to attend two courses — 'Archaeology' and 'Movement and Mime'. We also had some charming European girls from Germany and France. All came to learn traditional crafts, and heard about An Grianán through either Experiment in International Living or Rencontres sans

Frontières. Bord Fáilte has also helped to publicise our college. Our 1978 weekends were all featured in their 'Short Holiday Breaks' and the same will apply in 1979. Attendance by Northern Ireland WI's is very gratifying; some of these members come as guests of Federations or guilds. At Queens University, Belfast, David Rowlands is in charge of a project called 'Carry on Learning'. He brings together in groups, women of all classes and creeds and from various areas in Belfast. Those with talents help those who have not had an opportunity to develop any. David thought it would be a good idea to bring some of these women to An Grianán to acquire extra expertise. Two craft weekends were organised last year, and approximately thirty women attended each weekend. They were absolutely enthralled with the warm welcome, peace and relaxation, and understandably so, considering the stresses and strains they live through each day. It was wonderful to see women from what is termed 'the two communities' living and learning together in complete harmony. There is surely a lesson here for the advocates of violence. Two similar weekends are being organised for 1979. I must add that some of our ICA craft teachers travelled to Belfast to conduct a craft weekend for this project.

As present Administrator, what are my hopes for the future? I hope that we may always be mindful of the great generosity of the W.K. Kellogg Foundation and that we prove ourselves to be ever worthy of the trust placed in us twenty-five years ago by that Foundation. I hope that we will never forget the dedication, idealism and foresight of our members who were instrumental in making An Grianán become a reality — a dream come true — their dream. My last hope is less noble but it is an economic necessity — may we never have an empty bed.

11
1980 Onwards

In the 1980s there was growing acceptance by government and society of the broader economic, social and political role of women. Unemployment continued to soar and by early 1990 had reached 300,000. Over 70,000 people emigrated between 1980–86 and by the later part of the decade emigration had reached the 1950 level. Alongside this, increasingly active women's organisations and increasing numbers of female public representatives aired the problems experienced by women. Public attention was thus drawn to issues such as contraception, rape, single parenthood and abortion. In 1980, Mella Carroll became the first woman to be appointed High Court Judge, and the first women soldiers held their passing out parade. The effect of EC directives continued to have a significant resonance in Ireland ensuring 'the inexorable progress towards real equality'.[1]

Challenges Facing the ICA

Camilla Hannon became ICA President in 1979, at a very difficult time for the ICA — membership had dropped to 23,000 and whilst central office was breaking even, the Adult Education College and the Horticultural College were losing money, though both had plans for large extensions. In addition, the ICA magazine was not a success. Her first course of action was getting the Dept. of Education to sanction four full-time development officers. It was at this time that Commins, Spring, Carroll and McKinley were appointed and joined forces with Colhoun and Kennedy.

With renewed vigour, and supported by the development officers, the ICA had greater success and by 1980, membership had increased by 1,500. During Hannon's term of office the ICA celebrated its 70th birthday and An Grianán its silver jubilee. Ceremonies marked both celebrations, including the erection of a commemorative plaque on the slopes of Slievenamon, Co. Tipperary and a tree planting ceremony at Bree, Co. Wexford. The highlight of the jubilee dinner at An Grianán was the showing of *Irish Fashion 1760–1968*, loaned by the National Museum.

Despite the heavy workload of securing funding, overseeing the expansions of the ICA colleges and attending to members' needs, Camilla Hannon also had to defend the association on all sides. T.J. Maher, MEP called for an end to sexist organisations such as ICA and certain golf clubs, and Monica Carr wrote about young women, the greatest critics of ICA:

> Few of them remember an era when farm women were regarded as part of the furniture and taken entirely for granted. They were expected to sit outside licensed premises in country towns and villages on fair days and after Mass on Sundays when their menfolk were inside drinking and talking. 'Home people' pure and simple, their only pur-pose in life to slave and 'mullack' and look after the comfort of their families, Irish rural women whether this present generation recognises it or not, owe a great debt of gratitude to the ICA, which brought them gently and gradually out of the narrow confines of their own front gate.[2]

AN GRIANÁN

Camilla Hannon, ICA President, said at An Grianán's 25th anniver-sary celebrations:

> An Grianán is a trust handed down to us to carry on for the benefit of those who will come after us — our heritage to posterity. It is not only for the ICA, not only for women but for all the people of Ireland, North and South. It is, as its name proclaims, a happy sunny place with an atmosphere of welcome and shared enjoyment in work, and I look forward to the future, knowing there is an assured place for An Grianán in the life of the nation.

At the same function Joan Coady, an esteemed Buan Cara, said 'Let An Grianán continue to be the "Sunny place" that develops people by primarily fostering a love and appreciation of the finest things in a distinctively Irish way of life.'

James Creed was appointed director of An Grianán on 20 April 1981. He held that post until April 2000 and under his stewardship the college became a resounding success. At the same time, to provide the ICA with a vital means of communication, a newsletter was published with Creed acting as editor.

The increase in the number of horticultural students highlighted the need for improved facilities and, thanks to the continuing generosity of the Kellogg Foundation matched with grants from the Dept. of Agriculture, a new extension was opened by the Taoiseach, Dr Garret FitzGerald in November 1981. In the course of his speech he recognised the developmental role the ICA played in Irish rural life and said that this role had been a significant influence on the women's movement in the country. He went on to make two points. The first point was that there was a low level of representation of women on state boards and agencies, a fact drawn to his attention by women's organisations including the ICA, and he undertook to improve the situation. His second point was that much of the work which women carried out in agriculture was not adequately reflected in national statistics. He acknowledged that the ICA had played a key role in the enhancement of the quality of rural life and therefore a change was necessary on this undervaluing of women's contributions.

RECOGNITION FOR ICA

The ICA's involvement in many areas of national importance had not gone unnoticed. As far back as 1979, Brian Lenihan as Minister for Foreign Affairs appointed Camilla Hannon, as ICA President, a member of the Advisory Council for Development Co-operation, and in the same year Michael O'Kennedy as Minister for Finance asked her to serve on the Commission on Taxation. It was fitting that she was appointed to the board of Cospóir, as she was a former hockey interprovincial player for Leinster. In 1981 John Boland, Minister for Education, placed her on the newly formed Commission for Adult Education and in January 1982, the ICA's long campaign for recognition of the contribution made by women to Irish agricultural life was rewarded when the Minister for Agriculture, Alan Dukes, made her the first woman ever to have a seat on the board of ACOT.

Around the same period, individual members of the ICA brought honour to the association and advanced the cause of women in general. Joan Coady of Tramore Guild, Co. Waterford was the first Irish woman to be elected vice-president of ACWW, which had over 8.5 million members world-wide. Margaret Erraught of Ballymun

Guild, Dublin, was appointed to the EEC Consumer Consultative Committee as well as the Advertising Standards Authority of Ireland. Peggy Farrell of Roscommon was voted Business Woman of the Year for her initiative in setting up her own clothing factory and providing much-needed local employment. The first woman chairperson of a County Committee of Agriculture was Longford ICA member, Marcella Higgins. In addition, the ICA nominee to the Senate succeeded in actually becoming a senator — Senator Patsy Lawlor.

NEW CONCERNS AND CONTACTS

Among the resolutions causing concern to members at this time was the need to amend the Family Home Protection Act, with an ICA deputation meeting Senator Mary Robinson to discuss the subject. Other resolutions requested that the United Nations 1971 declaration on the rights of mentally retarded people be implemented, highlighted the need for trained ban gardaí to be available for rape victims, requested a review of farm inheritance law to make it more equitable, and Donegal guild was concerned about uranium mining. The Executive realised that members worked very hard to bring these resolutions to Council, and was aware of the disappointment when results were not apparent. Now and then, however, a resolution debated at a Council meeting initiated a groundswell of public opinion and led to improvements in the law, and this made the whole process worthwhile. Alternatively, one guild or Federation sometimes refused to abandon a resolution. One such case was the Dungarvan resolution on criminal conversation, an archaic law introduced in Britain in 1822 and repealed there in 1856, but removed from the statute books in Ireland only in 1982 after five years of campaigning by Joan Bailey and fellow guild members.

Mamo McDonald took over ICA presidency in 1982, which was declared the 'year of the aged'. At this time membership stood at 27,500. The Horticultural College was extended in 1982 and there were plans for the expansion of the Adult Education College. Issues to the fore included changing family structures, lack of childcare, women's health, environmental issues and Northern Ireland. In her inaugural speech, Mamo McDonald raised the question of whether the media would recognise that the complex problems of divorce, contraception, abortion and homosexuality were 'people issues' and not 'women's issues'. She wondered whether journalists sought the views of Donal Cashman of IFA and John Carroll of IT&GWU on these issues, as they had sought her views as ICA President.

She saw her term of office as a period when the association would inform itself, involve itself and achieve even more than before. It was a vibrant time, with membership rising and plenty of energy as well as dissension in the association. McDonald realised that right-wing sections of the ICA were trying to stifle debate, but she was determined that this would not happen.

In 1982, McDonald represented ICA at an International Conference on Women in Bonn, together with Mary Liddy from the CSW and Anne O'Donnell from the Well Woman centre. At first she was nervous of the 'radical' women's movement but she was surprised to find many areas of agreement, and alliances were formed that gave all concerned a new outlook.

The ICA submission to that conference summed up what life was like for the 1980s Irishwoman, with high unemployment and emigration, and a stagnant economy. It dealt with issues related to education, consumerism, childcare, social welfare, health and family law reform as these affected rural women. It recognised that the lot of women had improved, though these benefits were largely directed at women in an urban environment. In rural areas, improvement had been at a much slower pace. There was a lack of acceptance of a woman's right to work outside the home, a lack of recognition of her major contribution to the farm home enterprise and to the running of a family business in country towns. There was also a lack of opportunity for her to make her voice heard on local councils, health, education and housing boards where her input would be of great value.

The traditional approach to Irish education, according to the submission, had been to direct girls towards the domestic and academic subjects, and boys towards the sciences and technical disciplines. In rural areas particularly, this approach had been accentuated by lack of choice. Education was generally undertaken by the religious orders, and lay education was seen as second best. Even when breaking out of the traditional modes, the sexist approach had endured.

Efforts in the consumer field concentrated primarily on prices and complaints. There was a distinct lack of awareness of consumer responsibilities. The laws with regard to indiscriminate dumping, pollution of lakes and rivers and the protection of other consumers were largely ignored and seldom enforced. There was a passive acceptance too, of the widespread use of aerosol sprays and insecticides. In the production of cattle, sheep and poultry particularly, chemical injections to promote growth were accepted as the norm.

There was no organised state system of childcare. Health departments did subsidise some nurseries in urban areas but these were basically for the use of children who are 'deprived' or 'at risk' (children of lone parents fell into this category). This situation forced working parents to depend on sympathetic relatives and neighbours or private nurseries/child minders. There was no system of registration or inspection even for state-subsidised childcare facilities. Training courses existed for those working with pre-school children, but wages after training were very low. The cost of private untrained minders was prohibitive for most women and therefore, women tended to opt out of paid employment.

The presumption that a married women was dependent on her husband simply because she was married, created several anomalies in regard to social welfare payments. Personal rates of benefit in the areas of unemployment, disability, invalidity and occupational injuries were lower for married women than for men, and the duration of unemployment benefit was shorter. A man was regarded as a dependant of his wife only if he was an invalid and mainly maintained by his wife. Where separate payments were made, these were not divided equally between husband and wife, the wife getting the adult dependant allowance while the husband got the higher basic allowance. There were a number of anomalies in relation to pension rights for women, particularly in the State employment sector.

The Family Planning Act in 1979 allowed the legal sale of contraceptives for the first time, though on a severely restricted scale through certain pharmacies only. Although a means-tested free medical care system existed in Ireland, it was far from adequate in the area of women's health and particularly in relation to family planning. Because the Irish Constitution recognised only the family based on marriage, there was no legal recognition of families based on relationships outside marriage.

In conclusion, the submission noted that Irish membership of the EEC had brought about considerable legislative change in favour of women, but noted that the Court of Justice had not taken any action against Ireland where it had failed to implement EEC Directives on discrimination.[3]

As the modern feminist movement developed, the ICA was challenged and accused of not achieving enough for Irish women. Clearly, in the midst of the 'feminist' attack, the ICA felt that its size, its history, the geographical spread and the scope of its activities was not being taken into account. The 'New Wave Ravers' of the feminist brigade came in for a spirited dose of their own medicine when Mamo McDonald, in her address to Council meeting at Enniscorthy in 1985, posed the question: 'Who speaks for Irish women?'

She recalled that the recent debate on the Family Planning Bill was a spirited affair. There were political pronouncements, pastoral interventions, a spate of letters to public representatives and the papers and a large number of investigative articles and in-depth programmes on radio and television. Anticipating the Bill, the ICA carried out a survey of its 28,000 members to elicit their views. Among the questions asked of members was whether they thought contraceptives should be freely available, available to persons over eighteen years, or available to married persons only.

When asked to do so, the ICA made the survey results public. The reaction was prompt, pithy and predictable. The ICA survey was described as unrepresentative, the ICA's opinion was considered irrelevant and their attitude, they were told, was unrealistic. As a group of women, ICA members were variously described as being 'past it', out of touch, conservative, old, sexless and behind the times. One commentator put it succinctly when she said, 'I wouldn't expect anything else from the ICA — a bunch of middle-aged old bags.'

The people who spoke like this were, according to McDonald, usually in the communications industry, mostly women, as often as not belonging to, or at least in sympathy with, the 'radical urban women's movement'. For them the world began in 1970 when the big breakthrough of the Irish women's liberation movement took the country by storm. They were bold and belligerent, but the 'women's libbers' jolted the people's consciousness into a rethink of women and their place in society. Shock tactics were the name of the game — everyone remembered the talk of bra burning, the contraceptive train to Belfast and the invasion of the Forty Foot. Apart from these attention-getters, there was another side to their activities which many were inclined to forget. It was they who instigated the AIM group, looking into laws which discriminated against women. Resource centres such as Cherish, the organisation for

unmarried mothers, the Rape Crisis Centre and the Home for
Battered Wives — or Family Aid as it is now called — provided valuable and much needed support for women in stressful situations.

Whilst McDonald would not agree with all the activities of these
women's groups, in answering their criticism of the ICA she stated
that it would be unfair and churlish to discount them as merely a
bunch of agitators and protesters. However, what did grate was
their tendency to 'corner the market' on feminism, regarding theirs
as the only way and their view as the fount of knowledge on
women. She laboured the point that there was a women's movement started when most of them were not even thought of. She
briefly outlined the major achievements of the association since its
inception in 1910 and acknowledged that its revolution may have
been a gentler one than the high jinks of the 1970s, but enthusiastic and spirited for all that. One heard a lot about new women's
groups dedicated to consciousness-raising and mutual support, but
within its guilds the ICA had provided that facility over the years.

She went on to answer criticism of the ICA survey specifically,
under three headings — as it was labelled unrepresentative, irrelevant and unrealistic.

+ *Unrepresentative*: Since the ICA was tagged as an association of
  older women, four guilds were picked at random — one in each
  province — to ascertain the age profile. Ballinode, Co.
  Monaghan, was a rural guild with the youngest member aged
  twenty-two, the oldest in her sixties and the majority of members were in their thirties. Midleton, Co. Cork, was an urban
  guild where the youngest member was sixteen, the oldest in her
  sixties and the majority in their thirties. In Kilronan guild on
  Aranmore island off the Galway coast, the youngest member
  was in her mid-thirties, the oldest was seventy and the majority
  of members were in their forties. Blanchardstown was a Dublin
  guild where the youngest member was twenty-two, the oldest in
  her seventies and the majority of members were in their forties,
  though they had recently had an influx of younger women.
  Apart from their age profile, as the 28,000 ICA women came
  from all creeds, classes and political persuasions, it would be
  difficult to get a more representative group.

+ *Irrelevant*: When ICA chose to remain silent on contentious
  topics, they were accused of 'copping out'. If the organisation
  voiced an opinion at odds with trendy thinking, it was dismissed

as irrelevant. McDonald posed the question of who sets the parameters of what is relevant. Topics which might not be contentious in the ranks of radical feminism often prove daring in the mainstream of society. Those who took the trouble to read the survey would find that it indicated a significant development of opinion within the ranks — and ICA ranks number more women that the composite membership of other organisations.

♦ *Unrealistic*: ICA members lived in the real world — as wives, as mothers, as women, they had to cope with the same life problems that beset others. They accepted the inevitability of change and that modern technology and other influences have accelerated the pace of that change. Nevertheless, they believed that change for the better must take account of the natural law, the threatened environment, the cultural heritage and the generations still to come — and that it seldom does this.

Whilst the scope of ICA interests speaks for itself, people who stay in the middle of the road are constantly in danger of being run over. The ICA has long been a soft target for those who wish to criticise, always harping on the 'apple tarts and tweedy old dears' image. The ICA works on, confident in the knowledge that it plays a significant role in Irish society. The 'New Wave Ravers' were good for the ICA as it kept the association from growing complacent.

Those demanding contraception had made their point, said McDonald, but in 1910 poultry and not the pill had been foremost in the minds of Irish countrywomen and as far back as that, the ICA had been there to assist. 'For all the publicity which our more militant sisters can generate, the ICA has a more revolutionary and direct bearing on the vast majority of Irish women.'[4]

In the minute books for this period, the language used had become more positive as Diarmaid Ferriter recalled:

> The endurance and the relevance of the themes which necessitated the society's existence ensured that the challenge from a more radical feminist movement could be sustained.... ICA had always been there to lay more emphasis on provision rather than agitation, particularly in terms of providing a social outlet for Irish women. Perhaps what has not been recognised but what their history proves, is that to provide can often encompass as great a degree of radicalism, innovation and energy as to agitate.[5]

Attitudes of women in the 1980s towards work, family and lifestyle had changed radically. In 1984 among the issues causing concern to the members were:

— reduction in the Farm Home Advisory Service;
— the closure of Rural Home Economics Colleges;
— the selling off of ACOT kitchens;
— the deprivation of Maternity and Childcare services at hospitals throughout the country;
— the treatment of victims of rape.

This was also the period which saw the constitutional barrier to abortion copper-fastened in 1983. Since the passing of the Abortion Act of 1967 in England, the number of Irish women seeking abortion there had increased to 3,700 annually by 1987. In Ireland, a 1986 constitutional referendum to relax the ban on divorce was also defeated. In the 1980s Irish women were under-represented in decision-making, be it at government level, in the civil service, trade union, employer or farming organisations. This imbalance was equally evident in the media, educational and legal institutions.

The ACWW Triennial Conference was held in Killarney, Co. Kerry on 20-27 May 1986, hosted by the ICA. The theme of the conference was 'Focus on Family' and the official opening was performed by Dr Patrick Hillery, President of Ireland. Ina Broughall, ICA President, gave the welcoming address to 1,200 visitors. The conference was a great success despite been picketed by IRA sympathisers protesting against Mrs Thatcher, a situation which called on Broughall's skills of diplomacy. Delegates from the Women's Institute in England demanded rapid removal of the picketers and requested that the press be notified, but Broughall was able to convince them that this was exactly what the protesters wanted. While this reassurance was going on, Camilla Hannon negotiated with the protesters. An ugly confrontation was averted.

1986 saw the completion of the new Kellogg wing in the Adult Education College at An Grianán. It consisted of twelve bedrooms, an art room, leisure centre and demonstration kitchen cum lecture rooms, bringing the Kellogg investment to over $2 million since 1979 and enabling the college to cater for eighty-six visitors on a residential basis.

When Broughall was elected President her ambition was to improve communications between guilds and Executive and to give

Above: Attending a European Family Conference in Dublin in November 1996 were (*L to R*): Sally Ward, Brídín Twist, Lucien Bouis, President of COFACE (Confederation of Family Organisations in Europe), Nellie Dillon and Breda Raggett.

Below: Delegates to the Associated Countrywomen of the World Conference in 1965 attend a reception hosted by Bord Fáilte.

Above: The first visit to the Republic by members of the Executive of the Women's Institute, Northern Ireland, May 1971. Mrs Sheila O'Donnellan, President of Galway TA, presents souvenirs made by members of the Guild to Mrs Dorene Dawson, Women's Institute of Northern Ireland.

Left: Joyce Barrett, Barbara Haggart and Rachel Arnold, New Hampshire, US, at the Associated Countrywomen of the World Conference in Killarney.

Above: ICA members attending a Poultry Instructors Course in July 1963.

Below: Members of the Ballymun Guild of the ICA, winners of a first-round heat of the Eleanora Gibbon 'Siamsa' Competition. Holding the trophy are Anne Power (*left*) and producer Joan Collins.

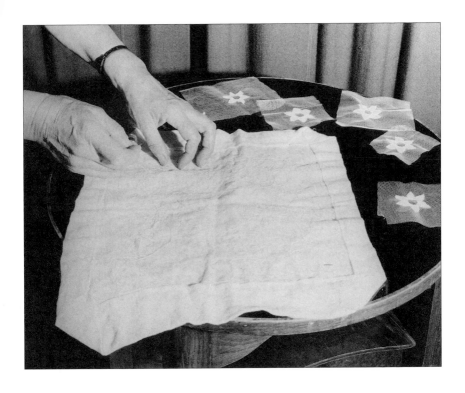

Above: Carrickmacross lace embroidery.

Below: Members of the Carrick-on-Shannon Guild on the ICA float at a Fleadh Ceoil.

Above: The cast of a one-act play peformed by ICA members in Ballyheigue, Co. Kerry.

Below: Members enjoy a class in shellcraft.

Above: Students in a wine-making class given by Mr Michael Allen, Clonakilty.

Below: A horticulture student examines plants in the greenhouses at An Grianán in 1979.

Above: Candidates for National President 1993:
Phil Brennan, Moira Meagher, Mary O'Reilly, Teresa Colhoun,
Phyllis Mulry, Bernadette Falvey, Brídín Twist.

Right: Mother and Child
Week at An Grianán in
the 1960s.

Above: The author (*right*) with (*L to R*) Liam Myles (Farm Apprenticeship Board), Breda Raggett and Ivan Yates, Minister for Agriculture, at celebrations in 1995 to mark the ICA's eighty-fifth year.

Below: (*L–R*) Monica Prendiville, National President of the ICA, the Nigerian Ambassador and National PRO Karen Carleton.

the ICA a better image. Among the resolutions during her term was one from Kildare Federation calling for an explicit poster campaign for schools on the issue of Aids. The resolution was reported in the media as 'ICA advocating the use of condoms'! Instead of receiving credit for being the first national organisation to have the courage to debate this issue, the ICA was disappointed to see it sensationalised. Broughall's aim of improving the ICA's image was severely tested. However, she had greater success with the Buy Irish Campaign which the ICA advocated at every opportunity — an initiative to stem emigration and flight from the land and also to support Irish industries. Broughall was very conscious of reaching out to other groups, such as the 'Ladies of Ballyfermot' whom she brought to An Grianán for holidays thanks to contacts made with Fr Michael Cleary. She also cultivated links with the All China Women's Federation (ACWF), resulting in at least two ICA visits to China. Unlike the ICA, the ACWF was not a voluntary body, but rather an extension of government into local areas to help and advise women on legal matters, marital problems or any difficulties concerning the home and the family. It was important to the ICA to have international involvement.

CHALLENGES FOR THE 1990S

By the time the ICA celebrated its 80th birthday in 1990, membership had dropped to 23,000. Kitty Harlin of Meath became President. She recognised the need for internal reconstruction due to problems such as the lack of communication between Executive and guilds. She also firmly believed that a national organisation needed its own magazine.

It was disappointing to the ICA to have resolutions raised again in the 1990s that were originally discussed in the 1960s — underage drinking and drugs, concern for the environment, the intolerant treatment of carers, rural policing, identification cards for teenagers, video nasties, conditions in women's prisons, the alarming increase in suicides, campaigning against cuts in health care, seeking the availability of breast cancer screening. Some Federations were more successful or persistent in their campaigns than others. For example, Meath Federation staged a protest on the issue of mammography, raising large sums of money and also collecting over 10,000 protest letters and holding marches.

Another area of concern to the ICA at this time was the increase in violence in all its ugly forms — especially against children, women, elderly and the infirm who were most vulnerable. Under the guidance of Kitty Harlin, a confidential and free Family Counselling Service was set up to give professional help to women coping with problems such as marital issues, illness, unemployment, sudden death, substance addictions, or problems with children and adolescents. A qualified psychologist was available for members and their families, and the high level of take-up has demonstrated the real need for such a service.

One of the most significant developments in Ireland was the election of Mary Robinson as President of Ireland on 7 November 1990, the first woman to hold that office. Her election gave Ireland a new confidence in itself and reinvigorated its image abroad. People regained a sense of their own role in politics and their power to effect change. At the same period, the second Commission on the Status of Women was initiated. Its report, published in 1993, identified many of the same areas highlighted by the first Commission as being in need of reform. This report paid much attention to rural women and made many recommendations for change, including improved transport plans for rural areas, the introduction of mobile health centres, that the work of women on farms be categorised and counted for statistical and policy pur-poses and that the training and education needs of rural women be met. The ICA has a representative on the monitoring committee but progress to date has been slow.

The Commission recommended introducing a quota system within political parties as the most important step in righting the imbalance. Whilst no such system has yet been introduced, the general election of 1995 saw a further increase in the number of female legislators, though they still made up only 13 per cent of the government. In 1992 a referendum on abortion gave women the right to travel for abortion and the right to information on abor-tion, and three years later another referendum led to divorce being legalised. In 1996, a means-tested carers allowance for relatives caring full-time for incapacitated or elderly people was introduced. This was welcomed by the ICA as they had campaigned for such an allowance for years, but the campaign continues to seek a non-means-tested allowance.

In the 1990s, there had been an increase in reported cases of violence against women and children and old people, a fact which justified the continuing existence of the ICA's counselling service. The ICA expressed great dissatisfaction with the leniency and inconsistency of sentences given to the perpetrators of these heinous crimes. It must be remembered that in 1991 the judicial service had no woman at a senior level in the civil service, no woman Supreme Court Judge, no woman Circuit Court Judge and only two women High Court Judges.

As attitudes changed slowly in Ireland, it has been an uphill struggle for an association such as the ICA to monitor the situation continually. In general, change is brought about, not by the initiative of legislators but due to pressure from strong lobby groups — farmers, teachers, trade unions. Marginalised groups such as women do not form a strong lobby group.

ECONOMIC AND SOCIAL CHANGES

Monica Prendeville from Kerry became ICA President in 1991, and was followed by Brídín Twist of Clare and then Eva Coyle from Donegal. As problems continued to occur with the right wing element within the ICA and the left wing outside, it became more difficult to effect significant change amid controversy. Attempting to chart a middle ground was often deemed to be the only realistic response.

The average member in the 1990s was involved in all sorts of activities — cheese making and similar agri-food production, dressmaking and knitwear, lacemaking, leather work as well as drama, dance, music and art. Many ran farm guesthouses and promoted tourism — achieved through their own efforts and through involvement with the ICA which encouraged them and gave them faith in their own abilities. At present, the economic needs of members are still being catered for through innovative 'Start your own business' schemes.

During the 1980s, a decade of vast changes and inequality, the gap between rich and poor had widened, unemployment was over 250,000 and crime had increased. The situation changed again in the 1990s, however, with the advent of the 'Celtic Tiger', when Ireland's economy was turned around making it the fastest growth area in the EU. Standards of living were raised, but not all citizens shared in that rise and the ICA continued to be mindful of the needs of the most vulnerable.

The 'Celtic Tiger' came with a changing social and economic landscape: divorce was legalised, as were the provision of information on abortion and freedom to travel for abortion. In addition, the prosecution of members of the clergy for child abuse contributed to the reduced influence of the Catholic Church. Emigration was halted due to the dramatic turnaround of the Irish economy. Ireland's reduced dependence on the British economy was countered by the setting up of franchised British retail chain stores. The decade also became the golden age for Irish language, music, theatre, art, film, and dance, with an Irish-made film winning Academy Awards, and Riverdance being performed world-wide, as well as a six-month exhibition of Irish arts and music in Paris. There were changes in legislation supportive of women. It seemed as if the greater the pull on Ireland's allegiance to Europe — which has given significant financial advantages to the Irish economy — the more a search for identity was beginning to bear fruit. Gaelscoileanna abound, and an Irish-language television station was funded by government in 1996.

As the time seemed right to broaden the sense of Irishness, Irish people came to a kind of maturity about themselves. It was a time of great creativity and vitality, replacing a worrying uncertainty and self-depreciation which had come from post-colonial inhibitions. As Ireland's history is one of subjection, Irish people lacked the confidence to decide for themselves, and traditionally Irish society had lacked a dominant middle-class who would have always questioned, but this has now changed.

Tolerance and pluralism could help to broaden public horizons, and Ireland should view emigration and migration positively, as mobility has always nurtured ideas. For thousands of years Ireland has been shaped by Celts, Vikings, Normans, Huguenots, Scots and English settlers; regardless of our view of history, all these people marked our island — to be truly Irish, one must be tolerant and understanding of a diversity of people, traditions and influences.

LOOKING TO THE FUTURE

Brídín Twist, ICA President, said in 1995 on the occasion of the association's 85th birthday:

> ICA started from a rural base but today it epitomises the interface between rural and urban life. It should be complimented on maintaining a balance and for providing a necessary social and educational outlet for 23,000 members. We were referred to recently by a government member as a 'sleeping giant'. That giant is very much awake and moving and the ICA will continue to face up to the challenges of the future and continue to address issues of importance to women and their families.

As the ICA grappled with changes in Irish society over the past decade, it has reacted in a number of ways, some inherently positive, others sadly inappropriate. There were many reasons why the association continued to lose members in the 1990s — the natural age wastage, the fact that more women were working outside the home and dedicating any free time they had to a single-issue group or activity. Some felt the ICA was top-heavy with structures and rules, and it had no magazine — a serious loss to many members since this was the only sure way to keep members informed of the association's activities. In 1912, the Executive considered a magazine vital — do the members in 2000 not have the same need? A serious factor related to the continual drop in membership is due to financial constraints, with ICA now having just one development officer, Margaret Kennedy, for the whole country. A voluntary organisation, the ICA depends on membership fees for its income. The minute books provide the story of development encompassing all aspects of community life — social, cultural, economic and educational — but for the ICA to survive in the future it must be active and outward-looking with a clear vision to effect change and bring about improvement. It must begin with its members, and rules and structures which no longer make sense must be changed — these remain the challenges for the future survival of the ICA.

CONCLUSION
DEEDS, NOT WORDS

ICA's CONTRIBUTION AND EXPERIENCE

The ICA contributed to changing a traditional and conservative society. Through its educational programmes it gave members skills to make them more employable; through its social aspect it gave them self-esteem and confidence to challenge existing archaic principles; as a feminist organisation it believed in equality for all, and through its resolutions to government, it became a vehicle for change in the society of the day.

In 1792, Mary Wollstonecraft wrote:

> It is time to effect a revolution in female manners — time to restore to (women) their lost dignity and make them, as a part of the human species, labour by reforming themselves to reform the world.[1]

Again in 1919, Mary Connery wrote:

> Women have very little to hope for from political revolutions. Social revolutions offered an opportunity for reforms which go nearer to the heart of things and affect the lives of women more closely than mere political revolutions.[2]

On the same theme, former ICA President Mamo McDonald said:

> It could be argued that the Ladies Land League, Suffrage Movement, Cumann na mBan etc, had a very narrow focus and could be termed 'flash in the pan' or 'fly by night' societies, while UI were in it for the long haul, and ninety years later ICA is still there educating and improving the lives of thousands of Irishwomen.[3]

The great proof of the ICA's success over the past ninety years is the fact that its achievements tend to be taken for granted. The range of women's roles in Ireland's countryside, villages, town and cities as daughters, wives, mothers and widows attests to the understated and frequently repressed energies of a struggling generation, women surviving despite the odds in an Irish state.

The dominant ideology of the Irish Free State, as exemplified by the 1937 Constitution, placed women in the home as mothers and housekeepers, yet provided no advice, no financial support or guidance on how women should fulfil that role. The state remained indifferent to women in the home, even in relation to violence against women and children. The reality of the violent and harsh nature of many Irish women's lives was not allowed to upset the imagined 'ideal of Irish family life'. As Joe Lee said, 'Irish people have a capacity for self-deception on a heroic scale.'[4] The notion that 'changeless and archaic practices in rural Ireland were inherently positive and enhanced the fabric' did not go down very well with ICA members. Olivia Hughes, ICA President from 1955–57, commented: 'This is a man's country in which women are not thought of, but they are the backbone of the country.'

Ireland's countryside is one of great interest and importance because of the character of its physical landscape and wildlife content, because of its heritage of historical features and folk traditions and because of its contemporary economic and social features. The richness and diversity of the countryside adds greatly to the quality of life in Ireland. Yet rural life has not always been a place of contentment and unchanging tranquillity — problems included inaccessibility of services such as shops, education, medical facilities, transport and entertainment, inadequate employment opportunities, low and uncertain income and long hours of hard work and travel. Technology, and economic and social circumstances, have brought many changes and therefore rural life should now balance development with conservation.

The ICA highlighted the contribution that women could make to Irish society as homemakers. Their work within the home should be not only acknowledged but justly rewarded. ICA submissions to Commissions on Vocational Organisations in 1939, Youth Unemployment in 1944 and Emigration in 1948 have manifested the association's sense of responsibility. The ICA shared the desire of other groups to improve the quality of women's lives and represent women as intelligent and responsible members of society. Aware of the loneliness experienced by many women living in the countryside, the association gave members the opportunity to meet

for weekly classes in domestic science, traditional handcrafts and
farming skills, lectures and debates as well as music, drama and
dance which were organised to recruit new members and provide
some light relief from the everyday drudgery of life. Women were
also encouraged to get involved in local government, and many
guilds campaigned for the introduction of school meals and nursing
schemes in their areas.

The ICA represented women who worked in the home, carrying
out a domestic role as wives and mothers, as well as women who
worked outside the home. Caitriona Beaumont stated that ICA and
others highlighted the contribution women as 'homemakers' could
make to Irish society. Working together, they defended the right of
all women to equal citizenship in the Irish Free State. They called
on the government to introduce social welfare reforms which would
enhance the lives of many thousands of Irish women. In doing so,
women's organisations which were active during the 1930s and
early 1940s provided a vital link between the suffrage campaign
and the women's liberation movement of the 1970s. It is crucial,
therefore, according to Beaumont that their achievements are
included in any history of Irish women and the politics of equality.[5]

The history of ICA guilds and its resolutions down through the
century enforces the view that ICA has been a vehicle for social
change. The basic themes emerging from research of the ICA
archives are: the endurance and continuity of the rural themes
which necessitated the organisation's inception; how the organisation defined itself and set its objectives, both internally and its
relationships with other bodies; how it instigated and adapted to
the process of modernisation in rural Ireland and finally the
degree to which these women have been depicted as mould break-
ers or solemn preservers of tradition in their contribution to the
fabric of national life this century. The history of the ICA is of vital
importance because its size, geographical spread, time-span, and
subject matter enable it to make a unique contribution to the documentation of Irish women's social history. Its value is further
enhanced by the fact that it records the progression of the largest
and most representative women's organisation in the country and
second oldest in Europe.

ICA's Image

Irishwomen have grown up in a society which believes women are
second-class citizens, leaving many with low self-esteem. This can

be seen in the way women wait to be invited, rather than thrusting themselves forward. Unfortunately, ICA has tended to reinforce this because of its fear of being too strident, fear of losing government and public respect, and apprehension of the press and how it might portray the ICA. The state, a patriarchal institution, defined an inferior position for women and, paradoxically, this was often reinforced and transmitted through ICA, even though many members viewed ICA as a road to liberation. However, when put in the context of its time, ICA is vindicated by comparing its achievements with those of other women's associations of the period.

In 1910, the founders of ICA, then UI, set themselves the objective of 'better living' through the development and education of women. They recognised that the theme of housework and family duties would foster unity, and therefore created the 'tea-makers' image. However, the discussion and promotion of women's broader interests has continued as an underlying theme, and in a way the ICA has hidden behind this conservative image while preparing other reforms for which Irish society was not yet ready. By its achievements, ICA has shown that it is not a conservative organisation but rather an instrument of change to benefit women.

Press and public alike have tended to categorise ICA at times, with various labels such as 'fuddy-duddy', 'old women chatting and making tea', 'the blue-rinse supp-hose brigade', or 'tweedy old dears with ascendancy notions'. Yet we must remember that the ICA is ninety years old, and it is true that the founders were women of the old ascendancy class – they were the women who had time and money, and the only ones who cared about rural Irishwomen at the time.

The ICA did much to improve conditions and give rural women independence through education and income-generating projects. In the modern context, does it still allow members to question and contest gender relations in Ireland, or has it stopped in time merely reinforcing women's domestic role? On the one hand, the ICA is seen to endorse a conservative, patriarchal establishment, reinforcing the naturalness of women's responsibility for domestic labour and childcare. ICA does not appear to question the economic power relations that trap women within the family and society at large. On the other hand, attendance at any Council meeting reveals the wider role of the ICA – acting as a shield for the exploration by individuals of the constraints of this conservative debate. Negative experiences of women's ascribed role and inferior position are not seen as the fault of the individual but are understood as part of the wider social circumstances. 'Personal' negative experience is seen as political in origin, and in this process a form of consciousness-raising is taking place.

An ongoing debate of patriarchy and conservatism, feminism and self-determination is evident within ICA. The organisation is a site where the meaning of existing structures of social institutions and the subject positions on offer to women are questioned, mainly though not exclusively, through language. Language is active and part of a revolutionary potential. It has therefore become my contention that ICA does have, and indeed has had in the past, a radical potential.

Could the revolutionary potential of language be used, despite the negative image of the ICA — 'old conservative tea-makers' — so that the organisation becomes more accessible to a wider and more diverse group of women? If ideas changed by this method in the past, why not again?

By using what a patriarchal society deems acceptable female activity, ICA has protected a platform for women since Suffragette times — a platform disguised by gardening, handcrafts and cookery. Beneath the 'tea-making' surface was an organisation discussing issues that affect the quality of life in Ireland, often well in advance of public discussion on issues such as education and health, violence against women, pornography, child sexual abuse, prison reform, impact of Aids on women, environment and ecology. (For example, over thirty-five years ago, at the ICA AGM in 1964, a resolution was passed calling for legislation to prevent the pollution of air, water and land.)

Given that ICA is a democratic organisation for all women, and cannot exclude those of differing ideologies, the process of consciousness-raising has been painstakingly slow, yet the association continues to work away quietly trying to bring all women along.

An ICA survey in the 1990s revealed that 39 per cent of members are aged between 35 and 50, thus disproving the image of an association of old women. Since members are drawn from all walks of life, from the radical left to the conservative right, many feel strongly about women's role in society but equally a lot of members are quite pleased with the status quo.

Change in the ICA is brought about in two ways — through its Executive members and through the fresh ideas of new members. An informed Executive can work through its Federation Presidents, who filter down more radical ideas in an acceptable form to the grassroots level for members to react. By building on members' confidence, and discussing the idea in order to awaken members' interest, they then get thinking and talking about it which helps them to see the issue differently. If the preparation has been done and the issue is presented in a non-aggressive, non-threatening manner, the average ICA member has a lot of common-sense and when well-informed will take a position on different issues and see them through to a successful conclusion.

ICA's conservative 'tea-making' image has two aspects: on the one hand this image is a safety net allowing women to confront issues and move forward; yet on the other hand it deters many women from becoming involved, thus failing to attract new members with new ideas.

Other issues facing ICA are its voluntary status and its lack of funding. The positive aspect of the voluntary sector is that it provides a vehicle for the involvement of a substantial portion of the population in caring for each other and promoting the welfare of local communities. But its limitations include its uneven coverage of the country, and its unreliability. Depending on individuals to participate, it cannot aim to reach all areas with equal vigour and consistency. Voluntary organisations are also notoriously reluctant to come together in pursuit of wider goals, and their very number, with their non-bureaucratic style of operating, makes it difficult to know what they do and how well they do it, or to remedy deficiencies in their work. As a voluntary organisation, ICA should recognise its limitations.

The way forward to improve the lives of women in Ireland lies partly in achieving change through legislation, with increased representation in decision-making areas. However, as Nuala Fennell, Minister of State for Women, said in 1986:

> The essential prerequisite for reaching levels of influence is the support of other women and greater self-confidence among women. Within Ireland, all women constitute a 'region' in need of development and it is up to all of us to exploit existing structures so that we bring to an end the exploitation of women.[6]

Even programmes which aim to develop infrastructures and institutions, in order to be successful, need to be aware of the special problems encountered by women. For if a woman is to set up a business, follow a training course, or otherwise advance, she needs access to affordable and reliable childcare and to transport facilities. Women require improved access to land, credit, training, advisory services, and adult and continuing education. Even in organisations which claim to represent the interests of women, women themselves are acutely under-represented at decision-making levels — in health boards, vocational education committees, farming organisations, consumer council, community councils and local development organisations.

The ICA did its work from decade to decade in a countryside where the lack of access to resources and facilities was a major factor. Alongside the lack of transport and childcare was the added burden of low incomes which limited rural women even further. Ann Byrne elaborated in 1993:

> There is a difference between living in the town and living in the country with particular disadvantages for women. These disadvantages prevent rural women from participating fully in community life and benefiting from some of the changes in attitudes and improvements in services for women that have been achieved within the past ten years ... Where are the centres for victims of family violence, or training courses which might contribute to the alleviation of some of the isolation that rural women experience?[7]

The ICA has always known about these women, because these are its members.

ICA AS A FEMINIST ORGANISATION

The ICA would never have been considered a radical organisation yet if one examines the archives, all its actions for the past ninety years as the largest women's association in Ireland have been for the betterment of women, and to empower women. Feminism aims to give each woman the freedom to explore her potential and the right to be accepted as a full person with responsibilities as well as the right to knowledge, self-determination and responsibility. 'Feminism in all its varieties has always insisted on the importance of women's ideas, feelings and experiences. It has valued women in their own right, and not according to male-defined ideas about worth. Over the years, feminists have come to celebrate women's strengths, abilities and intelligence and stressed the need to rediscover women's past and to re-evaluate present conditions.'[8]

Irish women are moving into the community and changing it in various ways so that it is more responsive to their needs. Male power seems to be designed to limit and control women as women in society. For instance, the powerful control of the media ensures that women are presented with distorted images of themselves that serve to reinforce a male-dominated society. Women should leave records of their struggles and achievements for future generations — for decades, unmarried mothers were perceived as 'letting herself and her family down' and were accordingly ostracised; marriage and the procreation of children assured a woman's adult status in society. Cullen, in explaining how our past has been ignored and packaged by historians and in urging women to create our own feminist history that will truly reflect women's contributions in all aspects of life, wrote:

F.S.L. Lyons, whilst knowing of the existence of the feminist movement does not consider it as significant a part of Irish history as nationalism, the cultural renaissance and the labour movement, nor did he see it as his responsibility to include it ... a self-perpetuating circle has operated, from patriarchal value-system to patriarchal history which in turn refuelled the value system.[9]

If one examines the key issues involved in the life, changes and development of a society, one cannot afford to ignore the contributions of 50 per cent of the population — to get the complete picture, one cannot ignore all the surviving evidence. The range and quality of women's contribution is very impressive, with the dominant pattern throughout history being one of women combining a caretaker role within families and households with a sharing of the breadwinner and provider roles. Women did not despise domesticity itself, but patriarchal society relegated women to the tasks which men did not want to perform and then devalued them.

The debate on the role of women, and whether they were equal to or subordinate to men within the family has gone on for two hundred years, according to Wollstonecraft:

For women in Western Europe who sought a role in civic life at the end of the eighteenth century, the biggest obstacle was society, based on the family, which sanctioned their subordination to men within the family by depriving them of access to education and the means for an independent life.[10]

From that standpoint, quite a lot has been achieved in the twentieth century. The ICA was the meeting ground for women from different social and religious backgrounds, and adopted strategies appropriate to the time, always being in a position to discuss issues of concern to all women in an environment free from religious and political supervision.

Feminism centres on people obtaining power over themselves, which is what the ICA has been trying to bring about. Its 1,000 guilds spread throughout the twenty-six counties have fostered a community tradition amongst members who organise in response to local needs. This community tradition still exists today, its strength and diversity adding to the broader political culture.

The education of women has always been the primary concern for the ICA, and the association always looked on it as a way of achieving some degree of equality and of bringing about social change. The ICA offered women an avenue through which to fight for a better life for themselves and their children, and the confidence to voice their opinions in the development of public policy.

What Margaret MacCurtain wrote of the IHA could be applied equally to the ICA:

> Conscious of the dual role of women in the mid-century, they presented to the public the solid frontage of the Irish Housewife; strategically they instructed their members on how to negotiate the complex maze of the Irish party machine.[11]

'Deeds not words' has always been the ICA motto. The association saw no future in head-on confrontation with radical groups, but rather continued to plough its own furrow, attracting 30,000 members in the 1970s – a figure that rests at around 18,000 today. It is interesting to note that many of the problems affecting women today were first identified by women so long ago. Very little has been achieved overnight. It has been a long, hard haul, with each generation building on the work of those gone before.

ICA down through the nine decades from 1910, experienced and expressed feelings of frustration and rebellion at the limitations artificially imposed on women's lives, principally through the range of resolutions they brought from Council year after year. Keeping true to their ethos of 'non-party political' the association played a significant role in politics in the public sphere. Their political agenda was aimed at changing the society in which they lived and in so doing they merged the public and private, the domestic and the political. They in fact conformed to Luddy's definition of politics:

> ... to include any action by an individual or group, in a formal or informal way, intended to affect or alter either the policy of government, or the behaviour or beliefs of individuals or groups within the local community, for the apparent benefit of a particular group or community.[12]

Declan Lynch perceptively estimated that the ICA's importance lay in its relevance to the reality of everyday existence for the women of rural Ireland and in the fact that it was articulating and remedying difficulties which in the past would have been offered up in prayer. He saw formidable, vigorous and capable women 'full of rude health, riotous conviviality, women scornful of the vicissitudes which assail their more delicate urban sisters'.[13]

The ICA showed a great degree of patience at the lack of recognition by the state, balanced by anger because so much time and energy was wasted. Women's experiences, ideas and feelings are very important, and the ICA has a history of conscious-raising and of a self-help approach, giving women a 'second chance', and valuing people in their own right. It has left a record of its struggles and its achievements through the immense documentation in its archives.

Through the ICA, women all over Ireland have made their voices heard on important issues that affect the quality of life. The association fought for and won improvements in education, health services, economic and local amenities, to name but a few of its achievements. For many years it provided the only social outlet for women; it changed and developed society for women; it campaigned in support of women's claims for civil and legal rights as evidenced by ICA resolutions. These campaigns are worthy of inclusion in history. In her essay, 'Telling it Our Way', Cullen elaborates why women's experiences should be included in historical accounts.[14]

Women's political activity and lack of rights are major issues of women's history. Contrast this with the usual treatment of men and women by historians. Quite different criteria are used to assess the historical value of men's actions and of women's actions — due to the mindset of historians rather than the evidence of the

past. Mainstream history has generally been written from a patriarchal perspective, and historians did not deem this evidence as
important enough to be included. This attitude begs the question:
Why should women's needs in their struggle to survive not be as
important as nationalist or labour activity? Women's needs are
seen as sectional, more trivial and less significant. As historians
bring their own baggage of assumptions and affiliations to their
work, this attitude has created an imbalance in their historical
judgement which has not been value-free. The writing of history
has therefore not been objective but has borne a definite distortion
based on a patriarchal world view which sees men as the sole
agents of change in society. Women have therefore not been seen
as active agents in the past, and historians are unlikely to search
for evidence of women's activity and on the contrary are likely to
underestimate or misinterpret any evidence that might slip
through. The fact is that there is only one society and everyone,
male and female, is part of it and the members interact and influence each other within it.

> Until women's historical experience is recognised by historians and incor-
> porated into their assessment of what is significant in the past it will not
> be possible to write anything approaching a valid human history.[15]

The ICA's history is vibrant and worth recording — its members
were survivors continually adapting to and exploiting the situations
in which they found themselves. Imagination and inventiveness were
important, as they had to be manipulative and active agents in the
process in order to survive. Women's experiences have been shaped
by class, culture, religion, marital status, opportunity to work, and
prevailing patriarchal beliefs. Traditional (mostly male) historians'
perceptions of what exactly that experience was, differed from the
realities of women's lives. Irish social history in general has been
less well served by historians than political and nationalist history
— a gap has existed around the role played by women, and which is
still played in communities. History has ignored women's great contribution to the formation of Irish society — they are after all 51
per cent of the population, the custodians and guardians of future
generations and the largest consumer group. Women's lives are
firmly connected to and dictated by the political, social, demo-
graphic and economic happenings of the time — they are a part of
its history and not on the fringes of it. The diversity of women's

lives, with their difficult and different life opportunities and experiences, all contribute to their ability to adapt and survive. Women's response to society and their participation in it on a public or private level was shaped by their background and their socio-economic class.

To date, many historians have talked, written and theorised at length about rural life — and Ireland for the greater part of the twentieth century was predominantly rural. Nearly all of these historians were men. In the contemporary historiographical climate, history is very much on the side of the ICA, both in terms of vindicating its role in rural life in the past and in helping its ongoing contemporary contribution to that life.

MEDIA ATTITUDES

The media has been blind to changes in women's lives, claimed Nuala O'Faolain in 1991,[16] though they have a central role to play in dispelling the myths prevalent in our society on various matters relating to women. Reporting is generally very lopsided and misrepresentative, to quote Maureen Keenan from the *Sunday Business Post*:

> It is official. The Women's Institute and the ICA have been hobnobbing for years. At a bash in ICA headquarters in Dublin, they came out of the closet and made a public announcement. President Robinson came along and the day was made. It was an historic and significant occasion. Although there would not have been a dicky bird from the Press if the President had put her feet up and stayed at home.[17]

Women's problems are often dismissed as boring, compared to politics, war, confrontation, disaster, crime and sport. How dreary something like childcare, or low pay or gender discrimination must seem! Yet women are running co-ops and starting literacy schemes and organising think-ins and setting up businesses and turning their hands very vigorously to whatever will enrich and protect their corner of the world. They are going to writing groups, taking charge of their own health, going back to school and opening their houses to visitors. There is hardly a part of Ireland where one cannot find women active outside the home giving their energy in new ways.

Nobody knows about all of this because each of the initiatives is local. None has a claim to national importance. Yet taken together, they may be the most hopeful thing about Ireland at present.

Women's initiatives are particularly susceptible to seeming trivial or unreal to the existing establishments.

Yet these initiatives have to look for funds from VECs, County Management, Health Boards, Partnership and Leader Projects, most of which are run by men of a certain age. Many of these men will be admirably progressive, but many more will be sincerely baffled by what women are revealing as their needs. There are 'new energies' at work. They will bring about change but because that change will be community by community, quite incidental, it will not be newsworthy. As Nuala O'Faolain wrote in 1991:

> Some day, the news media will wake up and see that something hap-pened, but how it happened and where and why, they won't be in any position to know.[18]

A VISION FOR IRISHWOMEN, PAST AND FUTURE

Policy makers need more and better information about the realities of women's lives. ICA's archives provide this information, tracing the reality of life for thousands of Irishwomen over the course of the century. The question at present is, 'Can ICA, which survived ninety years, now stand up and play its role?' — in the immortal slogan of its founders, 'Deeds not words'.

For so long the ICA seemed to be the sole voice for change for Irishwomen. The challenge as the association moves into the new century is to keep women on the political and social agenda and to prevent society from becoming complacent about this issue. A lot of work remains to be done to create a society of equals. Mamo McDonald spelt it out clearly at a Council meeting in 1983, and her words remain relevant in the new century:

> Let us women once and for all stop resisting our own emancipation. We are here in 1983 at a door that is not open, but ajar. We have out-lived our usefulness as doormats. We do not want to be just knockers, so let us aim to be bells — ringing out the good news: 'We're Here!'

The ICA's archives, tracing the lives of thousands of Irishwomen since 1910, will be an invaluable and rich source of the realities of women's everyday existence. The ICA has a duty to be concerned that women do not benefit equally from government policies, yet women have a crucial role to play in the survival of the country.

These unknown and anonymous women played a vital role in constructing society. They were active agents of change within society at large, shaping their own lives and the lives of their community. Change came slowly and then gradually women became more vocal and articulate as the century progressed.[19]

The history of the ICA reflects the activities of Irishwomen in the twentieth century, all their shared experiences — shared by large numbers of women — in the undervalued areas of common life and experiences, in their attitudes and values as they moved with vigour of their own in the spheres they chose. The social outlet element of the ICA helped them to cope and advance, gain access and open doors, and thus their history is women's story of survival in twentieth-century Ireland.

APPENDIX
PERSONALITIES AND PRESIDENTS OF ICA

UI, and later ICA, never had an abundance of tangible assets, but its intangible assets — its people, the devotion, vision and energy of its thousands of members — have enabled it to survive and prosper.

ANITA LETT, FOUNDER OF UI/ICA

The founder of ICA was Anita Lett, a vivid lady whose ambitions, ideas and caring community spirit could fairly be described as being ahead of her time. Perhaps this is the reason why the movement matured and prospered into the strong national movement that is now ninety years old. A woman who founded a movement in Edwardian Ireland which is still relevant today must have possessed special qualities

She was born Anita Georgina Edith Studdy at Waddeton Court, Devon, in England.

> She was the daughter of Commander Studdy of the Royal Navy, and was educated privately. Her passionate interest was in horses and hunting, and she was a skilled gardener and a talented artist.[1]

She came to Co. Wexford as a nurse to Captain David Beatty of Borodale, the father of Admiral Beatty of Borodale of Jutland. Captain Beatty had served in India and devoted a great deal of his life to horses. Beatty was widowed in 1896 and spent the remainder of his life at Borodale. Anita Studdy nursed the Captain well and soon romance was in the air. They married in England on 9 January 1899 and returned to live at Borodale until 4 April 1904, when Captain Beatty died. There was one child of the union, Henry 'Pat' Beatty, who became a flight Lieutenant with the RAF, and was killed in 1935 in an aeroplane crash off Marsina, Scilly.

Anita's marriage never really found acceptability among the Beattys, so when widowed she vacated the Borodale property. However, she was given a parcel of land on the estate where she built a comfortable residence. In 1908, she married Harold Lett, an extensive farmer and a very influential personality in the Enniscorthy area. They lived in Ballindara, Bree and Kilgibbon, Co. Wexford. Anita had two daughters by her second marriage, Eithne and Anita (Peggy). The fact that Anita was connected with these two prominent families, the Beattys and the Letts, coupled with her strong personality, her tenacity and her giftedness at crafts and gardening, ensured that her new-found ideas, inspired by a serious concern for the well-being of the community, were listened to and eventually accepted.[2]

She was an energetic person, a very practical farmer who knew what countrywomen wanted. Difficulties never daunted her but were there only to be overcome. She saw the UI firmly established and indulged in rural pursuits such as hunting with the Bree Harriers.

Anita Lett experienced the joy of seeing the organisation she had founded blossom in Bree and expand throughout Co. Wexford. Soon it was a national organisation with Anita Lett as the first President. There are two schools of thought as to why she had to resign after just two years. The first, according to the minutes, was because of the rule that missing three meetings meant obligatory resignation. Anita broke her leg in a riding accident and was unable to attend meetings. However, the second theory seems more feasible: her ideas were rebuked at top level and she became despondent. Her presence at national level was short-lived, as she was replaced by persons who believed in her philosophy but saw themselves best qualified to dictate the circumstances. Consequently, Anita devoted her best energies to the Bree guild and for the benefit of members in Co. Wexford. A national loss became a local gain.

She continued to devote her energies to the betterment of women and in 1928 assisted by Mabel Rudd set up a co-operative called Slaney Weavers. Spinning wheels were supplied to women who worked in their own homes. The tweed produced, which was of a high standard, was collected at the Enniscorthy Co-op each week and Lett found a sales outlet through her sister who lived in Newbury in England.

Anita's daughter, Eithne Hickey of Ballylane, New Ross, recol-
lects, 'I remember as a child that the whole of one's life seemed to
revolve around the UI — the house always full of strange people,
magazines, kid skins, cheeses, carving, weaving, etc!' She continues, referring to two letters Anita received from Roger Casement
about schools in Galway, 'About this time, there was a typhoid
scare in Letterfrack, and she with Miss Byron of Borromount went
down to see if they could find out what was going on and what help
the UI could give. They did not get very far as the local people
were trying to hide any signs of sickness. Roger Casement said in
his letter that he would get his friend Douglas Hyde to look into it.
But Anita Lett said that Douglas Hyde had done nothing to help as
far as she and UI were concerned.'

ICA's first President died in 1940, aged 68, at Ballinadare
House after a brief illness — almost thirty years to the day after the
great organisation she had founded was officially born. 'She is
buried at St John's Church of Ireland churchyard in Clonmore,
Bree. Her husband, Harold, predeceased her by two years and by
their own wishes their funerals were traditional. Their coffins were
placed on farm carts, straw-covered and drawn by horses without
pomp or ceremony.'[3]

SUSAN MITCHELL

(*From an account written by Cerise Parker in 1965*)
UI links with Susan Mitchell are two-fold: she was a member of the
first Executive Committee of UI, and indeed it was she who suggested the society's title. Perhaps more importantly, she was one of
the women actively interested in the co-operative movement which
through the inspiration of Horace Plunkett had come into being
by the end of the nineteenth century, and it was through her work
as assistant editor of *Irish Homestead* that she campaigned for
reforms for rural areas.

Born in Carrick-on-Shannon, she lived mostly in Sligo and
Dublin, was a writer and a poet, and one of the group that formed
the Irish Literary Movement. She had a fearless wit and did not
hesitate to satirise such personages as George Moore, yet she had,
more abundantly, a deeply spiritual nature. Mitchell composed a
song for the UI, 'To the daughters of Erin', in which she reminded
them of the hopeless struggle for freedom in the past and of the
pessimism and self-mistrust this had induced, but without quench-
ing the essential fire within, she cajoled:

Rise from your knees, O daughters rise!
Our mother still is young and fair,
Let the world look into your eyes
And see her beauty shining there.
Grant of that beauty but one ray,
Heroes shall leap from every hill,
Today shall be as yesterday,
The red blood burns in Ireland still.[4]

Susan Mitchell died in 1926 and is buried in Mount Jerome cemetery, Dublin.

ELLICE PILKINGTON,

Another Wexford woman, Mrs Ellice Pilkington, became UI's first honorary organiser. She was the second daughter of Sir John Esmonde and his wife Louisa. She was the sister of Sir Thomas Esmonde, 11th Baronet, and Colonel Laurence Esmonde, 13th Baronet, who succeeded his nephew. Her sister Annette married Sutherland Wilkinson, originator of Titania's Palace. The Esmonde family was very involved in the co-operative movement. Ellice and her sister Annette were educated in Paris and also studied art in Rome. In 1896, Ellice married Colonel Harry Pilkington, CB of Fore, Tyrellspass, Co. Westmeath, and went to South Africa after the Boer War with their daughter Ellice, where she taught in refugee camps. Their youngest daughter, Annette was born there. Later their home was at Llys-y-Gwinit, Holyhead, until her husband died.

Ellice was brought into the UI movement by Fr Tom Finlay, a Jesuit. UI's motto was 'Deeds, not words' and nobody lived up to that principle more than she, in her travels up and down the country opening branches of the society. She was co-author with Horace Plunkett and AE of *The United Irishwomen: their place, work and ideals* in 1911. Her health eventually gave way, and she spent time recuperating at Ballynastragh, Co. Wexford, later going to live in St Stephen's Green in Dublin. Ellice was also an accomplished water-colourist and for many years was secretary of the Irish Water Colourists Organisation which mounted exhibitions at Mill's Hall, Merrion Row in Dublin. She died on 24 August 1936 and is interred in the Pilkington family vault in Tyrellspass, Co. Westmeath.

CONSTANCE PIM

Constance Pim, a member of a well-known Quaker family, was the first honorary secretary of the UI and a member of its first Executive Committee. She was a niece of Lister, the surgeon and pioneer of antiseptics. She lived in Dublin until 1918 when she moved to Highgate in London, worked among the Quakers in the Welsh coalfields, and helped in the post-war years with the Friends for Refugees on the continent. She died in New York in 1946.

LADY FINGALL

Lady Fingall, President of UI from 1913 to 1942, was Daisy Burke from Moycullen in Co. Galway. At the age of seventeen she married the Earl of Fingall of Killeen Castle, Co. Meath, a first cousin of Horace Plunkett. Plunkett was the family name, and the family inherited a seat in the House of Lords, being heirs to the three peerages of Fingall, Louth and Dunsany. During penal days, the Lords of Louth and Fingall remained Catholic while the Lords of Dunsany became Protestant in order to retain the family lands. When the necessity had passed, the lands were returned to their Catholic kinsmen, but the religious distinction remained.

The couple had four children, Oliver, Gerard, Mary and Henrietta. Due to her busy schedule, Lady Fingall seems to have been a fairly absentee mother, seeing her children only about once a fortnight. When Lord Fingall died in 1929, Lady Fingall moved to a flat in Mespil Road, Dublin. She died in 1944 and is buried beside the ruins of Killeen Castle.

She was UI's second President — totally different in style to her predecessor, content to let committees work through their agenda, rarely offering an opinion and invariably arriving late for meetings. However, she had a stabilising affect on members, which was necessary when one considers the period. In her almost 500-page memoirs, she barely mentions the UI except to say,

The UI were always united and we never had a quarrel. After a great deal of work and with financial help from Horace and from the Carnegie Trust for our organising, we succeeded in forming about fifty societies through the country. Besides our practical doctrine of 'Better living', or included in it, was an aim at establishing social life in the rural districts, the dullness of which had sent the young flying to America. We had dancing classes and choral societies and organised outdoor games. Hurling for the boys, camogie — the feminine and milder form of the same dangerous game! — for the girls. Our fame spread and from England came people anxious to see what we were doing. They went back and started the Women's Institutes, an exact copy of what we were trying to do in Ireland. With help from the British government, very soon almost every parish in England had their Women's Institute. We flourished, with the inevitable ups and downs, enthusiasms and disheartenment of any such movement, until the 'Troubles' after the War. Then, when five little girls knitting together might be considered a seditious meeting, we almost ceased to exist. But we have come to life again. And we only need more support and more branches and more enthusiastic workers.

Also in her memoirs is a letter from Horace Plunkett dated 12 August 1930 in which he says:

The future of the Irish Free State depends absolutely upon the rural community — upon the improvement of the farming industry, the economical disposal of its products and upon the reorganisation of social life among all classes in the country districts. Young people must do the hard work of the UI, but you must guide it. No one else understands its importance as you do, nor grasps the necessity of getting people to understand that the rural problem has its three sides, expressed in the Irish formula, 'Better farming, better business, better living', which has gone all over the English-speaking world. Team work between these three lots of people who are working along these lines is absolutely essential. The 'Better living' is the crux. You know all the difficulties, and with patience and sticking to the fundamental principles which you can talk over with such 'wise men' as Father Finlay and AE, you can surmount them in time.

Lady Fingall remained in office until 1942, when the presidency moved to Lucy Franks.

Early Organisers

The first two nurses sent for training by UI were Nurse Cowman at Bree and Nurse Swain at Ballycarney.

Miss Nancy Brunton, a trained horticulturist, planted gardens and started tree planting schemes for schoolchildren, as well as being the moving spirit in the cottage garden scheme which was such a feature of Wexford county in those days. Later Miss Galbraith took her place and started the same kind of work in Donegal.

By 1916/17, two organising instructresses were at work. One was Miss Annie (Nan) O'Brien, who was an aunt of Michael Collins. She was for some time wholly engaged in the 'new and important work of demonstrating cheese-making'. She was in government employment as a poultry instructress in Co. Monaghan, and was an enthusiastic and ardent Irishwoman who threw herself heart and soul into the work of UI. When supplies became difficult during the war, she was sent to be trained in cottage cheesemaking under Mrs Dermod O'Brien of Cahirmoyle, Co. Limerick, herself an expert in that art. She also gave lectures in cookery, in intensive poultry keeping, and in rabbit keeping as a source of food. Lucy Franks, one of UI's most energetic women, credits Nan O'Brien as being the cause for her becoming a member in 1917, having listened to her speak with great eloquence of the need for co-operation amongst countrywomen.

The second instructress was Miss Mangan, to whose salary the CDB gave a grant. Her work lay in the more isolated districts of Co. Galway and the Aran islands. She had a hard assignment, and one report states, 'She is still working in Gorumna island and is slowly but surely bringing improvements into the cottages in that desolate district.' To those who know this district, the laconic remark that 'storms and bad weather in the winter make her work a matter of difficulty' seems to understate the case! It is difficult to envisage her journeys by currach, bicycle and donkey cart — never mind the inclement weather.

EVA GORE-BOOTH

Another UI member was the poet Eva Gore-Booth who was on her local committee at Lissadell, Co. Sligo. She was a sister of Sir Josslyn Gore-Booth (a staunch co-operator) and of Constance, later Countess Markievicz.

MARY SPRING-RICE

Mary Spring-Rice founded and was an active member of the local UI branch at Shanagolden, Co. Limerick. A daughter of Lord Mounteagle, she was an enthusiastic supporter of the co-operative movement and travelled throughout Ireland to make its aims and ideals known. She was one of the two women (Mrs Erskine Childers had been the other) who travelled on the yacht Asgard during its gun-running voyage to Howth, Co. Dublin.

LUCY FRANKS

Today's ICA is a living testimony to Lucy Franks' service to her country, to which she dedicated her life. To her must go the credit for bringing life back to an all but lifeless movement. AE said in 1926, 'The society of UI emerged like an emaciated kitten among a herd of elephants.' Due to Lucy Franks' courage, optimism and steadfastness, the society's fragments were held together. It was because of what she accomplished in those years of the late 1920s that UI did indeed come alive and flourish.

There are no records of how the seed of this service was nurtured. Was it while she watched her home burning to the ground during the civil war that she decided to give her life to building a new and happier Ireland? Was it that warrior in the fight for women's rights, Charlotte Despard — Lucy Franks' aunt by marriage, and to whom she was very attached — who encouraged her to fight for 'better living' for Irish countrywomen? Probably it was both of these, added to her own sense of justice and of right, her urge to be up and doing.

Lucy Franks' own account of these years is very interesting:

The years 1914–18 seem, as I look back, to be full of work for helping our Irish Regiments. I lived in Leix then, and my thoughts were taken up mainly with the appalling losses in France of many fine relatives and friends of my generation. This led to my first effort in public affairs and calling a meeting after consultation with the towns folk of Mountrath of all denominations. We arranged to start a War Work depot in the courthouse, to be called the Mountrath Workers and the object to supply comforts and garments to the men serving with the Leinster Regiment. This effort brought all the people of the town and country into closer contact than they had ever been before. I speak especially of the women.

During these years, we met every week, giving out garments cut out, and taking in. I acted as honorary secretary. We organised each year a sale and possibly a concert, which brought in sufficient money to carry on the depot. During these years I used to hear occasionally of a society called UI, the object of which I understood was to bring the

women of 'all creeds and classes together, to work for their homes and
for the country.' But it was not until 1917 that an organiser visited Leix
and that I was asked to attend the meeting. Annie (Nan) O'Brien was
speaking that evening and giving demonstrations in spinning to some
20 or 30 women in the town of Abbeyleix, and it seemed to me as she
spoke that of course all she said was absolutely true and exactly what I
felt myself was the trouble in our country, that we had never really got
together and there was no time like the present to see what the UI
could do in furthering this purpose, so Annie O'Brien was approached
and invited to come and speak at Castletown, if all authorities approved
of the idea, in that parish, and so in the autumn of 1917 the word went
forth and farmers' wives and all were notified of a meeting at the boys
school in the village and our parish priest attended it and Annie O'Brien
spoke, with her heart in her hand, to convince us how much happier we
should be if we were 'UI', and so we started during those war years and
the members of UI were drawn from those working at the War Supply
Depot. During the next year we held a village dance at one of the
schools and a concert, but our first need was a room or hall in which to
meet, in which to hold money-making entertainments. In 1918, we were
told of a corrugated iron shed for sale on the railway. We secured a
derelict building in the village on which to graft the iron shed and with
local help given voluntarily, we got sand and gravel and the local carpenter made a grand job of the roof and floor, so the little hall was
roofed but not floored nor plastered when we held our first Show on
17 March 1919. Every member of the committee gave 5/- towards
prizes and some other subscriptions brought in £5, our first prize
money. Every year since then a show has been held, even during the
troubled years of 1921–23. After that, I left the neighbourhood as my
home was destroyed and went to live near Abbeyleix for the remaining
period of my father's life, until October 1924 when I went to England
to stay with friends, then to South Africa, returning only in 1926.

Vaguely I had thought of settling in South Africa but again the ties
of Ireland were strong and always I hoped to be able to help the countrywomen to organise. Handcrafts suggested themselves as a way of
reviving the interest in the work and incidentally of providing pocket
money for the members.

Returning that September 1926 to Dublin, I was fortified with a
knowledge of making baskets as I had taken courses at a Glastonbury

summer school. Now I had to find a place to live. Meanwhile I had been requested to join again the Executive Committee for the UI, the secretary at that time being Maud Slattery, with Lady Fingall President and Nannie Ross honorary treasurer. The society was at a low ebb and very few branches were keeping up any activity, the notable exceptions being Bree branch where Anita Lett was carrying on weaving, Camolin had meetings at intervals and were doing knitting and sewing. Miss Deane carried on a goat farm and the UI-trained village nurses continued to live and work from their homes in Wexford. Two milk depots were carrying on with local UI committees at Fethard under Mrs O'Connell (Phyllis and Helen's mother) and at Abbeyleix, both doing good work in combating the milk shortage which was severely felt in some small towns. Gortloman branch had an embroidery industry where the members met at Ballyalla under the guidance of Mrs Vere O'Brien and her daughters. Nan O'Brien, organiser, was helping at Beltra in teaching marmalade-making, spinning and cheese-making.

I was given a free hand to teach basketry to any branch who might like to have me, and soon I was booked up to go to Beltra, Co. Sligo, and later to Camolin, Co. Wexford, where the constant attendance and great interest taken by the members assured me I was on the right track. Later I was asked to go to Gortloman, Co. Clare, and the following year I went to Fethard, Co. Tipperary on Olivia Hughes' invitation. After speaking at a meeting there it was resolved to expand the existing UI activities (i.e. a milk depot started in 1916) and to hold regular monthly meetings and so a new committee was appointed. Meanwhile, Maud Slattery had resigned for a period and went to join the 'Save the Children' work in Greece. Actually there was no money left to pay a secretary!

During that time we had no office of our own but we had a room at Miss Leigh's office at the Employment Bureau for Women, 33, Molesworth St, for £20 per year, in which we kept papers and Miss Leigh was responsible for getting our typing done. I was asked to keep the branches going in her absence while Nanie Ross saw to correspondence. The committee reviewed the finances — £370 in the bank and some small sums under different headings.

Although we sold work for the UI members at Beltra show and Gorey show and also at Mountbellew in Co. Galway, outlets had to be found to sell our members' work. In 1928 I had acquired a small second-hand car so that I was able to travel about the country and pile up handcrafts of all kinds in the dicky behind, to bring for sale in Dublin.

It was around this time that the idea of a summer school to study crafts was mooted, leading to Slievenamon, of which I have such great memories. The Spring Show in the RDS in 1929 was considered to be the ideal showcase for such crafts and to do justice to craft-workers from all over Ireland. It was here that Muriel Gahan offered her help, which was to become a lifetime commitment. Country Shop followed in 1930, this giving craftworkers renewed hope as at that period the country was going through economic depression. Our members were able to sell their work, we had a place in which to meet and have meals together, as the restaurant became a great resort for country members.

In 1936 I resigned from the post of honorary secretary after nine years and went back to the work I preferred — keeping in touch with ACWW and travelling around Ireland visiting guilds and encouraging handcrafts, becoming President of the association on the resignation of Lady Fingall in 1942.[5]

'To set out to bring life to an all but lifeless movement by learning to make baskets sounds improbable and perhaps ridiculous, but this in fact is what Lucy Franks did in 1926.'[6] She knew as a countrywoman that what countrywomen need for a start is something tangible and down to earth which will be of practical benefit to themselves and their families. At her own expense, armed with her new skill, she set off in a rickety second-hand car. She did round after round of visits to the half dozen despondent groups of countrywomen which were all that remained of a once widespread society, and as well as putting work into their hands, she put courage into their hearts and gave them a sense of community and of confidence in themselves.

Because of what Lucy Franks accomplished those years in the late 1920s, Ireland's countrywomen's movement did indeed come alive and flourish, and it is a measure of her fellow-members' esteem that for nine years she remained the association's honorary secretary, for ten years its President, and since then until her death its Buan Cara. In committee, her uncompromising integrity, her straight thinking and clear judgement brought truth and reality into every discussion. Throughout the country, no one had a greater influence for good and no one was more greatly loved. She always took trouble over her dress and her appearance, not from vanity but from that sense of responsibility to a social order into which she was born and of which she remained so much a part.

When latter-day countrywomen were busy changing their society's constitution under its new name 'ICA', it was Lucy again who made them turn from their own domestic problems and recognise that the problems of countrywomen the world over were also their concern. Her name is on the roll of honour of founder members of ACWW.

Although she was in her late eighties when she died, she attended meetings right up to her last illness, and, as *The Irish Times* reported, 'Miss Franks of Ashley cottage, Clyde Road, Dublin, bequeathed to the Association not only a large picture of Christ in Emmaus but also £1,000 — half of it to the Association itself and half to its college, An Grianán, at Termonfechin, Co. Louth.

Of all Lucy Franks' attributes, it was her gift for friendship that has left a gap never to be filled. She loved gardens and the countryside and especially (going back to her country roots) when they were blossoming and fruitful. She thought any kind of waste was wickedness and her own small garden where she worked indefatigably was a delight in its abundance. She was the brains behind the garden scheme to use up small crossroad plots around the country and turn them into roadside gardens. There is a garden house dedicated to her an An Grianán, recalling her interest.

One of Lucy Franks' last dreams for women in 1960: 'May you all have faith and courage to make and keep your homes the heart of country life, to give your mind and your hands to the development of our land and to take your part in beautifying our countryside and in preserving its traditions, its treasures and its arts.'

Lucy Franks died in 1964 and is buried at Deansgrange and remembered with great fondness by the association which will be forever in her debt.

OLIVIA HUGHES

Visitors to Fethard, Co. Tipperary are invariably drawn to the fine monument outside the town hall, erected in 1993 to the memory of Olivia Hughes — a fitting tribute to an exceptional lady whose life and achievements still generate great interest, especially in ICA circles.

Olivia Hughes was born in Dublin to Judge and Mrs Cruikshank in 1898, one of five children. She was educated in Alexandra College, Dublin. When only twenty, she married Major John Hughes, and came to Annsgift, an estate about four miles outside Fethard. The family were chased out by the IRA in 1922, but later returned. Major Hughes farmed extensively while Olivia made a point of becoming acquainted with the locality and the people, and soon saw the need for proper survival housekeeping and budgeting programmes among the women of the area.

With the courage and pioneering spirit so typical of her, as well as the social conscience and confidence of her class, she gathered a number of interested friends and reformed Fethard branch in 1926, its aim being to improve the lot of Irish countrywomen.

In the early years, meetings were held in the old school house in Barrack St, now the Tirry social centre. During the war years, she opened a milk depot in Burke St to ensure adequate nutrition for local people. With the help of Phyllis and Helen O'Connell, she organised a canteen serving tea, coffee, Bovril and sandwiches to all and sundry on fair days – a service run voluntarily on a rota basis by members, which continued well into the 1950s when marts replaced fair days. She was instrumental with others in organising the first summer school on Slievenamon. She was the creative inspiration behind the achievements of her colleague Muriel Gahan who was the 'doer' of the partnership. Olivia was married and lived in the heart of a rural community while Muriel was single and lived in Dublin, yet they bonded together in a common aim. Olivia was President of South Tipperary Federation from 1951–54, and indeed the idea of forming county Federations also came from her. In 1946, among her many achievements was the opening of the first branch of Country Markets in Fethard, enabling local members to earn income through the sale of produce at a small profit. She was also involved in setting up the National Council for the Blind. When the army Nissen huts became available for sale in 1946, it was thanks to Olivia Hughes' courage and decisiveness that Fethard guild took the then outrageous step of borrowing £200 from the bank to purchase one. Guild fund-raising efforts ensured the loan was paid back in record time, and the hut served the guild until 1990, when it made way for the O'Connell Hall, erected to the memory of Phyllis and Helen O'Connell whose generous bequest financed the building.

Olivia Hughes was ICA President from 1955–58, and was later made Buan Cara.

The Horticultural College was her brainchild, as she realised that there was no residential horticultural college in Ireland for girls and set about persuading the ICA to set one up in the grounds of An Grianán. Horticulture had always been one of her great interests. As a practical gardener she could see the value of producing vegetables and fruit for home use, and this led to the inauguration of Country Markets to sell the surplus. Flowers, too, were an abiding interest and the annual chrysanthemum show in Fethard was her idea.

Education of young people in its broadest sense was always her concern. She travelled to the USA on the invitation of the Kellogg Foundation and studied the work of rural youth clubs. On her return, she adapted these ideas to Irish conditions and the result was Macra na Tuaithe, founded jointly by the ICA and Macra na Feirme.

Her death in September 1989 left all who knew her with a great sense of loss. Up to the last months of her life, she continued to play the organ in the Church of Ireland, Fethard. Her spirit will live on in her achievements and in the fine example of courage and determination she left behind.

The dedication to her of the sports hall and the memorial gardens at An Grianán will keep her memory alive for future generations.

DR MURIEL GAHAN

Muriel Gahan (MG as she became known affectionately) was born on the outskirts of Donegal town, where her grandfather was County Engineer. Muriel's father also became a civil engineer, while three of his four brothers became Church of Ireland clergymen. Muriel's father worked first with the Cavan and Leitrim Light Railway Co., but when the Congested Districts Board was established to improve living conditions in the poorest areas of the west of Ireland, he was offered work there and the family moved to Castlebar in 1900.

The ten years Muriel spent as a small child in Castlebar played a crucial part in her later development. Mayo's extraordinary beauty was imprinted on her psyche at an early age, but the poverty she witnessed there marked her deeply. Her father's work also had a great influence on her, and she travelled with him to visit projects in the far reaches of Mayo. As they travelled, Frederick Gahan talked to her about CDB's attempt to develop crafts, a task which was no easier at the turn of the century than when Muriel tried to revive them forty years later. Her father had passed on the fostering touch to his young daughter at an early age.

Her ten magic years in the freedom of Mayo came to an end in 1910, when at thirteen she was sent to St Winifred's School for Girls near Bangor in North Wales. Three years later she transferred to Alexandra College, Dublin. Muriel always recognised that it was 'The Alexandra' that provided her education. 'They taught us to be leaders,' she would say, adding with a mischievous smile, 'leaders of what, I'm not quite sure!' Although the college was radical and progressive in educational matters, its politics were conservative and unionist. Here she made many friends including Olivia Cruikshank (later Olivia Hughes of ICA), who even at this early stage was sensitive to social issues and interested in co-operation as a way of encouraging people to help themselves towards a better life.

Muriel started work as a painter with a decorating firm, and it was for these skills that Olivia asked her to help Lucy Franks set up an exhibition at the RDS. This encounter led her to the UI, and those meetings in turn determined a life-long dedication to the people of rural Ireland. The 1929 Spring Show was an eye-opener for Muriel. There she got to know people such as Mainie Jellett, the modernist artist, and Vida Lentaigne, an active UI member who lived in the house at Termonfechin which would later become An Grianán.

In 1935, Muriel was elected first President of Dublin Town Associates of the newly-constituted ICA, and a member of the Executive. In 1941–46 and 1950–51, she was its chairman and was elected ICA Vice-President in 1945. She also served at various times as chairman of Country Markets Ltd, the Irish Homespun Society and An Grianán committee. She became managing director of the Country Shop, and made it her business to scour the countryside seeking weavers, potters, carpenters, iron workers and craftspeople of all kinds, and encouraged them to work to the highest standards using native materials as well as helping sell their produce through both the Country Shop and Country Markets Ltd.

Many tributes have recognised her life's work and its contribution to 'better living' for rural women. In 1974, Allied Irish Banks chose her for the community development award. In 1976, the RDS bestowed on her a great and wholly deserved honour when she was made a Vice-President of the society — the first woman ever to be appointed to this position. Trinity College, Dublin, awarded her an honorary doctorate in 1978, and in the same year she was made one of the Rehabilitation Institute's 'People of the Year'. In 1984, she won the Plunkett Award for Co-operative Endeavour.

She has fostered women's interests through long and devoted service to the ICA, being one of the main inspirations for many innovations and schemes that have been successfully pursued over the years. She has inspired people to give of their best. At her approach, petty feuds fade away, and she instilled in countless people the sheer fun of taking on great enterprises and working them out together.

The memory of grown women, young and old, tall or short, thin or fat, down on all fours in the drawing room at An Grianán taking part in 'The Bears' will bring a smile to many faces.

ALICE RYAN, ICA PRESIDENT 1952–55

(*From a tribute written by Olivia Hughes, helped by Alice's younger sister, Betty*)

In all the western area of South Tipperary, there was only one 'Miss Alice', and that was Alice Ryan of Emly guild. She came of a line of enterprising patriots and pioneers on both sides of her family. Daniel O'Connell and Bianconi were her great-grandparents, but even more remarkable from a woman's point of view were the pioneering works of her mother and her Aunt Helen.

Her mother died in 1914, aged 53, having reared ten handsome, healthy children. She found time to be on the Board of Guardians of the County Home, which she visited every Saturday to examine the food prepared for inmates in the kitchens — interviewing the butcher if she was not satisfied. She was a member of what was then the County Council. She also ran a Temperance stall at Tipperary fair once a month, spending the previous night at the house of her brother-in-law in order to be at the fair by 4.00 a.m.

Alice's aunt, Helen Ryan, lived in London. She worked with women prisoners and ran a hostel for women who had finished their sentences, work which proved so successful that the Archbishop of Liverpool asked her to set up a similar service for women prisoners in Liverpool.

Alice was engaged to be married and all preparations for the wedding had been made when her mother died. The wedding was cancelled as Alice was needed at home to care for the younger children. The Ryan family were famous masters of horses and hounds and led the 'Black and Tans' pack from 1600 to the present day. Alice loved the hunt, and followed the hounds in her pony and trap up hill and down dale, and especially through her beloved mountains. She had wished to train to teach dancing, and one of her few vanities was her neat feet and the shoes which set them off.

Until she joined UI in 1929, she looked after the younger children and supervised the stable boys, which gave her a firm and bossy manner and led to one of her nicknames, 'the Reverend Mother'. We were often glad of this authoritarian manner, as in the early days of the summer schools we often attracted neighbours in the evening to join in singing and dancing, and the young men were not inclined to go home. We called on Alice to disperse the 'cuckoos in the nest'.

I came to know Alice first when I was asked to talk about UI to a group of women at Knockcarron schoolhouse. I wondered how I would get on, as in those days there were very few UI branches and I had never before been asked to start one. At this meeting there was one lady who seemed well known and competent and ready to take on the job. This, of course, was Alice, and she had met with a life-long vocation. She had inherited public spirit, but had now met with a work for Ireland which suited her character and upbringing.

The next meeting with Alice was some months later when the first summer school on Slievenamon was planned At this summer school, we nicknamed her 'Valor Perfection', as she always had everything needed, from a boot button to how to stretch the morning's milk. She loved handcrafts and in those days was a first class glove maker, and always ready to learn anything new. We learnt together to re-cane a chair, knowledge which I have used over and over again to help the handicapped.

She made a little pocket money with her gloves, but was never well off and one friend said she had a 'patrician attitude' to the need for more money and she never complained. I think she probably spent every penny she earned working for ICA and backing up An Grianán which became her second home.

Fun and dressing up was her joy. Alice could do herself up as a 'speckled hen' or a 'bishop' with equal facility. I acted a murder scene with her once, when she was a poor invalid in a bath-chair and I had come to kill her. I shall never forget her trembling voice and abject demeanour.

She never missed an ICA function which she could possibly get to. She was deeply religious and went to Mass every day of her life, but never bothered other people with pious preaching. She did one great service for the UI and later ICA, and that was her determination to keep the organisation ecumenical.

She was a great woman and came of great people, and the ICA were lucky to have her as President for three years.

JOSEPHINE MANGAN, PRESIDENT OF CORK FEDERATION 1936–48

(Taken from the *History of Cork Federation 1936–94*)
Those who knew Josephine describe her as a formidable woman, an innovator and a perfectionist. It was she who established the first ICA guild in Co. Cork, in Clonakilty in 1930. She had worked for a while on a poultry farm in Sussex before returning to Ireland where she completed her training at the Munster Institute.

Following her appointment as a poultry instructress, she travelled extensively, particularly in West Cork, and she became passionately devoted to the cause of rural women. Her sister, a poultry instructress in Tipperary, told her of the work of UI, pioneered in that county by Olivia Hughes. It seemed an answer to prayer — here was an idea, here was potential, here was a movement which would help rural women to improve the quality of life for themselves and their children.

She persuaded the thirteen women in her poultry class in Clonakilty to form that first guild in Co. Cork and when there were seven guilds in the county the Cork Federation was set up in 1936 where she was unanimously elected President, and presided with energy and dedication until her retirement in 1948.

She guided the infant Federation through its growing years and established close contacts with central office in Dublin. She kept aware of the rules and regulations of the many shows to which members contributed, revised schedules and worked ceaselessly visiting guilds, giving help in gardening, growing vegetables, attending meetings in Dublin and Cork. She was also responsible for a monthly article in *Model Housekeeping* and in *Farmers' Gazette*, usually on poultry. In 1940 she attended the ACWW conference in London for eight days out of her annual leave.

A pioneer, an innovator, Miss Mangan worked and indeed fought for the improvement of rural living. She used every possible weapon in this fight, even the 'station Mass'. ICA members were encouraged to embroider and crochet, to experiment with cookery and colour schemes and spread the gospel of gracious living.

She saw the rural lifestyle transformed in her working life. Piped water, electricity and the updating of farm kitchens as designed by Lady Wicklow. These made her dreams become a reality for many women. Described by Lucy Franks as 'a woman of a thousand battles', Josephine Mangan was someone who never took no for an answer. Hundreds of women must have blessed her indomitable courage and her foresight in introducing ICA to Cork.

PHYLLIS O'CONNELL

Phyllis O'Connell of Fethard joined UI in 1933 and went on to become chief organiser, having served as county and local organiser. Her dedication to her task is proven by the recording in the minutes in 1945 that 'Phyllis O'Connell travelled from Fethard to Emly by bicycle to attend a meeting' (a distance of over thirty miles). In the early days of her outstanding work, the bicycle was her usual mode of travel to outlying areas, though she later covered the country by car. She and her sister Helen were experts in the art of Lumra rug-making.

The following tribute was paid to her by Olivia Hughes:

I must write about Phyllis because I know what she meant to Fethard, to Tipperary and to Ireland.

When she started working with UI, feminist movements were almost unknown. She travelled around on her bicycle meeting women, usually in comfortless sheds or schoolrooms, getting them to organise so that in some way or another they could better the circumstances of the community and help themselves to a livelier existence. Such organising was sometimes opposed. At one meeting we both attended, Phyllis told me that straw was lit in the chimney to smoke out the women. I have seen a goat thrown in through a window amidst shrieks of laughter. Phyllis persevered, and when I was national President (1955–58) she took me all over Ireland and we left behind a trail of women determined to better their lot. It was not always serious — there was dancing, singing and acting.

There was soon a team of organisers following in her footsteps and summer schools on mountains or in castles led to the luxury and inspiration of An Grianán. Governments and county councils began to take an interest in women's existence.

A countrywoman writes of Phyllis thus:

She worked very closely during the rural family conference in 1959 and the year leading up to it. She was a marvellously calm and efficient secretary and was so practical in her suggestions with officials from the Depts. of Agriculture and Education. She listened quietly and sympathetically to everyone and made helpful suggestions. She was sent by ICA to international conferences and we knew we could be proud of our representative.

She and her sister Helen were first-rate handcraft workers. I still have one of their rugs which was given to me twenty years ago. She never neglected Fethard. If a play was got up, Phyllis helped with the make-up, lent furniture and dresses and spent the week acting as prompter. Everything to do with the Church was her business and wherever she travelled she usually managed to get to Mass.

If I think of any text as specially suited to Phyllis, it would be 'Blessed are the peacemakers, for they shall be called children of God.'

THE ORPEN SISTERS

The contribution of the Orpen sisters to ICA was unique — four out of five sisters gave a lifetime commitment to the ideals and aspirations of the association.

Cerise

Trained as a Froebel teacher. Married Cyril Parker in 1932 and had twin daughters. She joined the ICA in 1935, served the association in many positions and was responsible for compiling a resume of the association for the ACWW conference in 1965.

Grace

Trained as a physical education teacher in England. Married Philip (Paddy) Somerville Large in 1933 and joined ICA in 1935. She held different positions within ICA, including honorary treasurer in the early 1940s. It was her view that visiting existing guilds should be as important for organisers as opening new guilds — it is useless to found a guild in an isolated district and expect it to fend for itself, since each ICA member should feel part of a united body of women. Grace is credited with sending out the paper pattern for shorts to each participant in advance of the summer school in the 1930s!

Kathleen

Born in 1910, Kathleen shares the birthdate of UI. She trained as an architect in UCD but left after four years to marry Hugh Delap. She joined Dublin Town Associates in 1937 and became its secretary. From 1947–55 she was editor of the ICA page in the *Farmers' Gazette*, a job she gave up only when she became honorary secretary of ICA in 1955. From then until 1958 she was at the same time secretary of the Counterpart Fund and the Finance and Appointment sub-committees. In 1958 she was appointed chairman of the Executive Committee and was also elected ICA Vice-President. Later elected Buan Cara, she is a very worthy recipient of the title 'our national treasure'.

Bea, ICA President 1974–76

Bea was educated at Alexandra College, Dublin, studied art in Academy School, Dublin and the Slade School of Fine Art, London. She became a freelance artist and was well known as an artist and designer. She also became an art teacher and lectured throughout Ireland to schools and adult groups under the Arts Council and the Shaw Trust.

She joined ICA in 1939, and in 1940 married C.E.F (Terry) Trench, the founder of An Óige. Their family consists of three sons and one daughter.

Leaving Dublin in 1942, she was co-founder of Drogheda Town Associates in 1947 and became President of Louth/Meath Federation in 1950. She was elected chairman of the Executive Committee in 1952 and was ICA President from 1974–76.

A very talented artist, her works grace the walls of An Grianán and central office, and she designed the cover of *Ár Leabhar Féin* since 1954. She also designed the President's chain of office — a large oval-shaped silver pendant encircling a Kerry diamond, with the names of all past Presidents engraved on the silver leaves of the chain.

Bea was honoured by being elected an honorary member of the Royal Hibernian Academy of Arts. She is also an honorary member of the Water Colour Society of Ireland. Particularly concerned with conservation of the environment, she was a member of An Taisce and urged ICA guilds at every opportunity to form local history groups and to have a sense of pride and protection for their own areas.

To quote a member, 'Mere words cannot convey her legacy to us all – but when we encourage beauty in our everyday lives, when we see our children conscious of their history and culture, we will remember her.'

As well as the four Orpen sisters, other past pupils of Alexandra College were Olivia Hughes, Muriel Gahan, the Cherry sisters who were founder members of Delgany guild in Co. Wicklow, and Barbara Thompson (née Miller) member of Dublin Town Associates.

VIDA LENTAIGNE

Vida Lentaigne was mainly instrumental in starting Termonfechin guild of the ICA in Co. Louth. She gave the use of a large basement room in her house for guild meetings, which later she fitted up as a kitchen, and·courses in cookery were given by Mrs Walsh. Glove making was a highlight in this guild, Miss Cahill being the presiding genius, and Tarmon gloves quickly made their own market after a display on the ICA stall at the RDS in Ballsbridge, as none were passed for sale unless they were technically perfect. In the Summer of 1933, Mrs Lentaigne lent her house for the summer school and provided the ICA with all amenities for games, etc. in the grounds. (The house later changed ownership and became the Termon Hotel.) Surely this was providence, for in 1954 the ICA purchased this very house which was to become An Grianán – there has always been a warm glow about this haven due in some small measure to its history, having welcomed the UI over twenty years previously.

MAEVE CURTIS

Born in Omagh, Co. Tyrone, Maeve was of farming stock and one of a family of six, all of whom made careers in education. She qualified as a domestic economy teacher and worked for a time in the north of England before returning to Ireland where she took up a post as 'itinerant teacher' with Carlow VEC.

Here, during the second world war, she became founder member of the Bagenalstown guild of ICA, and used to cycle out to little country schools night after night to teach and to get to know the countrywomen on their home ground. Out of her many and varied talents, she was concerned principally with making life better, easier and more rewarding for all. Her only impatience and her only anger was directed at the lack of dignity and recognition accorded to Irish women – whom she knew better than most and whom she respected for their qualities of tolerance and dedication to their families.

On marriage, she moved to Cork where she became a member of Bishopstown guild, as well as editing the women's page of the *Cork Examiner*. She established a communications course at An Grianán, which included creative writing as well as report writing and featured radio and television techniques. This course was greatly appreciated, as increasing numbers of ICA members needed media skills as local radio and local newspapers became part of community life.

She was Vice-President of the ICA in 1964 when *The Irish Countrywoman* was launched, and she acted as honorary editor for four years. She represented ICA on the Institute for Industrial Research and Standards, and organised day-long seminars on every aspect of consumer education. At the ACWW conference in 1965, she was convenor and principal speaker at a forum about 'The individual woman in society: freedom and the common bond'.

A Maeve Curtis bursary was set up in recognition of her wonderful contribution to the ICA, and it provides scholarships in communication courses at An Grianán. Maeve herself presented a speaker's table to An Grianán, and Mr and Mrs Crosbie of the *Cork Examiner* presented a matching chair.

DOROTHY SMITH, ICA PRESIDENT 1958–61

Dorry Smith worked as Administrator at the Irish Hospital in Saint-Lo, Normandy in 1945–46. Returning to Ireland, she joined ICA in January 1953 when a guild opened in Cavan. She acted as honorary secretary that first year and was guild President in 1954. She continued the following year to become President of Cavan Federation from 1955–57, then chairman of the Executive from 1956–57, and was elected ICA President in 1958 – surely a meteoric rise to the top.

JOSEPHINE MCNEILL, BUAN CARA 1959

A friend of Louise Gavan Duffy, Josephine graduated from UCD with a degree in languages. She was a member of Cumann na mBan, and was engaged to Pierce McCann who died in 1919. She later married James McNeill who became the first High Commissioner to London for the Irish Free State in 1927, then Governor General. Fianna Fail was determined to demean the office of Governor General to such a point that it would become totally meaningless. MacNeill was forced to resign and died out of favour. The UI was interested in these proceedings as MacNeill's wife, Josephine, was a prominent member of the association since the 1930s and later in her own capacity represented Ireland in many EU countries

When she was offered a position as the first official woman diplomat to Holland, she felt she had to resign her ICA membership. As a token of gratitude for her work with the association she was presented with a Hone panel purchased in Dawson Galleries. In her reply she stated, 'No part of my life do I value more than the past twelve years — it has been an inspiration to work with you.'[7]

KIT AHERN, ICA PRESIDENT 1961–64

The past is of particular importance to Kit, because she is the oldest surviving ICA President, having served as a guild member in Ballybunion, President of Kerry Federation, as well as senator, Dáil representative and member of the Council of Europe.

She is intensely proud of her humble roots, describing herself as 'the first pleb' to be elected President of the ICA. This deliberate self-deprecation is a way of staking her claim to be one of the few Presidents whose life was actually rooted in the machinery and people of rural Ireland. It is a simple persona — the woman with the common touch. But she feels its absence from the affairs of the ICA at present, and that the modern leadership has been more urban and image conscious — and even of lacking in vision. Her message, she said, had always been 'from small things come great things', not the other way around. As far as Kit is concerned, the ICA had vision in the 1950s and 1960s — with women like Kathleen Gleeson, Kathleen Delap, Phyllis Faris, Áine Barrington, Dorrie Smith and of course Muriel Gahan.

Kit was nominated for a seat in the senate by Taoiseach Seán Lemass. She accepted, she said, for three reasons: 'As a tribute to the women of Ireland, as a tribute to myself, and to try to create a base for a new North Kerry Fianna Fáil TD.' And what of those who balked at the idea of an ICA President inviting such a profile in national politics? That, for Kit, was not the issue. It was, she believed, ridiculous for women to remain detached from politics. The ICA needed to change its constitution to allow a President the freedom to accept this type of nomination as President of the association, not as a redundant ex-President. (This has been a contentious issue within ICA — the rule states that a President must resign her position upon nomination, while still remaining an ICA member. The premise has been that it is difficult to do these two jobs.) Kit feels it would have been hypocritical of her to decline the invitation, having cajoled women to get actively involved in politics. Again, she wonders whether the present generation understands the environment from which the women of her ilk sprang. They were, she passionately attests, creators with vision. There were no spin-doctors in North Kerry in 1944, only 'cute and seasoned rural hoors'. Kit and her future Kerry Federation had started guilds and spread guilds. They had not fallen into a ready-made ICA like so many later Presidents. Their surroundings were a countryside recovering from war-time scarcities, and an association which was solid but immobile. They had to oil the machine.

Creating did not leave time for the luxury of leisure. These women were not well off. There were no expense accounts and few had cars. They stayed with friends rather than in hotels, which kept them in touch with the grassroots – the people who mattered. They sought to supplement their income by making the most of what they owned, by promoting their own localities: 'we were there long before Bord Fáilte, even though we were doing the same thing they are doing now.'

Does she look back favourably on these formative years, coping without running water, electricity, transport? Of course she does, because she was directly involved in the front-line battle to make these facilities the norm. It was the self-creating and self-perpetuating optimism prevailing in times of hardship which galvanised these earlier sisters sick of servitude. They enjoyed creating new avenues.

Kit was the first women to be elected to Kerry County Council and the first woman to represent North Kerry in the Dáil. She muses over the fact that many ICA Presidents seem to virtually disappear after their terms of office, she obviously being the exception. She believes this is precisely because she was political and prepared to contest elections on her own. The key to her successful public life both within the ICA and outside it has been the way she has managed to mix and cultivate the image of peasant alongside that of President.

NORA BURTON, ICA PRESIDENT 1964–67

Nora Burton was a founder member of Ballinhassig guild and served as its President from 1954–57, as well as being President of Cork Federation from 1958–61.

As a poultry farmer, it is a measure of her great competence that she managed to carry out the arduous duties of an ICA President and also 'mind the hens' to use her own words.

A rural Cork woman, Nora was well used to the hopes, fears, uncertainties and problems of farm living. Her interests were naturally deeply rooted in the land, just as her sympathies were irrevocably bound to the farming community. She could speak at first hand on conditions in rural Ireland, and was therefore a valuable member of committees discussing emigration, migration to the cities, rural education, setting up local craft markets and improving the lot of rural dwellers in general. She was the first woman elected to the council of the Irish Agricultural Institute, a national body set up to deal with all aspects of agricultural research. When officially opening the Farm Home Research unit at An Grianán, she issued a word of warning to farming men — that unless they set about making life a little easier for their womenfolk they would find themselves ageing bachelors, and not by choice!

Her objective as ICA President was to ensure the success of ICA's five-year rural development programme, with its principal goals of expansion, co-operation and education. In her Presidential address, she said, 'Don't ever forget that one of the main aims of ICA membership is self-fulfilment through self-help and mutual help. What better way to attain fulfilment than through the development of our talents.' She proved a wonderful ambassador for Ireland during the ACWW conference in Dublin in 1965. Delegates from all over the world spoke of her graciousness, and she was later invited to accept a nomination as ACWW Vice-President. She declined this offer, but the proposed nomination remains a great personal tribute as well as a positive recognition of the contribution of ICA to this world-wide organisation of women.

In 1983, she was made a Buan Cara, which is the highest honour in the ICA.

Peggy Farrell, ICA President 1967–70

A native of Bantry, Co. Cork, Peggy was educated at the Convent of Mercy, Bantry, RDE School, Clifden and the Munster Institute in Cork, where she qualified as a poultry and dairy instructress. Working as a poultry instructress in Roscommon, she met and married T.P. Farrell. They have a family of four children.

With an abiding interest in handcrafts, Peggy holds ten brannraí awards and three demonstrators bars for handcrafts. She is also an avid reader, loves cookery and compiled the cookery book for the ACWW conference in 1965.

She is extremely interested in Western development and feels the need for supplementation of the small farmer's income. She is a founder member and vice-chairman of Slieve Bawn Handcraft Co-operative Markets Ltd.

As President, she was outspoken on practical patriotism, the importance of the homemaker, and the responsibility of professionals to repay the debt to their communities. She refused to take sides in the NFA dispute, feeling that it was the responsibility of ICA to inform its members and let them decide individually. She stressed the importance of conserving our inheritance and advocated displaying artefacts in local museums rather than storing them in the basement of the National Museum.

OONAGH CORBETT, ICA PRESIDENT 1970–72

Oonagh came from a farming background in Co. Kildare, and married Arthur Corbett, a farmer in Abbey Braney, New Ross. They have a family of four.

Oonagh was one of the founder members of Gusserane guild in Co. Wexford. She became President of Wexford Federation and represented ICA on the NFA national poultry committee. She was a committee member of the Joint Rural Organisations for Co. Wexford, of which she was a founder, as well as being its first secretary.

Her particular farm project is broiler production. She is interested in conservation and nature study, and is a member of An Taisce and the Georgian Society. It was fitting that it was during her presidency that ICA celebrated its Diamond Jubilee, with the theme of 'Our Irish Heritage'. 1970 was also European Conservation Year. It is not surprising that the theme of 'conserve and preserve' dominated many of her speeches as President. Arts, crafts, old buildings and monuments, prevention of air and water pollution, all figured high on her agenda as she urged members to become involved. Her keynote for the jubilee year was 'Preserve the things we cannot replace.'

Having handed over the reins of the family farm, she and her husband have now retired to a houseboat on the Shannon. During the winter months they are moored near Portumna where they participate in all the activities of the local community, but come

Spring they 'take to the river' to indulge their passion of dinghy sailing and boating.

JOSEPHINE CARROLL, ICA PRESIDENT 1972–74

Josephine Carroll is the first ICA President from Ulster. She comes from a very rural area in County Tyrone, near the shores of Lough Neagh, where her people are small farmers. She married a local government official with Monaghan County Council, and they have two children.

It was very apt that the President from 1972–74 should have been a Monaghan woman who was reared in the North. At all times through her presidency, she sought to get women involved in the search for peace in the North. Convinced that women could play a part, she encouraged them to get out, be friendly, be open, and by discussion bring the people with them and say, 'look, we have some control, on the basis of the slogan that the hand that rocks the cradle rules the world. Tell these fellas, your brothers, your husbands, your boyfriends or whatever, to stop it, to work by negotiation.' But the ICA were reluctant to get involved. 'They were working on the idea of arts and crafts and rural development, and they were afraid of offending anybody, particularly the Women's Institutes in the North.' Josephine felt the ICA was in a fog, afraid of what steps it might have to take. The ICA consulted with the Women's Institute, who themselves were very hamstrung by the Northern situation.

Through her speeches at Council meetings she made it clear that the most important thing was to get people united. She spoke about the onus being on women to put pressure on their politicians, local councillors, and others. There again, the ICA was reluctant, as it had difficulty dividing politics and party politics. Josephine tried to get them to become involved with local councils, if possible as independents or if not with the party of their choice, provided they did not bring that into ICA and did not do their canvassing in ICA. After her term as President she had to take a bit of her own medicine when she was approached by a political party to stand for the urban council, which she did, and described the experience as 'an eye-opener'.

Issues raised during her presidency included that of highlighting at every opportunity the value to be put on the contribution of women. Josephine felt that there was very little account of the huge amount of work that a woman puts into homemaking, rearing a family, providing furnishings, using her hands and acquiring skills to improve the standard of living, and of course she was well aware of how little time a woman had left to get involved in local politics.

While ICA was predominantly a rural association, not all members were farmers. However those who were tended to be very vocal and expected the ICA to support the farmers' dispute. When the Executive decided to remain neutral, this contributed to the urban/rural prejudice creeping in, and created a 'them and us' mentality. There was a feeling in the countryside of 'them ones' in Dublin running the association, which was untrue as an ICA President never came from Dublin Federation, and Dublin guilds have given great support to central office over the years, as well as doing a lot of entertaining and representing the association when necessary.

PATSY LAWLOR, ICA PRESIDENT 1976–79

Patsy Lawlor was born into a business and farming family in Kill, Co. Kildare, where she became a founder member of Kill ICA guild in 1961. Her widely-acknowledged commitment to the aims, objectives and activities of ICA did not preclude her from participating in other areas of local and national affairs. Elected member of Kildare County Council, she was also a member of the Arts Council, Chairperson of Kildare County Library Committee and a member of the local Health Board. She married Tony, an extensive farmer and member of the well-known family of caterers in Naas, and has four children.

'When I joined, I saw the ICA as a social outlet with something to offer a young married woman. It provided the opportunity for involvement with other women and there were leisure pursuits like arts and crafts. You have to remember that in the early sixties women were second-class citizens. There was no work outside the home; there was no women's movement worth talking about; there were very few women involved in politics; and there was no social outlet apart from golf clubs and even they were a bit elitist.' But having joined mainly for the outings and social gatherings, Patsy Lawlor soon realised, as did others, that the ICA had tremendous potential.

'In 1965, when the farmers were marching for the right to earn a living comparable to others, I and others felt that the ICA should support their cause. I began to see the ICA as a group which could have a huge voice if their influence was harnessed.'

Patsy found that 1976 was a good time to become ICA President, with the 'women's decade' under way, and groups such as the Council for the Status of Women, AIM and the Rape Crisis Centre tackling issues related to women's lives. However, the urban view of rural Ireland had not fully changed. 'You couldn't be a farmer's wife!' was the comment this tall, blonde, well-dressed and attractive ICA President often received. 'Maybe they expected that I should be wearing wellies and have my clothes tied together with bits of string,' Patsy laughed. More seriously, she believes that the ICA involvement in both town and country has done much to banish such images.

It was Patsy who proposed changing *The Irish Countrywoman* to a glossy format magazine produced by a commercial firm. She made a plea to members to 'look on change as progress and not as a threat', and put the motion forward at Council where it was carried. She found it interesting that the guilds not in favour of changing the image of the magazine were all Dublin-based.

Outside the ICA, Patsy Lawlor has had a busy career. She held a Fine Gael seat on Kildare County Council from 1974 to 1985, when she was refused the Fine Gael nomination and won her seat as an independent candidate. She chaired the Kildare VEC for six years, and also chaired Kildare County Council. She was elected to the Senate in 1981 as the ICA nominee on the cultural and educational panel.

Speaking of the ICA, she believes, 'Maybe we're a very humble organisation and maybe we're a little nervous of public reaction at times. Sometimes it's good to steer clear of controversy, but perhaps at other times it's not so good. I suppose it's all to do with women's poor image of themselves and of their place in our society. Certainly the ICA doesn't get anything like the credit it deserves for its achievements over the years. Having survived over eighty years, our roots go very deep.' And for the future, there is still plenty to be done: 'There are issues such as the environment and ecology. We have a responsibility to our descendants to pass on an achievement that they can enjoy. Then there is the whole business of leisure, which must be looked at in the context of early retirement, redundancy and unemployment.'

Support for career women and those who are setting up small industries is another area in which Patsy Lawlor feels the ICA has much to offer. And, perhaps most important in her view, there is the continuing need to make the ICA more attractive to younger women who are the potential new members. 'When you first join, you do so to get out of it what it can offer you. After a time you change to offering it what you can give.'

Sadly, Patsy's untimely death in 1997 leaves a gap that will never be filled. Her vibrancy, her enthusiasm and her charisma will live on in the memories of all who are privileged to have known her.

CAMILLA HANNON, ICA PRESIDENT 1979–82

Camilla was born in Ballymote, Co. Sligo, educated there and in Loreto Abbey, Rathfarnham. Her work included three years with the Blood Bank travelling to every corner of Ireland. Returning to a settled city life, she joined the advertising department of *The Irish Times* as a supervisor and remained there until marriage. Her Dublin-born husband Joe had gone to an agricultural college and opted for a career in farming with a family-owned 'outfarm' in Co. Meath. As well as rearing five children, she kept all the farming accounts and records.

She had no community involvement until she became a founder member of Kiltale ICA guild, Co. Meath. She went on to become a VCO and in 1976 Meath Federation President and chairman of the Horticultural Board of An Grianán. In 1979 she became the second Meath ICA member to become ICA President, and her first priority was to increase membership. Six development officers were funded by the Dept. of Education and with the VCOs the membership stabilised and soon began to increase.

She was appointed to numerous national boards whilst in office and is now a member of the National Agricultural, the Rural Development and the Environment committees and also on the National Steering Committee on Violence against Women. One month after her term of office as President was completed, she became the Taoiseach's nominee for the senate.

MAMO MCDONALD, ICA PRESIDENT 1982–85

Mary Frances Bowen McDonald was born in Tuam, Co. Galway and as her father worked in a bank her childhood was spent in various parts of Munster. She moved to Cavan in 1949 to work in the Hibernian Bank, where she met and married Eugene McDonald. They have eleven children, nine boys and two girls.

It was while living in Croom that Mamo first joined the ICA, an association that she saw as providing a service, an opportunity to develop arts and crafts, and a much-needed social outlet for women.

A founder member of Clones guild in Co. Monaghan since 1959, McDonald developed an abiding interest in issues concerning women, the family and consumer rights and responsibilities. She was elected ICA President in 1982, and during her three-year term the association conducted a constitutional review, considered but did not embrace regionalisation, and forged a relationship with radical feminism having found much common ground. A major task during her term was the preparation for the ACWW conference to be held in Killarney in 1986. Mamo's lasting memory of that time was of the energy, commitment and creativity of the members working on behalf of women at local, national and international level.

In 1989 she helped to found Age and Opportunity, of which she is cathaoirleach, and she is also a founder member of European Older Women's Network (OWN) established in 1993.

She has written poetry and fiction since the 1960s and at present is studying at UCD.

Mamo McDonald received a People of the Year Award in 1999 in recognition of her work as an activist on behalf of women, older people and her local community.[8]

Wild Geese (Mamo McDonald)

Sitting on a train in Ballybrophy
in 1944
watching a sad goodbye;
he, with belted coat and cardboard case
split at the edges
she, with anguish on her tearswept face
begrudging him to England
and the war.
I was just fourteen then.
It was a side of love and loss
I had not known,
yet, grieving with them,
wept all the way to Kingsbridge.

'Tis many years since then.
Such scenes a part of history;

Flight of the Earls
and Wild Geese gone,
but yet it comes to mind
each time I bid
my own Wild Geese goodbye
these geese who are my swans.
I live again
the sorrow of that scene
viewed from the railway train
at Ballybrophy.

INA BROUGHALL, ICA PRESIDENT 1985–88

Originally a member of Graigcullen guild, Co. Carlow, she now
lives in Co. Louth. Before her election as President when her
theme was 'The Media', she was the association's press officer
from 1984 to 1985. She was always of the opinion that so long as
women's contribution remains invisible, unrecorded, unpaid, so
long will the decision makers continue to ignore their needs. The
perception that women have of themselves is reflected in the perception of women by society. An organisation such as the ICA
encourages women to see themselves as equals in society.

Ina has since become an accomplished artist and has held successful exhibitions in between her extensive travelling.

KITTY HARLIN, ICA PRESIDENT 1988–90

Kitty Harlin is a native of Sligo, married to Michael, a farmer. They
reared a family of three and live in Kilmessan, Co. Meath. A member of Scurlogstown guild since the late 1960s, she was
Vice-President of Leinster which involved opening new guilds and
lobbying government ministers on social and consumer affairs. She
was appointed to the Board of ACOT and represented ICA on the
Consumer Committee in Brussels.

In 1991, she pioneered the ICA Counselling Service in order to
give members and their families in every county access to counselling for the price of a local call.

She was elected President of COFACE in 1991, the first
President to be elected from outside the major countries and the
first woman in that position. The presidency involved ninety
national organisations from member states — all with different

needs and different problems. It was a huge commitment and a great challenge and during that time Harlin was a founder member and Vice-President of the 'International Year of the Family' and was elected 'Meath Person of the Year' in 1994.

She would like in the future to see a woman as Minister for Health and to see the ICA revive its journal.

MONICA PRENDIVILLE, ICA PRESIDENT 1991–94

Since joining Castleisland guild, Co. Kerry in 1967, she has been actively involved at guild level, held most offices and progressed to Federation level as Treasurer for Kerry in 1979. As Federation President in 1983–86 she served on the Executive, then as elected member for Munster, Vice-President of Munster and ICA President from 1991–94.

Internationally, she led Irish delegations to the European Area Conference in Velden and to the World Conference of ACWW in the Hague in 1993. She was number one delegate to COFACE Administrative Council and sat on various COFACE commissions. She was honorary secretary of the co-ordinating committee for the ACWW World Conference held in Pretoria in 1997.

In all her activities over the years, what she enjoyed most and admired most was the commitment of the local organisations of the ICA, whether Federations or Council, or a meeting or a bigger event. In her opinion, the association's strength is the ordinary guild member, and its weakness is the non-attendance of guilds at Council where vital decisions are made.

BRÍDÍN TWIST, ICA PRESIDENT 1994–97

A member of Barefield guild, Co. Clare, one of the oldest guilds in the country. She held most positions at guild, Federation and national level. Among the highlights of her presidency was the very success-ful 'National Breast Cancer Awareness Campaign' which resulted in a commitment to a national breast screening programme.

Another highlight was being elected the first female member of the Irish Economic and Social Committee to the EU which allowed her to produce equality documents which were later voted into law.

She enjoyed being on the government delegation to Beijing for the fourth UN Conference on Women and seeing governments, world-wide, making commitments to new legislation. Above all, meeting the members countrywide who are 'the organisation' gave her most satisfaction.

SALLY WARD, ICA PRESIDENT APRIL–MAY 1997

Sally Ward joined Lakeview Guild of the ICA in Sligo in 1972. She served as Treasurer, PRO and President of her Guild and also as Secretary, PRO and President of County Sligo Federation.

At National level, she served as elected member for Connaught, Vice-President for Connaught, Chairman of the Committee for Social Affairs and Health and Chairman of the National Executive. She served on a number of Government Committees relating to the family, women and children. She represented the ICA on COFACE and is a member of the ACWW.

EVA COYLE, ICA PRESIDENT 1997–2000

Born in Longford, she has lived in Raphoe, Co. Donegal since her marriage, where she has reared her family of four. On taking up the office of President, her stated objective was the restoration of the ICA guild member at the heart of the association. During her term, *Rights and Responsibilities*, a major policy document, was published, bringing together all the strands of ICA policy, and in 1988 ICA went online with the creation of the association's website (www.ica.ie).

BREDA RAGGETT, ICA PRESIDENT 2000–

A member of Sevenhouses Guild, Kilkenny Federation, she believes ICA must adjust to Irishwomen's changing lifestyles and the challenge of new technology. She has served the Association at Guild, Federation and National level for the last twenty-seven years.

NOTES
___

INTRODUCTION: WOMEN WORKING TOGETHER THROUGH ICA

1 Margaret Ward, *Unmanageable Revolutionaries*, London, 1995. p. 39
2 Esther Bishop, *Bantracht na Tuatha*, ICA, Dublin, 1950. p. 21
3 Muriel Gahan, *The Countrywoman and Adult Education*, Annual Congress of Irish Vocational Education Association, Dublin, 1950
3 Pat Murphy and Nell McCafferty, *Women in Focus*, Dublin, 1986. p. 37

CHAPTER 1: BIRTH OF THE SOCIETY OF UNITED IRISH WOMEN

1 Sarah McNamara, *Those Intrepid United Irishwomen*, Limerick, 1995
2 Ibid, p. 10
3 M. Cullen, and M. Luddy, *Women, Power and Consciousness in Nineteenth Century Ireland*, Dublin, 1995. p. 14
4 *The United Irishwomen, their Place, Work and Ideals*, Dublin, 1911. p. 9
5 George Russell, IAOS AGM, Dublin, 1909
6 ICA archives
7 Horace Plunkett, *The United Irishwomen, their Place, Work and Ideals*, Dublin, 1911
8 Ibid.
9 Sarah McNamara, *Those Intrepid United Irishwomen*, Limerick, 1995
10 Ibid.
11 Ibid.
12 UI report in *Irish Homestead*, 3 December 1910

13 Ibid.
14 Ellice Pilkington, *The United Irishwomen, their place, work and ideals*, Dublin, 1911
15 Ibid.
16 Ibid.
17 Ibid.
18 O. Walsh, *Protestant* 'Female Philanthropy in Dublin in the early Twentieth Century', *History Ireland*, 1997
19 M. Cullen, and M. Luddy, *Women, Power and Consciousness in nineteenth century Ireland*, Dublin, 1995
20 Ellice Pilkington, *The United Irishwomen, their Place, Work and Ideals*, Plunkett, Pilkington and Russell (eds), Dublin, 1911
21 M.E. Collins, *History in the Making*, Dublin, 1993
22 P. Bourden, *The Emergence of Modern Ireland*, Dublin, 1986. p. 279

CHAPTER 2: THE EARLY YEARS

1 Minute book 1913–21 from the ICA archives
2 Ibid. (November 1913, Executive committee meeting)
3 Ibid. (July 1913, Executive committee meeting)
4 Ibid. (April 1914, Executive committee meeting)
5 Sarah McNamara, *Those Intrepid United Irishwomen*, Limerick, 1995
6 *Enniscorthy Echo*, Co. Wexford, August 1910
7 *Bean na hÉireann*, newspaper of Inighne na hÉireann, January 1911
8 *The United Irishwomen, their Place, Work and Ideals*, ed. Plunkett, Pilkington and Russell, Dublin 1911
9 Minute book 1913v21 from the ICA archives
10 April 1914, Executive committee meeting
11 *United Irishwomen*, journal of UI, 1925, in ICA archives
12 Caitriona Clear, 'The Limits of Female Autonomy' in M. Luddy and C. Murphy (eds), *Women Surviving*, Dublin, 1989
13 Ellice Pilkington, *The United Irishwomen, their Place, Work and Ideals*, ed. Plunkett, Pilkington and Russell, Dublin, 1911
14 Minute book 1913v21 from the ICA archives
15 Sarah McNamara, *Those Intrepid United Irishwomen*, Limerick, 1995
16 UI notes in *Irish Homestead*, 28 November 1912

17 Esther Rudd, 'United Irishwomen' in *Bantracht na Tuaithe, Ár Leabhar Féin*, Our Book, Dublin, 1960. p. 44
18 Ibid.
19 Minute book 1913v21 from the ICA archives
20 E.A. Bishop, article on ICA jubilee in *Farmer's Journal*, May 1960
21 M.E. Collins, *History in the Making*, Dublin, 1993. p. 187
22 E.A. Bishop, *Bantracht na Tuatha, Irish Countrywomen's Association*, Dublin, 1950
23 F.S.L. Lyons, *Ireland Since the Famine*, London, 1985. p. 325
24 Ibid p. 326
25 Ibid p. 328
26 M.E. Collins, *History in the Making*, Dublin, 1993. p. 229
27 Patricia Bourden, *The Emergence of Modern Ireland*, Dublin, 1986. p. 137
28 Esther Bishop, *Bantracht na Tuatha, Irish Countrywomen's Association*, Dublin, 1950. p. 4–5
29 Ibid.
30 M.E. Collins, *History in the Making*, Dublin, 1993. p. 187
31 M. Ward, *Unmanageable Revolutionaries*, Pluto Press, 1995
32 Ibid. p. 342
33 Ibid. p. 421
34 R. Cullen Owens, *Smashing Times*, Attic Press, Dublin, 1984
35 P. Bourden, *The Emergence of Modern Ireland*, Dublin, 1986. p. 284
36 Muriel Gahan, *And see her beauty shining there: The story of the Irish Countrywomen*, ed. P. Bolger, Dublin, 1986

CHAPTER 3: SUMMER SCHOOLS AND COUNTRY WORKERS

1 Lucy Franks, An account of the first summer school of 1929 from ICA archives
2 *Farmers' Gazette*, 11 July 1931
3 Pro-Quidnunc in *The Irish Times*, 1978
4 *Farmers' Gazette*, 14 October 1933

CHAPTER 4: 1930S AND THE BIRTH OF ICA

1 M.E. Collins, *History in the Making*, Dublin, 1993. p. 344
2 Diarmaid Ferriter, *Mothers, Maidens and Myths*, Dublin, 1995. p. 18

3   Ibid.
4   *Farmers' Gazette*, 4 November 1933
5   *Farmers' Gazette*, 9 December 1933
6   Esther Bishop, *Bantracht na Tuatha, Irish Countrywomen's Association*, Dublin, 1950
7   Diarmaid Ferriter, *Mothers, Maidens and Myths*, Dublin, 1995
8   Caitriona Beaumont, 'Women and the Politics of Equality,' in M.G. Valiulis and M. O'Dowd (eds), *Women and Irish History*, Dublin, 1997. p. 178
9   Patricia Bourden, *The Emergence of Modern Ireland*, Dublin, 1986. p. 153
10 M.E. Collins, *History in the Making*, Dublin, 1993. p. 366
11 A. Sheehy Skeffington, Lecture to NL Society, 1989
12 Caitriona Clear, 'The women cannot be blamed', in M. O'Dowd and S. Wichert (eds), *Chattel, Servant or Citizen*, Belfast, 1995. p. 182
13 Ibid. p. 183
14 Ibid. p. 184
15 Ibid. p. 186
16 Lucy Franks, Honorary Secretary, Minutes of Council, 1937, from the ICA archives

CHAPTER 5: STRUCTURE OF ICA

1   Esther Bishop, *Bantracht na Tuatha, Irish Countrywomen's Association*, Dublin, 1950

CHAPTER 6: THE 'EMERGENCY' AND ITS AFTERMATH

1   Diarmaid Ferriter, *Mothers, Maidens and Myths*, Dublin, 1995. p. 21
2   Hilda Tweedy, *A Link in the Chain*, Attic Press, Dublin, 1992
3   Patricia Bourden, *The Emergence of Modern Ireland*, Dublin, 1986. p. 267
4   *Bantracht na Tuaithe – South Tipperary Federation 1941–1996*, Duggan, O'Malley and Kiely (eds), Tipperary, 1996
5   ICA submission to the Commission on Emigration, 1948, from the ICA archives
6   M.E. Collins, *History in the Making*, Dublin, 1993
7   *Bantracht na Tuaithe – South Tipperary Federation*, 1941–1996 Duggan and O'Malley (eds), Tipperary, 1996

8   *Eadrainn, a History of Cork Federation*, M. Daly, and K. Gleeson (eds), Cork, 1994. p. 25

9   Caitriona Clear, 'No Feminine Mystique', in M.G. Valiulis and M. O'Dowd (eds.), *Women and Irish History*, Dublin, 1997. p. 183

CHAPTER 7: RURAL WATER, ELECTRICITY AND DEVELOPMENT IN THE 1950S

1   Senior European Women (SEW) Report, A. Kelly, ed., Maynooth, 1996. p. 34

2   Marianne Heron, *Fighting Spirit*, Dublin, 1993. p .37

3   Senior European Women (SEW) Report, A. Kelly, ed., Maynooth, 1996. p. 33

4   Patricia Bourden, *The Emergence of Modern Ireland*, Dublin, 1986. p. 249

5   Mary E. Daly, 'Turn on the Tap', from *Women and Irish History*, M.G. Valiulis and M. O'Dowd (eds), Dublin, 1997. p. 206

6   *The Irish Times*, 9 November 1952

7   Geraldine Mitchell, *Deeds not Words*, Dublin, 1997. p. 188

8   Mary E. Daly, 'Turn on the Tap', from *Women and Irish History*, M.G. Valiulis and M. O'Dowd (eds), Dublin, 1997. p. 206

9   Michael Shiels, *The Quiet Revolution: the electrification of rural Ireland, 1946–76*, Dublin, 1984

10 Geraldine Mitchell, *Deeds not Words*, Dublin, 1997. p. 170

11 Dermot Ferriter, *Mothers, Maidens and Myths*, Dublin, 1995. p. 38

12 Kit Ahern, 'Women and Agricultural Development', *Kerry Farmers Annual*, 1977

13 Diarmaid Ferriter, *Mothers, Maidens and Myths*, Dublin, 1995. p. 40

CHAPTER 8: AN GRIANÁN

1   Report on Summer School, 1945 in ICA archives

2   Bantracht na Tuaithe, An Grianán Silver Jubilee 1954–79, Dublin, 1979. p. 18

3   Ibid. pp. 24–26

CHAPTER 9: ICA IN A CHANGING SOCIETY: 1960S

1   M.E. Collins, *History in the Making*, Dublin, 1993

2   Ibid, pp. 396–7

3   1963 Annual Report

4   Interview with Kit Ahern, 1996, in the ICA archives
5   Sarah McNamara, *Those Intrepid United Irishwomen*, Limerick, 1995. p. 69
6   F.S.L. Lyons, *Ireland since the Famine*, London, 1985. pp. 692–3
7   Diarmaid Ferriter, *Mothers, Maidens and Myths*, Dublin, 1995. p. 50

CHAPTER 10: THE WOMEN'S DECADE: 1970S

1   Ita Mangan, 'The influence of EC membership on Irish social policy and social services' in S. Ó Cinnéide (ed.), *Social Europe: EC social policy and Ireland*, Dublin, 1993. p.72
2   *Commission on the Status of Women*, Report to Minister for Finance, Dublin, 1972. p.7
3   Aileen Orpen, profile of Josephine Carroll in *Farmer's Journal*, Dublin, November 1973
4   *Bantracht na Tuaithe, South Tipperary Federation*, M. Duggan and N. O'Malley (eds), Tipperary, 1996. p.61
5   Maurice Manning, 'Women in Irish National and Local Politics 1922–77' in M. MacCurtain and D. O'Corráin (eds), *Women in Irish Society, The Historical Dimension*, Dublin, 1979. p.95
6   Diarmaid Ferriter, *Mothers, Maidens and Myths*, Dublin, 1995. p.55
7   Kathleen Delap, 'Women in the home', in *Administration, Journal of the Institute of Public Administration of Ireland*, Dublin, Spring 1975. p.93
8   Senior European Women (SEW) Report, A. Kelly (ed.), Maynooth, 1996. p.51
9   Ibid. p.53
10   Report of MRBI survey on the ICA, 1979

CHAPTER 11: 1980 ONWARDS

1   Senior European Women Report, A. Kelly (ed.), Maynooth, 1996. p.54
2   Monica Carr, *The Farming Independent*, Dublin, 5 January 1980
3   ICA submission to an EU Women's Conference in Bonn, 1982
4   1985 Council minutes in the ICA archives
5   Diarmaid Ferriter, *Mothers, Maidens and Myths*, Dublin, 1995. p.61

CHAPTER 12: CONCLUSION: DEEDS, NOT WORDS

1   Mary Wollstonecraft, *The Rights of Woman*, London, 1792
2   Mary Connery, 'The Future of Feminism', in *Irish Citizen*, May 1919
3   Mamo McDonald, interview for this research, March 2000
4   Joe Lee, 'Women and the Church since the famine', in M. MacCurtain and D. O'Corráin (eds), *Women in Irish Society: The Historical Dimension*, Dublin, 1978. pp.37–45
5   Caitriona Beaumont, 'Women and the Politics of Equality: The Irish Women's Movement, 1930–1943' in M.G. Valiulis and M. O'Dowd (eds), *Women and Irish History*, Dublin, 1997. pp.185–187
6   Nuala Fennell, *Regional Women: The forgotten women*, presentation at CSW Conference, Limerick, 1986
7   Ann Byrne, 'Single Women in Ireland, A Re-Examination of the Sociological Evidence', in A. Byrne and M. Leonard (eds), *Women and Irish Society*, Dublin, 1997. pp.415–429
8   Liz Steiner Scott, 'Introduction', in L. Steiner Scott (ed.), *Personally Speaking: Women's Thoughts on Women's Issues*, Dublin, 1985. p.8
9   Mary Cullen, 'Telling it Our Way' in L. Steiner Scott (ed.), *Personally Speaking: Women's Thoughts on Women's Issues*, Dublin, 1985. p.258
10 Mary Wollstonecraft, *The Rights of Woman*, London, 1792
11 Margaret MacCurtain, 'Foreword' in Hilda Tweedy's *A Link in the Chain, Dublin*, 1992. p.7
12 Maria Luddy, 'Women and Politics in Nineteenth-Century Ireland', in M.G. Valiulis and M. O'Dowd (eds), *Women and Irish History*, Dublin, 1997. p.12
13 Declan Lynch writing in the *Sunday Independent*, 1990
14 Mary Cullen, 'Telling it Our Way', in L. Steiner Scott (ed.), *Personally Speaking: Women's Thoughts on Women's Issues*, Dublin, 1985. pp.254–264
15 Ibid.
16 Nuala O'Faolain writing in *The Irish Times*, 1991
17 Maureen Keenan writing in the *Sunday Business Post*, 1991
18 Nuala O'Faolain writing in *The Irish Times*, 1991
19 Mamo McDonald's address to the ICA Council meeting, October 1983

APPENDIX: PERSONALITIES AND PRESIDENTS OF ICA

1   Anna Kinsella, *Women of Wexford*, Wexford, 1998. p.79
2   Sarah McNamara, *Those Intrepid United Irishwomen*, Limerick, 1995
3   Ibid., p.104
4   Hilary Pyle, *Red Headed Rebel*, Dublin, 1998. p.135
5   *Ár Leabhar Féin*, Golden Jubilee edition, 1960
6   Muriel Gahan, *And see her beauty shining there: The story of the Irish Countrywomen*, P. Bolger (ed.), Dublin, 1986
7   Executive minutes 1950–53, in ICA archive
8   Article in *Irish Examiner*, 23 May 2000